The
Conscience
of the
Eye

The Conscience of the Eye

The Design and Social Life of Cities

RICHARD SENNETT

ALFRED A. KNOPF
New York 1990

THIS IS A BORZOI BOOK
PUBLISHED BY ALFRED A. KNOPF, INC.

Library of Congress Cataloging-in-Publication Data
Sennett, Richard, [date]
The conscience of the eye: the design and
social life of cities/
Richard Sennett.—1st ed.
p.   cm.
Includes index.
ISBN 0-394-57104-5
1. City and town life.   I. Title.
HT231.S458   1990
307.76—dc20   90-52945   CIP

Manufactured in the United States of America

FIRST EDITION

For Saskia Sassen

From early on I have suspected that the so important-sounding task "Know thyself" is a ruse of a cabal of priests. They are trying to seduce man from activity in the outside world, to distract him with impossible demands; they seek to draw him into a false inner contemplation. Man only knows himself insofar as he knows the world—the world which he only comes to know in himself and himself only in it.

GOETHE

Contents

Introduction:
The Conscience
of the Eye

THE ANCIENT GREEK could use his or her eyes to see the complexities of life. The temples, markets, playing fields, meeting places, walls, public statuary, and paintings of the ancient city represented the culture's values in religion, politics, and family life. It would be difficult to know where in particular to go in modern London or New York to experience, say, remorse. Or were modern architects asked to design spaces that better promote democracy, they would lay down their pens; there is no modern design equivalent to the ancient assembly. Nor is it easy to conceive of places that teach the moral dimensions of sexual desire, as the Greeks learned in their gymnasiums—modern places, that is, filled with other people, a crowd of other people, rather than the near silence of the bedroom or the solitude of the psychiatrist's couch. As materials for culture, the stones of the modern city seem badly laid by planners and architects, in that the shopping mall, the parking lot, the apartment house elevator do not suggest in their form the complexities of how people might live. What once were the experiences of places appear now as floating mental operations.

We could never recover the Greek past, even if we wished and we would not wish to; their city was founded on massive slavery. But the clarity with which they could literally see the fullness of life raises at least the question of why we cannot see as fully, a question this book attempts to answer.

One difference between the Greek past and the present is that whereas the ancients could use their eyes in the city to think about political, religious, and erotic experiences, modern culture suffers from a divide between the inside and the outside. It is a divide between subjective experience and worldly experience, self and city. Moreover, our culture is marked by hard struggle whenever people seek to make inner life concrete. This sets us off not just from our own origins but also from non-European cultures nearer in time whose masks, dances, ceremonials, shrines, sacred grounds, and cosmologies connect subjective life to physical things.

This divide between inner, subjective experience and outer, physical life expresses in fact a great fear which our civilization has refused to admit, much less to reckon. The spaces full of people in the modern city are either spaces limited to and carefully orchestrating consumption, like the shopping mall, or spaces limited to and carefully orchestrating the experience of tourism. This reduction and trivializing of the city as a stage of life is no accident. Beyond all the economic and demographic reasons for the neutralized city there exists a profound, indeed, "spiritual" reason why people are willing to tolerate such a bland scene for their lives. The way cities look reflects a great, unreckoned fear of exposure. "Exposure" more connotes the likelihood of being hurt than of being stimulated. The fear of exposure is in one way a militarized conception of everyday experience, as though attack-and-defense is as apt a model of subjective life as it is of warfare. What is characteristic of our city-building is to wall off the differences between people, assuming that these differences are more likely to be mutually threatening than mutually stimulating. What we make in the urban realm are therefore bland, neutralizing spaces, spaces which remove the threat of social contact: street walls faced in sheets of plate glass, highways that cut off poor neighborhoods from the rest of the city, dormitory housing developments.

In this book I shall try to show how fear of exposure came about, how the wall between inner and outer life was built. The wall arose in part from our religious history: Christianity set Western culture upon the course that built a wall between the inner and outer experience. The shadows cast by that wall continue to darken secular society. Moreover, attempts to unify the inner and outer dimensions simply by tearing down the wall, making the inner and outer one organic whole, have not proved successful; unity can be gained only at the price of complexity.

The exposed, outer life of the city cannot be simply a reflection of inner life. Exposure occurs in crowds and among strangers. The cultural problem of the modern city is how to make this impersonal milieu speak, how to relieve its current blandness, its neutrality, whose origin can be traced back to the belief that the outside world of things is unreal. Our urban problem is how to revive the reality of the outside as a dimension of human experience.

In battle, at the deathbed, or simply on the street, the ancient Greek was hardly a mushy, good-hearted sentimentalist, moved to tears whenever he or she witnessed the pain of another. The value of witnessing both difficulty and diversity was instead thought to be that through exposure to the world the individual gradually found his or her orientation, found how to keep a balance. This condition the Greeks called *sophrosyne*, which could be translated as "grace" or "poise." Today we would say such a person keeping his or her balance in the world is "centered." A city ought to be a school for learning how to lead a centered life. Through exposure to others, we might learn how to weigh what is important and what is not. We need to see differences on the streets or in other people neither as threats nor as sentimental invitations, rather as necessary visions. They are necessary for us to learn how to navigate life with balance, both individually and collectively.

This might seem a matter simply of reflecting upon what we see, of reckoning our places in the midst of others. But for the Greeks, to balance oneself one had to act as well as to look. The result of caring about what one sees is the desire to make something. The Greeks called this desire *poiesis*, from which we derive the English word "poetry," but their word was broader than one art in scope. The balanced person wants to make a speech, a battle, love, as well as a poem with the same qualities of grace and poise. As a result of his or her own engagement in making or doing things carefully, *sophrosyne* and *poiesis* were intimately related. While I do not go so far as to consider "the city as a work of art," as does Donald Olsen in a book of that title, the impulse behind his title seems to me right. To care about what one sees in the world leads to mobilizing one's creative powers. In the modern city, these creative powers ought to take on a particular and humane form, turning people outward. Our culture is in need of an art of exposure; this art will not make us one another's victims, rather more balanced adults, capable of coping with and learning from complexity.

The Conscience of the Eye is the last volume in a trilogy of books about urban culture which, at the outset, I did not know I was writing. The first of these was *The Fall of Public Man,* published a dozen years ago (1977), which explored the distinction between public and private life in terms of public behavior as a kind of ritual. In that work, I sought to show how the public realm lost its life when it lost these rituals. The second volume in this trilogy was a novel, *Palais Royal* (1986), whose theme is how a city's complexity enriches the lives of individuals who are failing, as the world measures success and failure. This present book seeks to combine the social criticism of the first with the more personal insight of the second. More than the first two volumes, it aims at relating architecture, urban planning, public sculpture, and the visual scenes of the city to its cultural life.

The
Conscience
of the
Eye

PART
ONE

Interior
Shadows

_____

chapter 1

The Refuge

Inner and
Outer

T H E   P E O P L E of the Old Testament did not separate spiritual life and worldly experience. Like the Greeks, their everyday existence seemed to them filled with divine plagues, the miraculous parting of seas, voices speaking from burning bushes. God was always present. But unlike the Greeks, the people of the Old Testament thought of themselves as uprooted wanderers. The Yahweh of the Old Testament was himself a wandering god, his Ark of the Covenant portable and, in the theologian Harvey Cox's words, "When the Ark was finally captured by the Philistines, the Hebrews began to realize that Yahweh was not localized even in it. . . . He traveled with his people and elsewhere."[1] Yahweh was a god of time rather than of place, a god who promised to his followers a divine meaning for their unhappy travels.

Wandering and exposure were as strongly felt to be the consequences of faith among early Christians as among Old Testament Jews. The author of the "Epistle to Diognatus" at the height of the Roman Empire's glory declared that

Christians are not distinguished from the rest of humanity either in locality or in speech or in customs. For they do not dwell off

[1] Harvey Cox, *The Secular City*, rev. ed. (New York: Macmillan, 1966), p. 49.

in cities of their own . . . nor do they practice an extraordinary
style of life . . . they dwell in their own countries, but only as
sojourners. . . . Every foreign country is a fatherland to them,
and every fatherland is a foreign country.[2]

This image of the wanderer came to be one of the ways in which Saint
Augustine defined the two cities in *The City of God*:

Now it is recorded of Cain that he built a city, while Abel, as
though he were merely a pilgrim on earth, built none. For the
true City of the saints is in heaven, though here on earth it
produces citizens in which it wanders as on a pilgrimage through
time looking for the Kingdom of eternity.[3]

This "pilgrimage through time" rather than settling in place draws its
authority from Jesus' refusal to allow His disciples to build monu-
ments to him, and His promise to destroy the Temple of Jerusalem.

Judeo-Christian culture is, at its very roots, about experiences of
spiritual dislocation and homelessness. The terrors of exposure are at
the heart of our religious imagination. Our faith began at odds with
place, because our gods themselves were disposed to wander. And
yet in Augustine's time this spiritual resistance to settling down modulated. Augustine's *City of God* was occasioned by Alaric's sack of
Rome in August 410. Augustine was deeply awed, as were most of his
contemporaries, that the Christian churches were largely unharmed
by the barbarians. In response to charges by Volusianus and other
pagans that Christianity had sapped the will of the Romans to fight,
he was at pains to defend his fellow believers; his defense was that
one could be both a good soldier and a good Christian, so separated
was the life of battle from the world of inner experience. And to the
charge that Christianity would flourish in the ruins of the Roman
Empire, Augustine responded that though God, through the instrument of the barbarian hordes, had struck down unbelievers, the

[2] Translated and quoted in Jaroslav Pelikan, *Jesus through the Centuries* (New Haven: Yale
University Press, 1985), pp. 49–50.
[3] Augustine, *The City of God,* trans. by Gerald G. Walsh, S.J., et al. (New York: Image, 1958),p.
325.

Christian had no call to install himself now as master and rebuilder of
Rome; his duty lay within his soul, not in his hands. Augustine's two
cities are therefore "two groups of human beings, which we can call
two 'cities,' according to the special usage of our Scriptures."[4] That
usage of city was to describe two forms of authority, "two pyramids of
loyalty,"[5] rather than places.

For the Christians of Augustine's day more generally, the conflict
between spiritual life and worldly experience was felt as a conflict that
occurs within every human being; the Christian engaged in this spiritual battle whether or not he or she lived in houses where pagans had
raised their children, bathed where they had bathed, indeed used
their temples to Minerva or to Apollo for prayer to Jesus. Yet Augustine's book would lay the theological foundation for a city whose
architecture and urban forms would give the restless spirit a home.
This was because Augustine believed in "religious vision" as a concrete, perceptual act, not simply as a verbal metaphor. "Religious
vision" would lead, eventually, to an inner life that took shape in glass
and stone. Our civilization from his time on has sought to cope with
spiritual uprootedness as much through the eye as through words.

The nature of vision Augustine takes up immediately after he announces his two cities. "A shadow, as it were, of this eternal City has
been cast on earth, a prophetic representation of something to come
rather than a real presentation in time." In this passage vision is first
given a distinctively Christian cast. To Augustine the "shadow" of the
eternal, which is an impalpable intimation of faith, casts in turn another shadow, one of darkness and light apparent to any naked eye,
whether the eye of a believer or not: "In the world community, then,
we find two forms, one being the visible appearance of the earthly
city and another whose presence serves as a shadow of the heavenly
City."[6] His sense of religious "vision" supposes something like the
perception, in slow motion, of an image bouncing along a corridor of
mirrors. This image has a peculiar property; the farther away the
image travels from its spiritual source, closer to everyday life, the
easier it becomes to see. The shadow is more defined than the light

[4] Augustine, *De civitate Dei* 14.1.12–18.
[5] Peter Brown, *Augustine of Hippo* (Berkeley: University of California Press, 1967), p. 314.
[6] Augustine, *City of God,* pp. 325, 326.

that creates it. This simple proposition suggested to Augustine the process by which unbelievers can become believers. Those most in need of God, the unbelievers, can find him by using their eyes. They should look for where the image is coming from, seek out the light that casts the clearly etched shadow. The source of light is defined as the end point of a long passage.

Augustine's modern biographer, Peter Brown, has characterized this "stereoscopic effect" as one principle of organizing the arguments throughout *The City of God*.[7] Augustine begins with something pagan and familiar, then adds to it other more difficult but still pagan ideas or images, until suddenly, as though one had looked down that tunnel of vision, one came to the end and a whole new, Christian, image was revealed. The Christian who follows his or her eyes will find God.

For Augustine the eye was an organ of conscience, as it was for Plato; indeed, the Greek work for "theory" is *theoria*, which means "look at," "seeing," or—in the modern usage that combines physical experience of light with understanding—"illumination." However, this religious vision was not a sudden illumination, like switching on a light in a darkened room. One had to engage in a lifelong search to find the source of light.

Among Augustine's pagan contemporaries life as a quest was understood in terms of acting in the world, as it was first understood by Homer. For instance, men would seek to exonerate the honor of their families, to avenge an ancient injury, through the lifelong pursuit of an enemy. The Christian quest, rather than a saga of action, sent a man or a woman in search of faith, a quest altogether more inward. In Augustine's *Confessions*, when the saint finally has his moment of illumination, he feels that something has happened to him that he has sought for all his life, without, when young, knowing at all what he wanted. Later, he argued himself intellectually into religious adherence while still lacking the full, sensate illumination of religious belief. One sees clearly only at the end.

The very notion of "finding" faith, as though God were hiding, creates a profound uncertainty. The pagan, like the ancient Hebrew, had no doubt of divine presences. These presences were to be felt in

[7] Brown, *Augustine*, p. 306.

the speech of the winds whistling through trees, in the descent of plague upon a city. For Augustine, finding faith instead involved a reforming of the human being's powers of perception; one had to relearn how to see. Yet there was no formula a Christian could be taught in school, in prayer, or by Socratic example that would teach him or her how to have religious visions. Each Christian would have to find his or her own way to the place from where light was shining.

The Greeks had conceived of "centeredness," as I noted, in what they called *sophrosyne*, which translates as *gracefulness* or *balance*. This Greek ideal is expressed in modern terms when a dancer is said to be well-centered in his or her body; the Greeks imagined a spiritual gyroscope to compliment the physical sense of balance. Augustine's spiritual center was not a point of balance; his was no quest for *sophrosyne*. The Christian searching for his or her spiritual center indeed would lose in the process any guidance from established things; the shadows were not to be trusted.

This Christian theology has had a profound and disturbing effect on the way our culture both believes in and suspects the reality of the senses. On the one hand, the eyes offer evidence of God. On the other hand, up to the moment of illumination most of this evidence is false. Unlike Plato, Augustine believed in the permanent necessity of physical searching and sifting of evidence; his own story is one in which illumination had to be prepared for by sensual indulgence, by the thirst for power, by innumerable (in his own mind) wrong turns. This is the Christian's tragedy: experience is necessary for faith, but the sensations of experience do not correspond to the truths of religion.

It was out of this disjunction that "inner" and "outer" came to be incommensurate dimensions. Nothing is more cursed in our culture than the continuing power of this separation. It makes connecting motives and actions difficult, since they seem to belong to different realms. Experiences like love become disturbed because feelings are kept inside, invisible—the realm where Truth is kept. And the places people live in become puzzling. The street is a scene of outside life, and what is to be seen on the street are beggars, tourists, merchants, students, children playing, old people resting—a scene of human differences. What is the relation of these differences to inner life? What is the spiritual value of diversity? Augustine recognized that the

Christian would have trouble assaying the value of human diversity. The very act of believing would deprive a person of the ability to make sense of the scenes of life outside.

Like Plato considering in *The Republic* those who were released from a cave of shadowy illusions, Augustine took seriously the fact that staring at the sun blinds the beholder. Once the Christian believes, he or she cannot look at the halftones and varied shapes of those worldly differences anymore, those shadows that are the forms of everyday experience; the Christian has been blinded by truth. It is in this truth-stricken condition that the Christian is in need of God's protection. He or she has ceased to be a secular adult and reverted to a simpler condition—that of a child of God.

Augustine thought God would make a promise to men and women in this condition, a promise that was not felt by even the most devout Jews in the Old Testament. It was the promise of security through faith. Through the very act of believing, God will protect you, even if his redemption of your martyr's soul is divorced from protection of your suffering body. To resolve the endless process of wandering among shadows by finding where the light comes from requires an act of surrender, however, as one follows these images with one's eyes— ever greater surrender of one's will, ever greater understanding of what one sees. Augustine's religious vision thus had a concrete political denouement. You are promised that you will be taken care of, if only you submit, if you do your duty to bishop or king or parent. Vision, then, leads the wanderer to a house of submission, in which the pains of exposure come to an end. The eye is an organ of both faith and domination.

Building the Wall between Inner and Outer

The conceiving of a Christian city in stone fell to Saint Isidore of Seville (ca. 560–636). He was a practical man. By force of arms he

converted the Visigoth tribes to Christianity; he erected a coherent
Church hierarchy in Spain. His scholarly labors also had a practical
aim; he wrote the *Etymologies,* a book about the origin of words, in
order to clarify their use. In this book he traced the word *city* back to
different sources. One is *urbs,* the stones of a city. The stones of a city
were laid for practical reasons of shelter, commerce, and warfare. The
other root of *city* is *civitas,* and this word is about the emotions,
rituals, and convictions that take form in a city.

Christianity, Isidore thought, cannot be practiced in a pagan *urbs.*
In this conviction the conqueror of the Visigoths took a step beyond
Augustine and the other early Church fathers, who saw no need to
tear down the temples of Diana, the baths, gardens, and markets of
unbelievers. Isidore believed a proper design for the *urbs,* on the
contrary, was necessary for the Christian in the difficult struggles of
spiritual life. The *Etymologies* do not say how to draw it, only that the
Christian must make a city to subdue the flux of the soul.

In the seventh century A.D., this faith in building was almost a
heroic act. All around Isidore cities were falling into ruins: the public
buildings of the Roman Empire were pillaged by marauding heathen
tribes for wood and stone; the streets no longer scuffed by crowds
were coated with slippery moss. Not all cities suffered this fate. Milan, Treves, and Paris grew as the Roman Empire disappeared, but
their growth was as strongholds—places in which people looked to
the Church hierarchy to protect them. In these circumstances only a
very strong set of beliefs, of values deeply and passionately held,
could serve as an ideal of renewal. To build in adversity required a
devotion that would sustain generation after generation of mason and
carpenter. What sustained them was building that ideal of the inside,
in which the children of God were made safe from the street. Inside
the light of faith would dispel the shadows of difference.

The Church of Isidore's time became a congregation of builders.
From the sixth to the tenth century the Christian obligation to provide shelter was put into practice, and a network of cities developed.
However, it is easy to imagine as a modern tourist that the builders
before and during the Middle Ages put into practice Augustine's
command of indifference to the physical *urbs,* for these cities appear
to lack any design behind the walls. Streets intersect haphazardly, or

expand and contract in width without reference to the buildings lining them. In towns like Aosta in the north of Italy or Nantes in France
which inherited the regular grid pattern of the Roman city planners
and were continuously inhabited, the advent of medieval building
meant the old Roman forums were filled in with structures without
any regard to placement within the grid or in relation to one another—
seemingly a smudge of development over the ancient systems of
rectangles. In fact, the medieval town operated according to another
set of rules.

The medieval builders were masons and carpenters, not philosophers. As Christians, they knew only that secular space had to look
unlike sacred space. This happened as the secular buildings of these
cities grew jumbled together, the streets twisted and inefficient,
while the churches were carefully sited, their construction precise,
their design elaborately calculated. Though no design theory produced this difference, still the result was to give Augustine's religious
faith a concrete form. A center was the place of definition in the city,
a precisely made place where the Word ruled, in contrast to the flux
of the secular. Furthermore, it offered refuge and sanctuary from the
violence that infected the rest of the city. The Christian builder created a center with these qualities in a particular way.

Lao-tzu: "The true reality of a room is not its walls but the emptiness they contain."[8] Both Chinese and Japanese cities have centers
defined by sacred places. The Imperial Palace in Tokyo, for instance,
is also an orienting point for a city that has shifted around it over the
centuries. However, this Eastern sacred place, like the Forbidden
City in Beijing, was conceived of as a void, the center forbidden to
the outside world, a place where the profane is absent. Catholic
doctrine, on the contrary, conceived of the sacred as in some way
visible to the spiritual seeker. This beckoning sign translated into the
massiveness of medieval churches.

One of the pronounced differences between the churches first built
in the time of Isidore and those built in the 1100s was the gigantic
enlargement of their scale. Some writers have tried to explain the
massiveness of these structures in purely functional terms, as a way to

[8] Quoted in Paul Zucker, *Town and Square* (New York: Columbia University Press, 1959), p. 94.

make physically apparent the power of the Church in relation to the
secular life around it. But this is a modern uncertainty imported to
the Middle Ages. God's power was in no need of advertisement; the
problem was how humankind, pitiful and sinful as it is, can approach
Him, a problem of how to bring the congregation to an apprehension
of His presence rather than an affirmation of His existence. The very
immensity of mass of the church building, its vast space within filled
with colored light, incense, and song, was to do this work of apprehension. That is, rather than being simply places of external display,
these cathedrals were large because of what happened in their interiors. By an enveloping of the senses, the devout would experience
God as an overwhelming presence rather than, as in the austere
temples of Tokyo or Beijing, an empty sign.

The built mass of medieval churches betrays a mathematical precision far more refined than that of much modern engineering. Gothic
building was in fact a highly efficient system to create high vaulting
with the minimum use of materials; the price for this economical
building was that the least misstep in the laying and cutting of stone
would have caused the arch to collapse. The ingenuity of vaulting in
such religious structures as Freiburg Minster or Chartres is entirely
absent in the secular buildings around them, a difference in construction quality that comes from more than a difference in size. In ex-
quisitely crafted structures like these churches, set seemingly at
random in relation to other more indifferently built secular structures, engineering became part of religious effort. Precision took on
a spiritual meaning.

A center visible because immense and solid; a center of clarity, in
contrast to the mess of worldliness: in the medieval city, where a thing
with these qualities is to be found, there is an emanation, a shadow of
the shadow of the presence of God. Here was Augustine's religious
vision translated into urban design. The first Christian cities contrasted
sacred and secular into terms of clarity versus diversity in the *urbs*.

There are two ways to draw attention to a physical object, as there
are in language: through emphasis or through discontinuity. Emphasis is an act that veers toward exaggeration. The italicized word, for
instance, serves as a marker that it is *important*. Emphasis is a concentration of meaning. In modern spaces, design often adds emphasis

by creating a marker that exaggerates a common pattern; the pitch of a roof is made very steep, or the fenders of a car are sloped like a penis. The eye, remarking the heightened effect, notices the object. The medieval builder commanded attention by creating a contrast between ordered and disordered spaces, but had no need to emphasize, as we understand it. The church neither emphasized nor concentrated within its walls all the activities of the city. Instead, the builder drew attention to the spiritual center by creating a discontinuity.

This discontinuity would perhaps have been easily comprehensible to Augustine, though he might well have been offended that theology had become so physical. At the end of that "stereoptic effect," when the shadows and reflections have led one along a twisted secular route, suddenly there stands revealed Truth, belief in itself, apart—and clear. Again, it offends modern common sense in turn to speak of building at random; however, permitting squares and houses to sprout randomly created the necessary contrast to make clarity speak as an experience of faith.

In the nineteenth century, the churches and cathedrals of the medieval city were romanticized as quiet, tomb-like retreats. Thanks to the work of Alain Erlande-Brandenburg and other modern scholars, we know this romantic picture of sacred isolation to be false. The cathedral and its associated buildings were involved in the economy and politics of the city—but as a city within a city, as an element discontinuous from other, secular forms of life.

In the town of Cordes, in the French province of the Tarn, we see this process of orchestrating sacred clarity take place in the course of a century. Cordes was a *bastide*, that is, a fortified garrison, separate from the castle of the lord who was the founder of the *bastide*. Cordes was begun by Count Raymond VII of Toulouse in 1222 in the wake of the Albigensian wars, which had decimated the local population. In its original plan houses hugged an oblong wall; for a few years they filled in, Roman fashion, in regular grids. By 1273, however, the wars were a distant memory, the town received the right to hold a market, and now the Church of Saint-Michel was begun on the summit of the hill on which the original *bastide* had been laid. It is one of the most exquisite churches of the later thirteenth century; the quarter of

houses around it in this rich, peaceful new town were scattered randomly about.

Such a contrast in the horizontal relation of focus to unfocus was
reinforced vertically. The association of height with faith is not
uniquely Christian, nor is the contrary of depth and evil. Early Is-
lamic writers imagined the universe as funnel-shaped with circles of
heaven and hell rather similar to those of Dante's *Divine Comedy*.
The difference between the medieval mosque builder and the Christian architect had to do with representation. The religion of the
mosque builder forbade the painting of sacred images, to prevent
idolatrous worship of them, and this prohibition extended to buildings, which must not seek to mimic the Godhead. Whereas the Christian builder, like the religious painter, attempted to make faith
explicit to the eye. The cruciform shape of every church of course
mimics Christ's suffering on the Cross; equally explicit was the Ascension, registered in the extraordinary efforts to build upward.

The spires we see on many medieval churches are nineteenth-
century additions; height as it was originally conceived was a matter
of looking up from within, in the act of prayer, and so of having a
visual experience of the Ascension. It is interesting to compare the
effect of those nineteenth-century additions to the original heights
within. The additions were evidently added on the principle of emphasis; the more the better, in this case the higher the more spiritual.
In fact, the additions simply render the structures top-heavy; the
spire is out of scale to the base. Within, however, the lower ceilings
often achieve precisely the desired effect sought later outside; the
vaulting is perfectly calibrated in scale so that the eye looking up
travels very far indeed, but arrives at a destination, an inner roof, still
legible in detail. You can see the bottom of Heaven. It is the precision
of the structure's form rather than building for sheer size that achieves
this. Or, to take the case of an entirely modern building, the interior
of the nave of the Cathedral of St. John the Divine in New York is
perceptibly higher than the interior of the nave of the medieval cathedral at Rouen. The nave of St. John's is immense, the nave at
Rouen is awe-inspiring. In the original medieval churches, precision
in height was sufficient to establish visual dominion over the flat
horizontals of the secular. Moreover, horizontal and vertical clarity

were related. Medieval Lübeck, for instance, had five major churches, unrelated to one another at the flat street-plane level but related in the height of their roofs, so that anywhere in Lübeck it was possible to look up and locate a church.

As in any era, specific forms of medieval city building varied immensely. More of an effort was made to organize the mercantile center in early Bremen, for instance, than in towns farther inland, simply because of the volume of commerce. Italian medieval towns kept Roman habits as well as pagan memories: Todi in the eleventh century deployed more geometric logic in the making of its market squares than the Hanseatic city of Rostock. Still, making space sacred through definitions that contrasted to secular irregularity became a mark of Western urbanism. Contemporary Muslim cities did not draw a sharp distinction between sacred and secular, mosque and market, in the same way; in the Roman past of many Christian cities, aqueducts were designed with as much care as temples.

St. Augustine promised that as the religious wayfarer saw ever more clearly, he or she would come under the care of God. The religious center of the Christian city was to do this promised work of protection. Christian rules of sanctuary date back to the Dark Ages: enemies cannot be pursued within church walls; those within a church or monastery have the right to be fed, and cared for if sick. In Isidore's age the urban fabric was lightly woven; fields and woods were often contained within the city's walls. By the eleventh century the fabric of the city was more tightly knit (save in wall-less cities like Canterbury or Gloucester). The expanding sacred city pushed against the expanding secular city. Indeed, all of the secular medieval city outside the church was a marketplace. People bought and sold everywhere, on the street, in houses, as well as in open squares. These market squares were not, moreover, secular centers in the city—that would have accorded to secular space a kind of balanced parity to the sacred center. Market squares were seldom designed; they were simply more of the same receiving, bargaining, and shipping that buzzed in every open and closed cranny of space. Indeed, medieval guilds had their reserved spaces in churches since they frequently were the sponsors of church building. Under these conditions of expansion, how could the church serve as a bulwark against the world?

In cities that began as monasteries, like Magdeburg in Germany or Saint Gall in Switzerland, one way to establish sanctuary was in the spaces directly outside the churches; these became no-man's lands. Though the bulk and height of church buildings generated shade and protection from wind, which might have facilitated commerce, the gulf between the sacred and the secular forbade such practical use. The band of emptiness showed that the terms of life would change the moment one stepped within. This break established around the church what has been called a locality of immunity. Here beggars established themselves, here the still-living victims of plague were carried from their houses and laid upon the ground. Here also was the place where babies were abandoned. It was the place in which all those in need gained the right to be cared for. Originally the parvis in front of the church was part of this zone of immunity (the parvis, in its regular form and stepped height, is more an extension of the narthex within the church than space belonging to the outside). In time the parvis would become a place of public rituals, plays, and political speeches, while the zone of open-space sanctuary resolved itself to the gardens behind or on the sides of the church, in the nooks among its buttresses. These were the transition zones, the outside that was yet withdrawn from the city, creating silence at the center.

The word *cathedral*, which first appears in the High Middle Ages, referred not simply to a church building but also to the residence of its bishop and his administration, to a specialized market serving the needs of these ecclesiastics, and to the *hôtel-Dieu* that cared for the sick. This ensemble of buildings operated by the same rules that governed the open zone of immunity. If a modern city dweller asks where he or she could go in order to find help, it is first necessary to define the exact condition of one's distress—a person with AIDS might first discover this from a doctor, then define the specific services required from a social worker and a lawyer, then seek out where to find this help. In the medieval city the open space and the buildings of sanctuary reversed the search. First a person in need went to the place where help was obligatory; then the nature of the hurt was sought, and if possible, a remedy was found. It took no knowledge of one's own condition to ask for help, and the logistics of building churches was such that it was clear where to go.

In one way the zones of sanctuary are a minor footnote in the

history of urban form. Certainly the relation of the castle to the town
raises larger and more overtly political issues of the meaning of protection. In Avignon, as in Granada and medieval Mannheim (before
the wall between castle and town was removed), the castle functioned
as a separate realm from the church, as well as occasionally from
rebellious subjects. Occasionally, castles served as the strongholds
from which the lords preyed upon their own townsmen. But these
bulky fortress sanctuaries depended only upon their stones, whereas
the Church was protected by magic: God put an invisible barrier
around these zones where the buttresses loomed, where nuns held
bewildered babies, where lepers begged, in order to make clear that
here, need spoke.

The corrosive dualism between the inside and outside first became
visible as urban form in this medieval way of marking territory. For
the space of sanctuary also, necessarily established where charity and
regard for others was absent: charity does not exist on the street.
After prayers one might stroll outside to witness someone being
drawn and quartered. Magic spaces do not always or necessarily have
this divisive result. The zone of immunity around the medieval church
was far different in character, for instance, from the enchanted ground
protecting the Greek temple. That sacred ground protected the physical temple, but the revelations the devout received in it were to be
carried into the city and acted upon. This was far different spiritual
news from that spread by the ritual pageant passing through the
streets of the medieval town. When the pageant had disappeared
from sight, the street, in the words of a thirteenth-century Parisian,
"returned to the wolves." During an era when sacred and secular
pressed upon one another in the fabric of the city, a vigorous attempt
was therefore made to define sacred space within which profane activity had no claim. The theater of the Middle Ages shows a striking
example of this: the passion plays, originally staged within the
churches, were gradually moved outside during the twelfth century
as the Devil and his attendant devils became comic, human-size figures rather than terrifying, primal forces engaged in sacred combat.
Though monasteries in the countryside were under the same obligations of sanctuary as those in the towns, the compacting of human
beings together in a town made this contrast between sacred awareness and secular indifference. The zone of immunity protected people

from the city, yet left the *civitas* of the secular world amorphous, violent, undefined, a space of moral amnesia.

Here, then, is one historical root of the modern fear of exposure. Pain could be seen, tolerated, and indeed therefore enjoyed in those places where people were exposed. It had no aversive moral value in the "outside"; if one paid much attention to those who were suffering in an exposed place, it was mostly as spectacle. Whereas once one stepped onto the grounds of a temple, suffering suddenly acquired a gravity; the sight of it suddenly put upon the viewer an obligation of charity. Only on sacred ground did pain become real. Ethics became concrete in terms of place, a place whose visual character was marked by precision.

Augustine imagined a pilgrim immersed in the world. During the pilgrim's quest, all of his or her senses were plunged into chaos, and only when the pilgrim experienced the profundity of spiritual illumination would it be evident where he or she was—this sense of place that Augustine imagined as one's place in a hierarchy. But now the optics of faith had produced physical buildings. The nature of the pilgrimage had been altered thereby. In a city which articulated the relation of Man to God clearly in physical terms, the spiritual traveler had less need to search the street, less need to fathom what lay behind human differences. One had only to use one's eyes to know where to go to stop traveling. In becoming a matter expressed in stone, the difference thus grew greater between the spiritual inside and the worldly outside. And of all the modern consequences of this story a thousand years old, none would prove more destructive than this divide: the outside as a dimension of diversity and chaos has lost its hold upon the human mind as a dimension of moral value, in contrast to an inner space of definition.

The Modern Fear of Exposure

One branch of a famous auction house in Manhattan sells family junk as well as important loot. Dusty watercolors Aunt Ethel bought on a trip to Venice forty years ago from a perfectly charming young artist, the collection of silver ice picks Uncle Herbert amassed in the decades since that fatal voyage—all such signs of extinguished life are displayed for a day before auction to a peculiar public of devoted voyeurs. A few years ago the firm mounted a bizarre display of these wares. Next to a rowing machine was placed a Victorian bath chair; a collection of art deco cocktail shakers was laid out in a row on the foreground, perhaps as a warning of how drink might make the buyer change seats. And on the sides of the display were stacks of paintings and framed photographs of people who could not possibly have been related, a miscellany of noses, jaws, paunches, and bare shoulders.

Among these I thought I had found something of commercial value. It appeared to be a sketch in oils for William Orchardson's *The First Cloud*, a painting of the 1890s now in the collection of the Tate Gallery in London. Orchardson's is the story painting of an elegant young woman walking from a room as her young husband, formally attired, his hands thrust into his cummerbund, watches her retreating back. He looks angry and puzzled; evidently they have just argued and it is their "first cloud."

The painting easily puts in mind, to anyone with a taste for the Victorian era, a famous declaration of faith in the virtues of the home that John Ruskin made in *Sesame and Lilies*, first published in 1865:

> This is the true nature of home—it is the place of peace: the shelter, not only from all injury, but from all terror, doubt and division. In so far as it is not this, it is not home; so far as the anxieties of the outer life penetrate into it, and the inconsistently-minded, unloved, or hostile society of the outer world is allowed by either husband or wife to cross the threshold it ceases to be a home; it is then only a part of the outer world which you have roofed over and lighted fire in. But so far as it is a sacred place, a vestal temple, a temple of the hearth . . . it is a home.[9]

In the course of *Sesame and Lilies*, the dream of a safe interior spoke to Ruskin ever more strongly, as it spoke to his age. The sketch

[9] John Ruskin, *Sesame and Lilies* (New York: Metropolitan Publishing Co., 1891), pp. 136–37.

of Orchardson's painting before me, a painting equally celebrated in its time, showed a couple awakening from Ruskin's dream.

Of course it is burdening this modest painting with unfair symbolic duty to say it shows the denouement of Christian faith made buildable. And yet it shows, I think, the mundane reality of a larger difficulty, the difficulty of making Christian vision work in the secular world. The words "sacred" and "secular" are of course not simple opposites. The coming of the Industrial Revolution aroused a great longing for sanctuary, and the workers who first faced the Industrial Revolution quite naturally turned to religion for words to express their grievances and to sustain them in their trials. Something of the same resource occurred more broadly in society when people sought for images of protection; they drew upon religious images of places of sanctuary. Stated baldly, "home" became the secular version of spiritual refuge; the geography of safety shifted from a sanctuary in the urban center to the domestic interior. However, just as industrial workers found that God's wrath at Mammon could not quite encompass the evil of machine-based labor, so those who sought sanctuary in a home found often that the very act of taking domestic refuge only increased their miseries. This is what Orchardson's painting shows: suddenly the young people at home see one another too clearly.

The long shadow religion has cast over the world created by the Industrial Revolution was first of all a matter of connection between the interior and inner life. Augustine had begun this connection by supposing that the person who found faith would require God's protection from the world; the medieval builders sought to separate the life of the street from spiritual life, protecting the spirit within church walls. Now, in the secular dimension, it was psychological understanding that seemed to crystallize and define itself when one had withdrawn inside from the world.

A century before the Industrial Revolution which prompted Ruskin's dream, the notion of a spiritual interior was not as compelling to an age that celebrated Nature. It seemed perfectly plausible to understand someone by looking at him or her outside. In the eighteenth century, painters like Gainsborough sought to reveal the character of sitters by placing them in the open air: the lady posed in a simple dress lounging on the grass, her face framed in bramble and leaves, the gentleman leaning at her side with his shirt open at the neck; she looks at us, amused; he talks to her, his expression animated. Nature has revealed them. To convey what people were really like a century later, the portrait painter placed them inside a room in the midst of a family scene. Orchardson's contemporary James Tuxen, called upon to paint Queen Victoria celebrating her golden jubilee in 1887, places the elderly queen in a chair that she shares with two little girls who are her grandchildren, the old and young bodies crowded into a seat meant for one surrounded in turn by other little girls to the left and right, another grandchild behind them, the old woman peacefully surrounded by squirming bundles of soft flesh; the dignitaries of the British Empire are all background in this official portrait, which was painted in the queen's private apartments rather than in a state chamber. The reason Tuxen orchestrated his sitters this way is perfectly plain. Here, inside, in the bosom of her family, you see what your queen is really like.

One might peer into interiors much less exalted to see the same process of psychological definition. There is, for instance, a famous photograph of Sarah Bernhardt supposedly caught unaware in her boudoir. Under a tasseled sultan's canopy, the actor reclines on her bed, lying upon Oriental cushions. The bed is covered in shaggy fur. At its foot there is more fur, an entire bearskin; the bear, his eyes wide open and his jaws apart, exposing two long white fangs, guards his mistress. In the foreground next to the bear is an elaborate Moroccan iron lamp covered with a domed fringe shade. The guardian bear lies on more Orientalia, Persian and Berber rugs overlapped. This horizontal splendor continues up the walls. Over the mantel the actor has placed a pair of mounted gazelle horns, behind which there is an enormous painting. At the top of the photograph of this boudoir we see a chandelier and the tips of a hanging plant.

The room itself does much more than keep her warm. The real woman exposed is exposed by her decor; she herself is impeccably, indeed primly dressed. Yet this is no revelation like Manet's *Olympia*, another boudoir scene in which a naked woman is attended by a black slave. Madame Bernhardt instead seems but one more object in her interior, and less remarkable an exhibit than her stuffed protector. This cave of sensuality is a space divorced from the outside: eros is revealed by the interior in which the human figure is placed.

My sketch by Orchardson also belongs to this pairing of inner revelation with an interior. For Victorian viewers the wealth of these young people would have been a salient visual fact, to be seen as a lesson about how riches can spoil the character of young people. Now one notices not so much the pearls against the woman's swanlike neck or the man's gleaming diamond shirt studs as simply the fact of where they are. They have doubtless spent many evenings together at dinners and balls. For an elegant couple of the old regime these sorties in society would have been occasions of truth. It was necessary for Orchardson's newlyweds to withdraw. At last, at home, each is revealed to the other. It is the same territory as Ruskin's dream, this room the painter assumed as the proper setting in which the meaning of his story would be revealed.

The defining power accorded the interior was, equally, how socialists like the Comte de Saint-Simon literally saw their dreams of a better society take shape. Saint-Simon attempted to build small, intimate communities where workers, owners, and distributors could all live together; daily communion through face-to-face exchange, Saint-Simon was convinced, would overcome class hostility. When Saint-Simon's followers sought to gain popular support in 1848, they prepared a poster to illustrate the master's principles. It showed a factory scene that looks like a friendly gathering in a large living room, the machines clean and sofa-size, the workers decorously moving among them. His answer as to what made a home-size interior a refuge was all about scale; the alienations of capitalism are muted the smaller, and hence more personal, the space in which labor occurs.

The vision of an interior in whose warmth people open up was enshrined in the jargon of the social sciences by Ferdinand Tönnies when he coined the opposition between *Gemeinschaft* and *Gesellschaft*. *Gemeinschaft* represented to him a "face-to-face" social relationship in a place that was small and socially enclosed, while *Gesellschaft* was a more exposed, mute exchange. Buying a stewpot in a corner shop where you chat and bargain was an experience suffused with *Gemeinschaft*, whereas buying the same stewpot in a department store in silence was an operation in the domain of *Ge-*

sellschaft. Tönnies, like Ruskin and Saint-Simon, translated these two terms into space. He made them contrasts between villages and cities, and within cities between homes and streets, little cafés and large cafés, a knot of neighbors and a large crowd. The more enclosed and inward in each is supposedly the more sociable. Images of people touching and talking, their communion as their bond, are scenes of subjective life at last established and opened up: *Gemeinschaft* could literally be translated as "sharing what is within me." The image revealed within would not be, Saint-Simon thought, the worker in the rags of his or her wretchedness, but a clear-eyed human being. This noble figure had been there all along, inside, waiting for the mantle of oppression to be lifted.

The coming of the Industrial Revolution brought with all its horrors a strong need for secular sanctuary. But the ideal of sanctuary is rooted, in Western culture, in something more than physical protection. Sanctuary seems to offer, as we would now say, the possibility of psychological development, in the same way a monk sought spiritual enlightenment sheltered in his cell. We think by seeking refuge from the garbage of power in the world to understand more about ourselves. In withdrawing, we will find that things become clearer. What will be revealed in sanctuary is our true, best self—this is the weight of the medieval past on the present. In a secular society, however, such expectations of sanctuary ask for too much.

It was apparent almost from the beginning that the full expectations of sanctuary could not be fulfilled in a secular world. For instance, in 1830 the old French noble families were called upon to swear an oath of loyalty to the new king, Louis Philippe, scion of the House of Orléans but representative of a new bourgeois era. The July Revolution that had brought the king into office was brief, relatively nonviolent, and full of hope; people of all stations of life had united to demand a more evenhanded government than had ruled under the Restoration of 1815–1830. Louis Philippe disappointed these hopes; he became the creature of stockbrokers and corrupt jurists. When the king called upon the aristocracy to lend their prestige to the new coterie of wealth, many of the old families refused to submit; they resigned the offices they had held under the previous regime, retired to their estates, or abstained from public involvements. This voluntary aristocratic withdrawal was called at the time an *émigration intérieure*. Its terms were quite different from the exile of aristocrats during the more radical Great Revolution of 1789–1794. Rather than the fear that drove their parents, these aristocrats were animated by disgust.

The *émigration intérieure* seemed at first sheer lunacy; no sane man voluntarily gives up power. But within a few years the public found the actions of the old families more understandable—especially the younger public. In France, as in England, Prussia, and America, the first signs of the new industrial era were making their impress on the consciousness of young people; the vacuity of living life as though it were an accountant's tally of gains and losses was beginning to affect their impressions of everyday life. Echoing the old nobles, they felt an ever-stronger desire to retreat from the world, even though the wealth of the new order furnished them, too, great opportunities. They sought sanctuary through a wilfull act of psychological withdrawal.

This generation of 1840 knew how to make signs of how estranged it felt: the shrug of irony about studies or careers, the jeer at the old men who, like the king, became pear-shaped from too much rich food and too little intellectual nutrition. Chronicles of ambition shifted from those of Balzac's young men to Flaubert's, from Balzac's depiction of Rastignac's passionate desire to conquer Paris, shaking his fist on the height of Montmartre at the glittering, inaccessible prizes below, to Flaubert's portrait of Frederic Moreau's ambivalence about similar desires. Frederic was a young man of the 1840s; he had learned he ought to at least show some shame about his strivings. He sought to understand his true self in those moments when he felt disgust with the world. However, unlike the *émigration intérieure* of the landed aristocrats of 1830, the affirmation of a decade later of one's inner integrity was burdened with a certain self-loathing. One was denying the circumstances of one's childhood, denying those parental dreams that in the early years sing as one's own truth. The psychological aristocrat was seldom at home in his own past. The search for a refuge ended in unease. There was no clarification in the withdrawal; one lost instead one's moorings.

It was this cultural difficulty of enacting sanctuary in a secular society which then appeared as a problem of visual design. Designing sanctuary posed a specific problem: how could the qualities of an immense structure like a cathedral be transposed to the scale of a house? More, the cathedral was a place of precision in a chaotic world; what rules of precision could provide people their moorings in a house? The importance of these questions to the Victorians continues today, both in a continuing puzzlement about the qualities of shelter in house design, and more broadly in how a building can serve as a means to its inhabitants' self-understanding. That, after all, was the promise made by the cathedral.

Medieval houses had few specialized rooms, for love or any other purpose. Even among the affluent the same room could serve as a place to eat, to defecate, to do business, and to sleep. The furniture necessary for each of these activities was carried in and out of a room, if light enough, or simply shoved against a wall when not in use. This pattern continued well into the eighteenth century for most rooms, though by the eighteenth century only the children of the poor continued to sleep in the same rooms where their parents slept and made love, as had been true more widely across the social spectrum before. Privies were in widespread daytime use by the middle of the eighteenth century, relegating the chamber pot to the necessities of the night, but people continued to urinate during the day within even grand houses or in courtyards wherever they found a seemingly suitable spot. The *ancien régime* house was like a covered street.

During the course of the nineteenth century, interior domestic designs more and more separated the members of families and hid away the necessities of the body inside the house. The house had its own division between public and private areas, between its parlors and its bedrooms. In houses that could afford many servants, the domestics were for the first time sequestered in their movements in the late-eighteenth-century townhouse through the construction of backstairs. The nursery was invented so that children had a place to play. If poor families acquired some increase in wealth, the changes they made in their houses mimicked these more affluent patterns: the houses were partitioned or enlarged by the addition of specialized rooms. Thus, in practice Ruskin's dream of the family kingdom meant that subjective experience was divided into domestic duchies: love, play, sociability, each with its own distinctive interior, each of these subjective spaces in turn removed from the spaces of the body—the kitchen, the toilet, the bathroom.

The domestic interior that became characteristic of industrial New York, the so-called railroad apartment constructed in a tenement building, exemplified this logic of division. In these apartments the rooms are in a line, their doors giving on a side corridor. Each room is neatly designated for a separate activity, a living room followed by a dining room, followed by a bedroom or bedrooms, and at the end a kitchen. Or nearly neatly. In its early, bourgeois form, the railroad flat doors were cut between certain of the rooms: living room and dining room, or living room and small parlor. The reason for this adduced at the time was not greater ease in communication but greater privacy; a person could move from the formal parlor to the informal sitting room without having to appear in the common space, which is the narrow side corridor.

In retrospect we see the tenement as a devil's construction. As these apartments were abandoned to the poor, each railroad flat became like a city of its own. The corridor became an internal street; families crowded into the individual rooms. In its original version, however, the tenement revealed why Ruskin's dream of sanctuary could not be brought to life by building a new kind of interior.

The public world of the street was harsh, crime ridden, cold, and above all, confused in its very complexity. The private realm sought order and clarity through applying the division of labor to the emotional realm of the family, partitioning its experience into rooms. The logic is one of breaking something into its component parts; then you know what it is. However, unlike the medieval discontinuity between chaos and clarity, the process of fragmentation begun in the public realm simply continued into the private sphere via the division of labor. Separation created isolation in the family as much as it did on the street.

The signs were evident to our forebears that they had failed to create the shelter they sought. A German critic of architecture writing in the 1850s, the first fervent decade in the worship of the domestic, put the matter emphatically about the divisive effect in old houses when cut up according to new principles:

Our private town-houses of the sixteenth and seventeenth centuries opened to the visitor at once larger areas, halls, and courts
. . . those large spaces were for the use of *all* the members of the
household . . . in the modern residences of the wealthy citizen,
however, all the spaces belonging to the *communality* of the
family and household have been reduced to the least possible
compass.[10]

In the words of a modern critic, the logic of enclosure and partition
did not "work to encourage domestic intimacy." The hearth was supposed to give warmth, yet the division of labor, embodied in the
interior as the search for ever more specific interiors for the various
forms of subjective life, gradually also cast its own chill. In this way
the visual clarification of the interior failed to provide sanctuary.

The home failed as a refuge in a second, equally consequent way.
It failed to keep out inequality. In church, all became equally worthy
of charity. The sacred interior expanded the moral value, as it were,
of those who were weak and poor. As "home" took form in the nineteenth century, women instead entered a kind of secular purdah that
would have been unthinkable and economically impracticable in earlier ages. Home was the moral refuge where women were secluded,
while men were permitted the street. It would be inaccurate, however, to conceive simply of men suffocating women within in the
interior. Women dominated women in the same way, forcing others
into an interior space.

Working-class women in London, for instance, could not afford to
dream Ruskin's dream. Domestic necessities like hanging out the
laundry took them into the streets. Poor women who worked shared
the pleasures of male laborers, drinking after work in cafés or pubs.
In the eyes of middle-class women, these laundresses, cleaners, and
seamstresses were exposed to moral as well as physical danger; moth-
ering would suffer from exterior exposure. Of the origin of the home
visit by social workers, Christine Stansell remarks that

---

[10] Donald J. Olsen, *The City as a Work of Art* (New Haven: Yale University Press, 1986), p. 102
for both his own and the contemporary's words. In the latter quote I have taken the liberty of
substituting *visitor* for *comer,* which was Professor Olsen's undoubtedly correct literal translation
of the German.

the ideology of domesticity thus provided the initial impetus for
what would become a class invention, the movement of reformers into the working-class neighborhoods and the households of
the poor between 1830 and 1860.[11]

The more generous-minded felt it only proper to intervene in the
lives of the poor to take them inside, into a sheltered domesticity,
where at last their lives would supposedly become more orderly.
Orderly, therefore moral. This dominion was far from the upheaval of
faith Jesus sought to arouse among the poor.

These were the two perverse consequences of the search for refuge
in secular society: an increase in isolation and in inequality. In the
modern industrial order, as it first took form in the nineteenth century, the labor process accentuated unequal, isolating divisions among
people. This process invaded the building of interior space. As a
result, there was ever greater *émigration intérieure* rather than *Gemeinschaft* in the home. Yet an important caveat needs to be entered,
if we are to understand the shadows the nineteenth century casts over
our own. Despite the intimate isolation, "The deep belief in the home
as the locus of moral reform remained unshaken."[12] In an article
called "A Further Notion or Two about Domestic Bliss" appearing in
Appleton's Journal in 1879, an angry writer declared that the home is
not a woman's

> retreat but her battleground, her arena, her boundary, her
> sphere. To a woman, the house is life militant; to a man, it is life
> in repose. . . . She has no other sphere for her activities. . . .
> Woman by the very necessities of her existence must have a
> different idea of home than what a man has.[13]

The interior is a compelling place because it is the place of truth, a
good housewife's place of truth as much as Sarah Bernhardt's. The

[11] Christine Stansell, *City of Women: Sex and Class in New York, 1789–1860* (New York:
Knopf, 1986; University of Illinois Press, 1987), p. 65.
[12] Gwendolyn Wright, *Moralism and the Model Home* (Chicago: University of Chicago Press,
1980), p. 292.
[13] Quoted in Ibid., p. 99.

rooms of her house appeared as a magnetizing "arena . . . boundary . . . sphere."

The belief that the interior is the true scene for inner life is a legacy, in secular society, of an older Christian ideal. But now this interior space of the soul had become a space for a new kind of inner life. The home has come to seem so necessary a refuge because of the modern secular idea of human character: that it is malleable, and that its most significant molding moments happen early in the life cycle. To mold a young human being, you must protect it from destructive outside influences. This belief, self-evident to us, was not at all self-evident to earlier ages, who practiced what would seem to us a shocking disregard of the young.

The fact that so many children died in the *ancien régime* before reaching adulthood had tended to mute intense feelings about them. With improvements in child care and through medical advances like vaccination, it had become less emotionally dangerous to care intensely about one's children. And economics dictated that one do so. In ages governed by the inheritance of property and place, bloodlines are how the family relations are impressed upon property, position, and power. Ruskin's was an age in which inheritance of social position and property had cracked apart; it was instead animated by entrepreneurial striving; the formation of that strength of aggressive, tough character in the male child was an urgent matter. Moreover, the length of time that both boys and girls seemed to need in order to develop themselves stretched out from ten years to twenty. The time of childhood was divided, like the space of the house, ever more elaborately. All the stages of human development seemed, by the time Freud wrote, to proceed in a gradual unfolding, physical, mental and psychological, each step consequent for the future.

The notion that character develops and reveals itself in an interior marked by the division of labor spoke logically in the nineteenth century from the new importance placed on childhood development; partitioned shelter was necessary for this prolonged, difficult, perilous process. By contrast, the mixed confusions of a crowd, a street, a smoke-filled bar, seemed no place for the protracted process of developing a baby into an adult. The stimulations of the street lacked the sequential order of the rooms of a house. Self-development and the exposure to the city's differences thus became opposed in visual terms: the linear, interior order of unfolding, distinct scenes as in a railroad flat, versus the outside chaos, the street like a collage; the shelter of the sequential versus exposure to the synchronous. As shall appear in a later chapter, we still see in terms of these oppositions.

In sum, the *émigration intérieure* was a voluntary withdrawal dictated by dislike of a shoddy, materialistic society. Saint-Simon's workroom was a place of social engagement in which laborers would show the dignity hidden beneath the grime. The home visitor sought to save the poor from moral ruin by stoking the fires of the hearth, while in her boudoir Madame Bernhardt luxuriated in the furnishings of depravity. Ruskin dreamed of an end to strife within the home. Orchardson's worldlings, who had doubtless spent evening after chaperoned evening in polite society, suddenly found at home that they were on the field of battle. Louis XIV showed himself to his people in paintings as Mars, even as Jove; Queen Victoria showed herself as a grandmother. Each of these reinforced the very value of the interior, charged it as a space of life. But the design was unequal to the culture's need, an interior which could not do the work of protecting and promoting inner life.

One could imagine how an early Christian would explain this gap between the powers of design and human needs. The antagonism felt in the first modern age of industry between the collage of the street and the serial unfolding of the interior reverberates with an ancient opposition between chaos and definition. However, an early Christian would read the modern design as bound to fail because our culture is in pursuit of self-development rather than a faith transcending the self.

Spaces of Authority

The other picture I found in the auction house seemed to have little to do with Orchardson's sketch. It was a yellowed photographic print, valuable only for its age, of the corner of Fifth Avenue and Twenty-first Street, a picture probably taken before 1893 and familiar to amateurs of New York history through Mary Black's classic compilation of photographs of old New York in the collection of the New-York Historical Society.[14]

This print simply shows a row of prosperous houses on the small Twenty-first Street capped at Fifth Avenue by the Union Club. This club was a ponderous, square edifice with Palladian windows marching in perfect order all around it. In the photograph, there is not a single person or animal visible on the street. Moreover, the blinds of the Union Club are drawn, their opaque, flat white seeming even more to shut out the gaze of the viewer from the dining and snoozing gentlemen within. The trees on Twenty-first Street are bare, and the townhouses visible must have been built as a block, for they are all alike.

The photograph, as I say, is well known, perhaps because this empty uniform street corner may arouse in many viewers, as it does in me, a strong response. Though there is just an ugly building at the corner of a street of locked doors, the scene is reassuring—solid and weighty. Of course, one shouldn't respond so. Here is the bourgeoisie triumphant; the absence of street life means they have kept out the masses choking in tenements only a few blocks away to the west, near the docks.

Here, also, was definition. The technical qualities of the photograph in part explain the viewer's response. Whoever took *The Union Club* (probably Samuel Marksville, a society photographer with a studio nearby at the time) was a master of his craft. The light on the buildings appears crisp, the camera has been well positioned to frame both corner and street, and the printing is excellent. Whereas, in my sketch, as in Orchardson's actual painting, the brushwork is bad, the composition sloppy. The visual contrast was suggestive: a well-defined exterior versus an ill-made interior. The resolution of the Union Club photograph was part of its comfort, whereas the sloppiness of the Orchardson sketch made for part of its disturbance. This contrast could have something to do with the subjects depicted: a scene of

[14] See Mary Black, *Old New York in Early Photographs, 1853–1901* (New York: Dover, 1973), plate 111, p. 131.

protection versus a scene of personal truth and desire. The clarity of
the photo makes one see the Union Club as a place that can be cut off
from the confusion, smoke, and noise of the city; the building's security against the city's complexity.

In a way, of course, the photo represents every portly burgher's
fantasy: you find sanctuary at your club rather than at home. Yet one
can make this photograph just as heavy as Orchardson's painting: here
is what authority looks like in modern urban space.

In a study of how people see the city of Boston, the urbanist Kevin
Lynch has asserted how important it is to "concentrate especially on
one particular visual quality: the apparent clarity of 'legibility' of the
cityscape." In *The Image of the City*, Lynch elaborated what he
meant by clarity, as follows:

> By this we mean the ease with which its parts can be recognized
> and can be organized into a coherent pattern. Just as this printed
> page, if it is legible, can be visually grasped as a relational pat-
> tern of recognizable symbols, so a legible city would be one
> whose districts or landmarks or pathways are easily identifiable
> and are easily grouped into an over-all pattern.[15]

He invoked the idea of "imageability" as a guide to what planners
should strive for, because in everyday life, he believed, people are
constantly struggling to take these clear photographs of urban scenes
for themselves. He asserted thirty years after his original study that

> people had [then in Boston, before its building boom] a rela-
> tively coherent and detailed mental image of their city, which
> had been created in an interaction between self and place, and
> this image was both essential to their actual function, and also to
> their emotional well-being.[16]

These assertions call upon the planner to set himself or herself against
towers equally buildable in Rangoon, Poitiers, or Boston. They seem

[15] Kevin Lynch, *The Image of the City* (Cambridge, Mass.: MIT Press, 1960), pp. 2–3.
[16] Kevin Lynch, "Reconsidering the Image of the City," in Lloyd Rodwin and Robert M. Hollister,
eds., *Cities of the Mind: Images and Themes of the City in the Social Sciences* (New York:
Plenum, 1984), p. 155.

to assert that the ills of the modern city can be remedied by defined imagery, the planner opposing his or her legible picture of what the city should look like to the "unintelligible mess," as Dickens long ago described London, an image in place of the "non-plan of the non-city," as Lewis Mumford has described the modern, expanding metropolis.[17]

The photograph of the Union Club makes evident the modern dimension of clarity. It shows a place from which the viewer was excluded; there was—to use Lynch's words—no "interaction between self and place here." Not a church, open to all, rather, an exclusive men's club. The very legibility of the photographic image contributes to the sealed qualities of the place.

It might seem easy to deduce, therefore, what a space of authority looks like. It might seem a place, scene, or image which radiates privilege. But this would be to commit a sociological error with one's eyes: it would make power and authority look the same.

In New York today the distinction between the way power and authority look can be seen in the design of that complex of skyscrapers which for fifty years has defined the modernity of the city: Rockefeller Center, built in the 1930s and 1940s by a team led by Raymond Hood. In drawings made for the Regional Plan Association in 1931, Hood, Hugh Ferriss, and Thomas Adams presented two alternatives for the increased growth of skyscrapers in New York. One drawing shows the towers of the city becoming so dense through random development that New York looks like an "artificial mountain range." The other illustrated what the members of the Regional Plan Association then preferred: the image of a controlled city in which the towers are kept distinct, the buildings clear in form when seen from any direction, the towers combining to form a logical whole rather than a disorderly mass. This is what Hood built.

Rockefeller Center's historian, Carol Krinsky, traces the "sobriety" of its forms in part to one of Hood's collaborators, Harvey Wiley Corbett. He had designed the criminal court buildings in the city and applied the same rules of monumental authority to the new center of the city, making the skins of both "vertically emphatic limestone piers

---

[17] Both quoted in William Sharpe and Leonard Wallock, eds., *Visions of the Modern City* (Baltimore: Johns Hopkins University Press, 1987), p. 17.

and dark spandrel strips."[18] The people drawn sociably to Rockefeller Center, particularly to its pedestrian mall and skating rink, are mostly tourists. The tourists are to be found at all hours in the esplanade above the skating rink. The scene here is lively enough, but its picture-postcard pleasures have not proved very attractive to natives; "sobriety" does indeed characterize the more ordinary, everyday life of the place. The superbly somber buildings are organized in such a way that their true center is behind the tourist's postcard front; this place is invisible from Sixth Avenue, difficult of access from Fifth; in this center in the very center of New York the snapping of flags flying in the breeze is audible. All around these structures in the heart of the city there is pressure, too many people walking too fast on the streets, yet the internal grounds of Rockefeller Center are seldom used as a shortcut. On its sides between Fifth and Sixth Avenues these superbly calibrated spaces are much more empty at night than streets north or south. Over the years there have been various proposals to bring the streets in and around Rockefeller Center to life at night. In New York, people on the streets are what keep streets safe, but even more, it has seemed a waste for the very center of the center of the city to go dead once working people go home. The design, however, has defeated these efforts to enliven the space; every temporary change seems to be a stamp without glue. In creating a masterpiece of precise and formal economy, Hood and his colleagues seemed to have made an abscess in the city.

Yet Rockefeller Center does not prompt the word that comes easily to mind in looking at much modern architecture. Rockefeller Center is not "inhuman." It is not experienced as a space of domination, it is not perceived by New Yorkers as a space of power. Like the Union Club, this much-loved ensemble instead arouses a sense of comfort. It is by walking from the deadly stillness of Rockefeller Center's side streets at midnight into the noise and hustle of Sixth Avenue that one feels suddenly exposed and vulnerable, even though the dark side streets are in fact more dangerous than the swarming open spaces around the nearby bars and hotels. What is most important about this

[18] Carol Krinsky, "Architecture in New York City, 1940–1965," in Leonard Wallock, ed., *New York: Culture Capital of the World, 1940–1965* (New York: Rizzoli, 1988), p. 91.

space is that it is empty—like the old Union Club. This visual emptiness arouses a peculiar sensation of authority.

The root Latin meaning of *auctoritas*, from which *authority* is derived, is protector, the guardian who cares for those who cannot care for themselves, or the advisor of those who are uncertain. Authority in this root sense is about much more than sheer domination; it implies the protection parents afford to children, the shelter laws provide to adults. In Roman times a protector like the emperor Augustus, far from being a humiliating figure of oppression, made it possible through his power for those who obeyed him to flourish. And conversely, a regime like that of the emperor Caligula, which failed to provide protection to those who obeyed its rules, was thought to have lost its authority even during the height of Caligula's power. Above all, authority, in the sense of a rule or judgment being considered authoritative, involves the establishment of values and meaning. Authority establishes the weight of what matters for those within its orbit. It is a formulation of conscience; one person or institution serves as the conscience for others. The history we have traced culminates in how authority is established visually today.

The space of authority, in Western culture, has developed as a space of precision: that is the guidance it gives to others. In the Christian cities were to be found the root of the desire for legibility that Kevin Lynch celebrated. Those who have dreamed Ruskin's dream or followed in the path of the first *émigrés intérieure* sought for this legibility in a domestic interior. Its sequence of spaces was to provide moral orientation: in a home, adults were to be disciplined in the same way as children in their rooms, trained how and where to separate the functioning of their bodies from contact with other people; how to make love in the silence and darkness of a room furnished to that end; how to behave when received into a parlor as opposed to a more informal sitting room. It might be said that those who sought to interiorize attempted to build a space of authority for themselves, and they failed.

Sacred interiors were spaces of the Word, of confession and prayer, of submission to God, who would, as Augustine first promised, protect his children. Precision and charity, definition and refuge were indissoluble. Today the secular space of authority is empty; it looks

like the side streets of Rockefeller Center, or the closed windows of
the Union Club. The visual forms of legibility in urban designs or
space no longer suggest much about subjective life or heal the wounds
of those in need. The sanctuary of the Christian city has been reduced
to a sense of comfort in well-designed places where other people do
not intrude. Safe because empty; safe because clearly marked. Authority is divorced from community: this is the conundrum of sanctuary as it has evolved in the city. Any New Yorker looks at this
conundrum when passing the city's most famous landmark, across
from Rockefeller Center.

St. Patrick's Cathedral in New York City is a twentieth-century copy
of a medieval original, or many medieval originals. St. Patrick's is
coated with flying buttresses, rose windows, elaborate carving
throughout in styles that hover around the Gothic but never quite
come to rest. The cathedral sits smack in the middle of New York,
occupying an entire city block, its raised parvis fronting on Fifth
Avenue. To the north, on Fifty-first and Fifth, stands Olympic Towers, a sleek, perfectly smooth box of black glass and steel rising sharply
some thirty stories. To the south of the cathedral, on Fiftieth and
Fifth, the windows of Saks Fifth Avenue department store are filled
with colorful swimsuits on the ever-trim bodies possible only for
mannequins. Across from the cathedral, Rockefeller Center's tourist
esplanade fronts on the parvis of the church. St. Patrick's Cathedral
is a massive medieval fantasy set inside a most modern box.

This confection cannot be said to be loved by all New Yorkers, at
least not by many who are black or sick. A generation ago the cathedral was the site of protests for racial civil rights. Many people then
felt the archdiocese of New York was not helping vigorously enough,
or at all, in the struggle of blacks to cross the bars of discrimination in
schools, in public places, and in the Catholic church itself. In this
generation the cathedral has become a place to protest the church's
response to AIDS, the disease of deficiencies in the immune system,
whose sufferers in New York are mostly homosexual men or drug
users. The current cardinal is a prominent opponent of the large
homosexual community in New York. His enemies charge that his
morality has led him to neglect charity—charity directly to the

patient, real concern for those who might be at risk of disease, since the cardinal refuses to encourage the use of condoms during sexual intercourse.

There are many spontaneous, disruptive events around and within the cathedral now. But there is also an annual march which passes in front of the cathedral; and, like the civil-rights marches of an earlier generation, it takes a more ritual form. A line of protesters parades down Fifth Avenue, the side streets cut off by police barricades behind which church supporters cheer and protesters heckle. In the old days the action behind these barricades was not pretty: racial insults were hurled at the marchers as they drew closer, block by block, to the cathedral, and frequently blacks and whites began to argue and sometimes fight behind the barricades while the police guarded marchers on the street. The annual parade on behalf of the sick is more decorous; behind the barricades there are signs like GOD HAS DECIDED YOU SHALL DIE! but little verbal exchange—there are no apparent grounds for discourse—and at the least sign of trouble the police are all over the troublemakers.

What occurs on the block in front of the cathedral is even more silence. Surprisingly so, since this is a moment of intense confrontation. The entire front of the church parvis stands guarded by a line of police officers, many of them mounted on horses, as is normal for this kind of work. The opposing face of Rockefeller Center is once a year cleared of tourists; Saks is deserted, as is the fashion store on the ground floor of Olympic Tower; the doormen of the tower have retreated within the lobby, their faces pressed against the smoked glass and dimly visible as patches of frightened white; the noise of the marchers five or six blocks to the north seems farther away.

In the civil rights marches, on a signal from the parade leader a group of blacks and whites turned toward the cathedral, knelt in the streets, and began to pray. In the annual AIDS march, at the signal a group of people with AIDS, their doctors and nurses, and their families turn their backs to the cathedral, sit in Fifth Avenue, observe a minute of silence, rise, and go on. During this minute what is most audible is the snorting of the police horses, or their hooves occasionally striking on the hot pavement.

But it is also in this moment once a year that St. Patrick's suddenly looks like a real medieval church. The police barricades seem to have cast the magic spell of the old zone of immunity, the empty streets around the cathedral seeming to transpose it into a space of its own—in the very center of the city but at this moment divorced from it. Olympic Tower, Saks Fifth Avenue, and Rockefeller Center fall away, no longer enclosing the Gothic front as the fourth side of a much-photographed square; the doormen behind the plate glass of the Olympic Tower lobby stare at a terrible drama far away. Suddenly one sees how high the cathedral is, whereas when traveling past it in a bus it looks like a toy dwarf amid the skyscrapers. For some reason, the days of protest during the civil rights marches seemed always days of intense sun, so that the play of light and shadow on the deep-carved front dramatized to the eye the cavernous relieving coolness within the doors of the locked cathedral. And the street filled then with black and white bodies praying, now with healthy and sick bodies contemplating, suggested even more that something was happening outside that was obscene when exposed to the sun, that these protesters should go inside, if only the doors were not shut, shut then in social distaste, now in moral revulsion; those in need belonged within.

It is, as I say, a moment like this when St. Patrick's becomes the church it looks like. The presence of authority is no empty gesture at this moment. It shows, as Augustine declared, the denouement of clarity and precision in submission to a higher, severe law. In the age of faith, you identified with a space in order to identify with another human being. You could see them, morally, only when they were exactly, correctly, placed in relation to you. Only those who believed were admitted within this space, and all those who entered submitted to its authority. The building of Augustine's city set culture upon a disastrous course in which the spiritual has become discontinuous with the physical. Nietzsche spoke of this divorce with wonder: "the strange contrast between an inner life to which nothing outward corresponds, and an outward existence unrelated to what is within."[19] Yet the cathedral is closed.

This is also why my photograph of a men's club on a shuttered

[19] Quoted in Erich Heller, *The Artist's Journey into the Interior* (New York: Harvest, 1965), p. 103.

street is both comforting and disturbing. The photographer has done the work of clarifying and resolving. Here is a space defined, by a lens, it is true, rather than in stone, but with the same aura of authority. Yet it is not by chance that this is the picture of an inaccessible interior, a scene of locked doors and closed blinds, like the cathedral uptown. Clear and closed. If the doors were opened, the picture might be out of focus.

chapter 2

The Neutral City

Nowhere

IN THE CANTERBURY TALES, Chaucer portrayed a priest who well understood the boundaries of his own faith:

> And though he hooly were and vertuous,
> He was to synful men nat despitous,
> Ne of his speche daungerous ne digne,
> But in his techung discreet and benygne.
>
> [And yet, though he himself was holy and virtuous,
> He was not contemptuous of sinners,
> Nor overbearing and proud in his talk,
> Rather, he was discreet and kind in his teaching.][1]

Chaucer meant to evoke a sense of place when he described the priest's virtues as those of a "good man of the church": they were the virtues of the parish rather than the virtues of the wandering mystic. Yet the Christian impulse to wander was not tamed by promises to bring the journey to an end in a refuge. There were those who remained ever restless in the spiritual quest. This inner turbulence

---

[1] Geoffrey Chaucer, *The Canterbury Tales*, ed. and trans. R. M. Lumiansky (New York: Pocket Books, 1971), original p. 357, translation p. 10.

41

denied them the comforts of the parish; more faith-hungry, their lives in the world were more unbounded, indeterminate. It was from this source of unhappy energy that, eventually, an unlikely logic of space would appear in secular society: the logic of neutral space. Nietzsche's perception of the Christian discontinuity between inner and outer life would take a new twist: the world would appear not as a veil of tears but as a silent wilderness.

This change in Christian imagery which appeared in the coming of Protestantism connects to a modern way of seeing. It is the way the planner sees who designs neutral, sterile environments. The planner never meant to, of course. Still, it is curious how the designers of parking lots, malls, and public plazas seem to be endowed with a positive genius for sterility, in the use of materials and in details, as well as in overall planning. This compulsive neutralizing of the environment is rooted in part in an old unhappiness, the fear of pleasure, which led people to treat their surroundings as neutrally as possible. The modern urbanist is in the grip of a Protestant ethic of space.

It may seem both fitting and odd to take the small band of American Puritans as first instances of this compulsion to neutralize. Odd, because the places in which the Puritans lived would have been instantly recognizable to their contemporaries as traditional European villages recreated in America, a nucleus of houses packed tight around a green. Beyond this traditional village the pastures and fields extended out to the township lines.

While they lasted, these nucleated villages were conceived as spiritual centers, the knot of faithful human beings tied tight in the wilderness. The Salem Village Church Covenant of 1689 states, in part:

> We resolve uprightly to study what is our duty, and to make it our grief, and reckon it our shame, whereinsoever we find our selves to come short in the discharge of it, and for pardon thereof humbly to betake our selves to the Blood of the Everlasting Covenant.
>
> And that we may keep this covenant, and all the branches of it inviolable for ever, being sensible that we can do nothing of

our selves, We humbly implore the help and grace of our Mediator may be sufficient for us.[2]

Yet the faithful were to find this tight knot of community to be choking. These pilgrims perhaps dared more than Chaucer's parish priest: they scorned security; the wilderness began to tempt them. In the late seventeenth century, therefore, the traditional village pattern started to give way; once the village nucleus was established, "In land division the settlers abandoned the conservatism which had characterized their street plans. The allotment of wilderness seemed to ridicule humble European field systems."[3] And by the eighteenth century these tight-knit villages had unraveled, as the bulk of the population moved out to live on the land they worked.

The lure of the wilderness had a spiritual meaning as well: The American Puritan imagined himself in need of removal from the Europe in which he was born because of the unhappy warfare within his breast. His salvation or damnation was predestined by God, who had also, with a twist of the divine knife, made it impossible for the Puritan to know whether he would be saved or damned. A Puritan was obliged, in the words of the American Puritan Cotton Mather, "to preach the unsearchable Riches of Christ." But a Puritan was also human: he was a man who wanted to know his fate, a man in search of evidence.[4] The world's daily sins and temptations were not within his power to control, and he lacked the Catholic relief of absolution for sin. Nothing could be known ultimately, nothing could be absolved—his God was like a sadistic Fortune. Conscience and pain became, therefore, inseparable companions. Perhaps the most graphic expression of this inner conflict was a popular poem of the early seventeenth century by George Goodwin, which reads in part:

I sing my self; my civil wars within;
The victories I hourly lose and win;

[2] Reprinted in Charles B. Rice, *Proceedings at the Celebration of the Two Hundredth Anniversary of the First Parish at Salem Village* (Boston, 1874), p. xxv.
[3] Anthony N. B. Garvan, *Architecture and Town Planning in Colonial Connecticut* (New Haven: Yale University Press, 1951), p. 52.
[4] Quoted in Kenneth Silverman, *The Life and Times of Cotton Mather* (New York: Columbia University Press, 1985), p. 24.

> The daily duel, the continual strife,
> The war that ends not, till I end my life.[5]

From such misery the Puritan was tempted by the wilderness, by a place of emptiness which made no seductive demands of its own upon him, in order that he try to get his life under control, however forlorn that hope. Cotton Mather's father, Increase Mather, one of the first generation of Puritans to set sail, wrote the following on the title page of his diary:

> Give me a Call
> To dwell
> Where no foot hath
> A Path
> There will I spend
> And End
> My wearied years
> In tears[6]

Mundane labels like "the first colonists" or "English adventurers" don't account for the motives that would drive people to make hazardous voyages to a cold, mosquito-infested, rocky landscape to live out their lives. The first settlers were ravaged human beings. They suffered the dual need to "get away from it all" in order to attempt to "get control of their lives." It was an early sign of a duality in modern society: flight from others occurs for the sake of self-mastery.

In that flight are to be found the seeds of certain of our own attitudes about the physical environment. The churches in the centers of traditional European villages and towns made evident to the eye where to find God. These centers defined a space of recognition. God is legible: he is within, within the sanctuary as within the soul. On the outside there is only exposure, disorder, and cruelty. The

[5] George Goodwin, "Auto-Machia"; this version, with modern spelling and without Goodwin's capitalization and italics, is adapted from the original reprinted in Sacvan Bercovitch, *The Puritan Origins of the American Self* (New Haven: Yale University Press, 1975), p. 19.
[6] Increase Mather, *A Sermon concerning Obedience,* in "The Autobiography of Increase Mather," ed. Michael G. Hall, *Proceedings of the American Antiquarian Society* (1961): 352.

Puritan "inside" was illegible, a place of war, conscience at war with itself; this terrible business of "finding oneself" only becomes more confusing if the outside, other people, other confusions intrude. The Spaniard came to the New World as a lord, conversion, and conquest all of a piece; he came as a Catholic. The Puritan came as a refugee; conversion was a duty, conquest a necessity for survival, but neither was his reason for coming. Yet this search for refuge produced a vision of the outside different from the pleasure-filled, violent, bear-baiting outside of the medieval Catholic town. The place the Puritans arrived at had to be treated like a blank canvas for the double compulsion to play itself out, for a man or woman to get more self-control by starting over somewhere else.

Language frequently failed the people embarked on this purifying experiment to conjure what passed within their breasts. The failure of words to reveal the soul was tied to a heightened self-awareness in an immense, alien place. Lacking a language adequate to inner experience, the life of each would be more and more locked within, impossible to declare, perhaps at best intimated by the rendering of an impression. The inner space of medieval Catholicism was physical, it was a space people could share. The inner space of Puritanism was the space of the most radical individualism and was impalpable. The Puritan eye could only see within itself. Outside there was nothing. It exists, this wilderness self, in the space Beckett imagined in *Endgame* or *Waiting for Godot*, an empty space in a time without narrative. If the strange creatures who were American Puritans thus gave the first signs of a certain form of modern sensibility, they also suggested what would be its environmental consequences.

The search for physical sanctuary expressed, as we have seen, a desire to place oneself in the hands of authority. The Protestant imagination of space, on the contrary, expressed a desire for power. Most obviously, a kind of egoistic power. Obsessive inner struggle may imply a deep hostility toward the needs of other people, a resentment of their very presence. Others interfere; to get in control of oneself, nothing "out there" can count. This hostility marks now the way the homeless or mentally disturbed are seen on the streets; they are resented because they, who are obviously needy, are visible. The very sight of their need is an intrusion upon the self. To ward them off, one wants to treat the outside as neutral; then one is alone with oneself at last. But neutrality can organize power in a more systematic way, one which more deeply implicates the eye.

The cultural problems of the city are conventionally taken to be its impersonality, its alienating scale, its coldness. There is more in these charges than is first apparent. *Impersonality, coldness,* and *emptiness* are essential words in the Protestant language of environment; they express a desire to see the outside as null, lacking value. They are words that express a certain interest in seeing; the perception of outer emptiness reinforces the value of turning within. Certainly one does not imagine a shopping-mall designer wracked by Cotton Mather's anguish. But that old unhappiness has left its residue as a certain practice of visual denial, as the acceptance of sensory denial in everyday life to be normal. More than normal—reassuring. Nothing as important as the inner struggle to account. Therefore, one can deal with the outside in purely instrumental, manipulative terms, since nothing outside "really" matters. In this modulated form, neutrality becomes an instrument of power. I should like to show how this instrument can be wielded by looking at the modern forms of an ancient urban design.

The Grid

The Egyptian hierograph that the historian Joseph Rykwert believes was one of the original signs for a town is

transcribed as "nywt."[7] This hierograph, a cross within a circle, suggests two of the simplest, most enduring urban images. The circle is a single, unbroken closed line: it suggests enclosure, a wall or a space like a town square; within this enclosure, life unfolds. The cross is the simplest form of distinct compound lines: it is perhaps the most ancient object of environmental process, as opposed to the circle, which represents the boundary defining environmental size. Crossed lines

---

[7] Joseph Rykwert, *The Idea of a Town: The Anthropology of Urban Form in Rome, Italy and the Ancient World* (Cambridge, Mass.: MIT Press, 1988), p. 192.

represent an elemental way of making streets within the boundary, through making grids.

The Babylonians and the ancient Egyptians made cities by planning straight streets to meet at right angles, thus creating regular, repeating blocks of land on which to build. Hippodamus of Miletus is conventionally thought the first city builder to conceive of these grids as expressions of culture; the grid expressed, he believed, the rationality of civilized life. In their military conquests the Romans elaborated the contrast between the rude and formless camps of the barbarians and their own military forts, or *castra*. The Roman camps were laid out as squares or rectangles. The perimeter was at first guarded by soldiers, and then, as the camp grew into a permanent settlement, the four sides were walled. When first established, a *castrum* was divided inside into four parts by two axial streets, the *decumanus* and the *cardo*; at the meeting point of these two principal streets the principal military tents were placed in the early stages of settlement, and later the forum was placed just to the north of the crossing. If the encampment did indeed prosper, the spaces between the perimeter and the center were gradually filled up by repeating the overall idea of axes and centers in miniature. For the Romans, the point of these rules was to create cities on the pattern of Rome itself; wherever in the world a Roman lived, the Roman soldier was at home.

In its origins the grid established a spiritual center. "The rite of the founding of a town touches on one of the great commonplaces of religious experience," Joseph Rykwert writes in his study of the Roman city; the ancient writer Hyginus Gromaticus believed that the priests inaugurating a new Roman town must place the first axis in the cosmos, for "Boundaries are never drawn without reference to the order of the universe, for the *decumani* are set in line with the course of the sun, while the *cardines* follow the axis of the sky."[8]

In the subsequent history of Western urbanism, the grid has been of special use in starting new space or in renovating existing space devastated by catastrophe. All the schemes for rebuilding London after the Great Fire of 1666, Robert Hooke's, John Evelyn's, and

[8] Ibid., p. 90.

Christopher Wren's, made use of the Roman grid form; these schemes influenced Americans like William Penn in conceiving of making a city from scratch. Nineteenth-century America seems a whole nation of cities created on the principles of the Roman military camp, and the American example of "instant cities" in turn influenced new city building in other parts of the world. No physical design, however, dictates a permanent meaning. Grids, like any design, can become whatever particular societies make them represent. If the Romans saw the grid as an emotionally charged design, the Americans were the first to use it for a different purpose: to deny that complexity and difference existed in the environment. The grid has been used in modern times as a plan that neutralizes the environment. It is a Protestant sign for the neutral city.

The Roman military city was conceived to develop in time within its boundary; it was designed to be filled in. The modern grid was meant to be boundless, to extend block after block after block outward as the city grew. In contriving the grid plan of 1811 which has since determined modern Manhattan above Greenwich Village, the planning commissioners acknowledged, "It may be a subject of merriment, that the Commissioners have provided space for a greater population than is collected at any spot on this side of China."[9] But just as Americans saw the natural world around them as limitless, they saw their own powers of conquest and habitation as subject to no natural or inherent limitation. The conviction that people can infinitely expand the spaces of human settlement is the first way, geographically, of neutralizing the value of any particular space.

The Romans imagined from the sense of a distinct, bounded whole how to generate a center, at the intersection of the *decumanus* and the *cardo*, and then how to create centers for each neighborhood by imitating this crossing of principal axes in each subsection. The Americans tended more and more to eliminate the public center, as in the plans for Chicago devised in 1833 and those for San Francisco in 1849 and 1856, which provided only a handful of small public spaces within thousands of imagined blocks of building. Even when the desire for a center existed it was difficult to deduce where public places should be, and how they should work, in cities conceived like a map of

[9] "Commissioners' Remarks," quoted in William Bridges, *Map of the City of New York and Island of Manhattan* (New York: n.p., 1811), p. 30.

limitless rectangles of land. The humane civic spaces in colonial Phil-
adelphia created by William Penn and Thomas Holme, or at the
opposite pole, the brutal slave-market squares of antebellum
Savannah—both workable spaces for organized crowd life—faded as
models during the era when vast sums were poured into urban development. The loss of a center is the second geographic way an
urban space is neutralized.

The American grids imposed, it is true, a certain intensification of
value at the intersections of streets rather than in the middle of
blocks; in modern Manhattan, for instance, tall buildings in residential neighborhoods are permitted at the corners, whereas the middle
of the block is kept low. But even this pattern, when repeated often
enough, loses the power of designating the character of specific places
and of their relationship to the larger city.

Perhaps the most striking grids made in this fashion were in the
southern rim of settlement in America, in the cities developed under
Spanish rule or influence. On July 3, 1573, Philip II of Spain laid
down a set of ordinances for the creation of cities in his New World
lands, the "Law of the Indies." The key provision is the decree that
towns take form through the planning of their centers, a decree the
king expressed simply and rigorously:

> The plan of the place, with its squares, streets, and building lots
> is to be outlined by means of measuring by cord and rule, be-
> ginning with the main square from which streets are to run to
> the gates and principal roads and leaving sufficient open space so
> that even if the town grows it can always spread out in a sym-
> metrical manner.[10]

Beginning with cities like St. Augustine, Florida, this royal decree
was meticulously obeyed, as it was along the entire Spanish rim
during the course of nearly three centuries. An early plan for Los
Angeles in 1781 would have looked familiar to Philip II or for that
matter, to Julius Caesar. Then, suddenly, with the coming of rail-
roads and massive doses of capital looking for a home, there came a

[10] "Royal Ordinances concerning the Laying Out of New Towns," trans. Zelia Nuttall, quoted in
John Reps, *The Making of Urban America* (Princeton: Princeton University Press, 1965), p. 29.

break in towns on the Spanish rim with the principles enunciated in the "Law of the Indies." The square ceased to be a center; it no longer was a reference point in generating new urban space. Town squares became random dots amidst the block after block of building plots, as in a plan for Santa Monica as part of the "new" Los Angeles in 1875, and then entirely disappeared, as when the "new" Los Angeles on paper became a fact a generation later.

The twentieth century completed both these geographic processes at work in the making of grids, even when development occurred by building a thousand houses along arbitrarily twisting streets, or by digging out lumps of industrial park, office campus, and shopping mall on the edges of highways. In the development of the modern "megalopolis," it has become more reasonable to speak of urban "nodes" than of centers and suburbs. The very fuzziness of the word *node* indicates the loss of a language for naming environmental value: *center* is charged with meanings both historical and visual, while *node* is resolutely bland.

This American pattern is in many ways the extreme toward which other forms of new development tend; the same kind of settlement has occurred in Italy and France, in Israel, in Russia beyond the Urals. In all of these, development lacks a logic of its own limits and of form established within boundaries; the results of amorphous building are places without character. The grid in particular doesn't, as I say, "cause" this blandness; neutrality can take the form of an endless city of regularly intersecting lines or winding housing developments, shopping strips, and clots of offices or factories. But the recent history of the grid reveals how modern neutrality is constituted, as a Protestant language of self and space becomes a modern form of power.

In April 1791, Pierre Charles L'Enfant was courageously engaged in combating Thomas Jefferson's plan to create the new American capital according to a gridiron plan. L'Enfant wrote to President Washington:

> Such regular plans . . . become at last tiresome and insipid and
> it [the grid] could never be in its origin but a mean continuance

of some cool imagination wanting a sense of the real grand and truly beautiful.[11]

A capital should reverberate with symbolic power, and L'Enfant imagined the regularities of the grid as empty of such reverberations. The century after L'Enfant was to show, however, that grids would organize power precisely by stripping away the character of a place.

A generation after L'Enfant, the young Alexis de Tocqueville's family were among the band of aristocrats of 1830 who refused to participate in the new regime, and made the *émigration intérieure*. He arranged his famous voyage to America as a way out of his own difficulties in taking the regime's oath of loyalty. He saw this new, character-less form of power in the making when making his first visit to New York.

In his time the usual way for a foreigner to journey to New York was to sail into the harbor from the south, a route that afforded the voyager a sudden view of the crowd of masts along the packed wharves, which spread to offices, homes, churches, and schools. This New World scene appeared to be a familiar European one of prosperous mercantile confusion, like Antwerp or the lower reaches of London on the Thames. Tocqueville instead approached New York from the north, through Long Island Sound. His first view of Manhattan was its bucolic upper reaches, still in 1831 pure farmland dotted with a few hamlets. At first what excited him about the view of the city was the sudden eruption of a metropolis in the midst of a nearly pristine natural landscape. He felt the enthusiasm of a European coming here who imagines he can plant himself in this unspoiled landscape just as the city was planted, that America is fresh and simple and Europe is stale and complex. And then, after that fit of youthful enthusiasm passed, New York began to disturb him, as he later wrote to his mother. No one seemed to take where they lived seriously, to care about the buildings in which they hurried in and out; instead the city was treated simply by its cit-

---

[11] Pierre Charles L'Enfant, "Note relative to the ground lying on the eastern branch of the river Potomac. . . ," undated but necessarily written between April 4, when Washington forwarded Jefferson's ideas to L'Enfant, and April 10, 1791, when Jefferson accepted L'Enfant's control of the planning of the new national capital. Text reproduced in E. L. Kite, *L'Enfant and Washington, 1791–1792* (Baltimore: Johns Hopkins University Press, 1929), pp. 47–48.

izens as a complicated instrument of offices and restaurants and shops for the conduct of business. Throughout his American journey Tocqueville was struck by the bland and insubstantial character of American settlement. Houses seemed mere stage sets rather than buildings meant to last; there seemed nothing permanent in the environment. The reason was that these "new men" were too driven to settle, too driven for stone. They wanted nothing to get in their way.

The grid can be understood, in these terms, as a weapon to be used against environmental character—beginning with the character of geography. In cities like Chicago the grids were laid over irregular terrain; the rectangular blocks obliterated the natural environment, spreading out relentlessly no matter that hills, rivers, or forest knolls stood in the way. The natural features that could be leveled or drained, were; the insurmountable obstacles that nature put against the grid, the irregular course of rivers or lakes, were ignored by these frontier city planners, as if what could not be harnessed to this mechanical, tyrannical geometry did not exist.

Often, this relentless imposition of a grid required a willful suspension of the logical faculties. In Chicago the grid created immense problems of transport across the river that cuts through the center of the city; the lines of the streets suddenly end at one river bank only to continue on the other side, as though the river were spanned by innumerable, if invisible, bridges. A visitor to the new town of Cincinnati noticed in 1797 the "inconvenience" of applying the grid to a similar river topography; further,

> if they had made one of their principal streets to face the river and the other at the brow of the second bank . . . the whole town would have presented a noble appearance from the river.[12]

Cincinnati bore an ancient name but was no Greek city; these urban plans imposed arbitrarily on the land rather established an interactive, sustaining relation to it.

Though it is one of the oldest cities in America, New York's plan-

---

[12] Francis Baily, *Journal of a Tour in Unsettled Parts of North America in 1796 and 1797* (London: n.p., 1856), p. 226, quoted in Richard Wade, *The Urban Frontier* (Cambridge, Mass.: Harvard University Press, 1959), pp. 24–25.

ners treated it during the era of high capitalism as if it, too, were a city on the frontier, a place required to deal with the physical world as an enemy. The planners imposed a grid at one blow in 1811 upon Manhattan from Canal Street, the edge of dense settlement, up to 155th Street, and then in a second stroke in 1870 to the northern tip. They imposed the grid more gradually in Brooklyn east from its old harbor. Settlers on the frontier, whether from fear or simple greed, treated native Americans as part of the landscape rather than as fellow human beings; on the frontier nothing existed—it was a void to be filled up. Planners could no more see life outside the grid in New York than they could in Illinois. The farms and hamlets dotting nineteenth-century Manhattan were expected to be engulfed rather than incorporated as the grid on paper became building in fact; little adaptation of the plan was made in that process, even when some more flexible arrangement of streets would make better use of a hill or better suit the vagaries of Manhattan's water table. And, inexorably, development according to the grid did abolish whatever existing settlement was encountered. In this neoclassical age, the nineteenth-century planners could have built as Romans, or nearer at hand, like William Penn, laying out squares or establishing rules for where churches, schools, and markets were to go. The land was available, but they were not so minded. Instead, they aggressed against the environment; their victories lay in neutralizing it.

There is a closer connection between neutralizing space and economic development. The New York commissioners declared that "right angled houses are the most cheap to build, and the most convenient to live in."[13] What is unstated here is the belief that uniform units of land are also the easiest to sell. This relationship between the grid city and capitalist economics has been stated at its broadest by Lewis Mumford thus:

The resurgent capitalism of the seventeenth century treated the individual lot and the block, the street and the avenue, as abstract units for buying and selling, without respect for historic uses, for topographic conditions or for social needs.[14]

[13] "Commissioner's Remarks," p. 25.
[14] Lewis Mumford, *The City in History* (New York: Harcourt Brace Jovanovich, 1961), p. 421.

In the history of nineteenth-century New York, the matter was in fact more complicated because the economics of selling land were very different in New York in 1870 than they were in 1811. The city at the beginning of the century was a dense cluster of buildings set in the wilderness. Land sales were of empty space. After the Civil War they were of places that would soon fill up. To sell land profitably required a social reckoning: where people should live, where transport should most efficiently be located, where factories should go. Looking at a map that shows only blocks all of the same size answers few of these questions. The grid was rational as an urban design only in an abstract, Cartesian sense. And, therefore, as was true of investments in rails and industry, the latter economic history of the grid is as much the story of disastrous investments as of large profits. Those who sought to profit from a neutral environment shared the same necessarily blank consciousness of its character as those like L'Enfant who hated it.[15]

The economic history of the grid points to a simple, large truth. Possessing power is quite different than using it to one's own advantage. This large, simple truth is important in understanding the power to neutralize a city. Those who could do so were disturbed in their pursuits by a set of difficulties inherent in the very act of treating the world neutrally. These difficulties the sociologist Max Weber took up in his famous study of the "Protestant ethic." Weber connected self-doubt of the sort the Puritan felt to competition with others; he sought to explain how in winning against others a person wanted to prove something about his own worth. But then, Weber thought, the truly hard-driving competitor is afraid to enjoy what he has gained: he is aggressive in making money and then denies himself its use for comfort, elegance, and amusement. "Christian asceticism," Weber wrote in *The Protestant Ethic and the Spirit of Capitalism,*

> at first fleeing from the world into solitude, had already ruled the world which it had renounced from the monastery and

[15] Though notes in this book are restricted to giving the sources for quotations, the reader interested in the irrational course that was the actual process of "the logic of capitalism" might want to read Peter Marcuse, "The Grid as City Plan: New York City and Laissez-faire Planning in the Nineteenth Century," *Planning Perspectives* 2 (1987), 287–310.

through the Church. But it had, on the whole, left the naturally spontaneous character of daily life in the world untouched. Now it strode into the marketplace of life, slammed the door of the monastery behind it, and undertook to penetrate just that daily routine of life with its methodicalness, to fashion it into a life in the world, but neither of nor for this world.[16]

Christianity, that is, thus took to the streets to find its truths. Perhaps people might make gains in this world that would bear on their life in the next. Just before he wrote *The Protestant Ethic and the Spirit of Capitalism,* Weber traveled to the United States, in the age in which the Vanderbilts had dinners for seventy served by seventy powdered footmen. The luxury-loving capitalists of Weber's day seemed to him an aberration of the species. Instead, he thought, economic drive was much more connected to questions of identity, questions first raised by the Puritans and other Protestant sects. The ghost from the past hovered: Who is worthy? This contains the hidden question Who is worthier?, which was answered by the believer and the hard-driving businessman alike: the worthiest person is the least self-indulgent.

The story the Protestant ethic tells is not a happy one. It is a story about value scarcity: there is not enough worth to go around. More-over, one might go soft and lose control if one stops struggling—and so to prevent this, one treats things and other people as instruments of one's own drives and needs. In themselves they are nothing. Yet the result of this instrumental relation to the world is ever greater confusion about the purposes and the value of what one is doing.

And here is where the grid found its place. It was a space for economic competition, to be played upon like a chessboard. It was a space of neutrality, a neutrality achieved by denying to the environment any value of its own. And, like the Pyrrhic victory earned by the person who competes and wins only to feel he or she has not yet achieved enough, the grid disoriented those who played upon it; they could not establish what was of value in places without centers or boundaries, spaces of endless, mindless geometric division. This was the Protestant ethic of space.

---

[16] Max Weber, *The Protestant Ethic and the Spirit of Capitalism,* as translated by Martin Green and quoted in Martin Green, *The Von Richthofen Sisters* (New York: Basic Books, 1974), p. 152.

Whenever Americans of the era of high capitalism thought of an alternative to the grid, they thought of bucolic relief, such as a leafy park or a promenade, rather than a more arousing street, square, or center in which to experience the complex life of the city. The nineteenth-century construction of Central Park in New York is perhaps the most bitter example of this alternative, an artfully designed natural void planned for the city's center in the expectation that the cultivated, charming territory already established around it—as bucolic and refreshing a scene as any city-dweller could wish for within a few minutes drive from his house—would be razed to the ground by the encroachments of the grid.

Its designers Frederick Law Olmsted and Calvert Vaux wanted themselves to obliterate the simplest reminder that Central Park was located in the midst of a thriving metropolis. This reminder would occur, for instance, in seeing or hearing the traffic crossing it. These Americans therefore built contrary to the makers of the Bois de Boulogne, who made traversing the Bois a pleasure, even for those who had business that required the journey. Olmsted and Vaux hid such people away, literally: they buried the traffic routes in channels below the grade of the Park. In their own words, these roads are to

> be sunk so far below the surface. . . . The banks on each side will be walled up to the height of about seven feet . . . and a little judicious planting on the tops or slopes of the banks above these walls will, in most cases, entirely conceal both the roads and the vehicles moving in them, from the view of those walking or driving in the park.[17]

These, then, were the dualities of denial: to build you act as though you live in emptiness; to resist the builder's world you act as though you do not live in a city.

Some of this denial of meaning to the built environment has a uniquely American source, derived from the sheer visceral impress of our natural landscape made upon all those who traveled in it, Americans and visitors alike. This natural world once was immense, un-

[17] Frederick Law Olmsted, "Description of a Plan for the Improvement of the Central Park, 'Greensward,' 1858," in Frederick Law Olmsted, Jr., and Theodora Kimball, Frederick Law Olmsted (New York: n.p., 1928), p. 214.

framed, boundless. The impress of a boundless world comes clear, for instance, in comparing an American painting of wilderness, John Frederick Kensett's *View near West Point on the Hudson* of 1863 to Corot's *Souvenir of Volterra* of 1838, two paintings organized around roughly similar views. What we see in Kensett's painting is limitless space, a view bursting its frame, our eyes going and going and going without obstruction. All the rocks, trees, and people in the painting are deprived of substance because they are absorbed into immensity. Whereas in Corot's painting, we feel the vivid presence of specific things in a bounded view, or, as one critic puts it "a solid architecture of rocks and even of foliage to measure the deep space."[18] It seemed that only the most arbitrary imposition could tame American vastness: an endless, unbounded grid. This effort of will, however, rebounded: the arbitrary spoiled what it tamed, the grid seemed to render space meaningless—and so sent an eye like Olmsted's searching for a way to recover the value of nature seemingly free of the visible presence of man.

In a classic American text of our Western movement, the novel *The Little House on the Prairie*, the family uproots every time another house becomes visible on the horizon, without anyone in the family being able to explain why another rooftop is an intolerable sight, and yet they all feel threatened, they keep moving. Only without interference from others can the psyche wrestle itself. Later observers who wondered at the relentless push westward of people who could have been richer, and more content, cultivating what they already possessed, were observing the secular, environmental refinement of the Protestant ethic—the inability to believe that whatever is, is sufficient.

This may seem a special story, limited to nineteenth-century American practices and perceptions geographically. The twentieth century, however, also deploys the grid. It is vertical and more universal; it is the skyscraper. The older geographic modes reappear in this architectural form. More, it is in the building of skyscrapers that the cracks became evident in the edifice of neutralizing power.

[18] John W. McCoubrey, *American Tradition in Painting* (New York: George Braziller, 1963), p. 29.

In cities of skyscrapers, Hong Kong as much as New York, it is impossible to think of the vertical slices above street level as having an inherent order, like the intersection of *cardo* and *decumanus*; one cannot point to activities that ought particularly to happen on the sixth floor of buildings. Nor can one relate visually sixth floors to twenty-second floors as opposed to twenty-fifth floors in a building. Nor do skyscrapers have the necessary height. The vertical grid lacks definitions of both significant placement and closure.

The tall building sliced into stories depends upon the elevator as a means of internal transport. The elevator has existed since 1846. Originally, it was a platform within a vertical frame, rising or descending by the operator's manipulation of counterweights built within the frame, and that original idea has endured. In 1853 in the Latting Observatory in New York, steam was employed to push and pull on the counterweights; the Dakota Apartments in New York and the Connaught Hotel in London used water-hydraulics instead of metal chains a generation later; the most modern elevators use magnetic calibration to regulate the force exerted on the weights in terms of the mass of people within the elevator, so that speed is always constant. The biggest innovation in this machine was making it safe when it failed to work; this honor fell to Elisha Graves Otis in 1857. His Haughwout building in New York contained an elevator fitted with automatic brakes; in case of loss of energy, the brakes would lock the elevator cab to the guide rails.

Yet, as the architectural critic Ada Louise Huxtable has remarked, modern tall buildings have not for the most part explored the possibilities of being tall: "Today architects are looking at some very big buildings in some very small ways. The larger the structure, the less inclination there seems to be to come to grips with the complexities of its condition and the dilemma it creates."[19] The reasons for this have in part to do with commerce, and also in part with visual design. Skyscraper designers have focused their expressive energies on the exterior forms and upon the skin of the tall building at the expense of experimenting with inner volumes.

The elevator was the necessary but not the sufficient condition for the creation of the tall building. What made these buildings feasible

[19] Ada Louise Huxtable, *The Tall Building Artistically Reconsidered* (New York: Pantheon, 1984), p. 9.

was the extensive use of metal framing. The quickness of this kind of construction was first demonstrated in the London Crystal Palace of 1851, where a building larger in volume than Chartres cathedral was designed by Joseph Paxton in a few weeks and put up in a few months; the cast-iron frame held panels of glass used instead of bricks and tiles for both walls and ceilings. The early skyscraper makers put this technology to vertical use, but not quite confidently. The Monadnock Building in Chicago, for instance, was a metal-framed structure that continued to use masonry bearing walls. The economical use of steel in construction inspired a greater confidence in the frame, as more recently reinforced concrete did, and so freed the wall as a medium for experiment. This freedom gradually engaged the creative attention of the makers of skyscrapers much more than the volumetric possibilities opened up by the elevator. This century has seen experiment in the skins of buildings, and increasing uniformity in the inhabited spaces within the building itself, which consists of repeating open floors served by a central service stack. They are big but simple structures.

From the vantage point of non-Western concepts of space, easy mechanical levitation may, in itself, seem to destroy the meaning of height. In making the contrast between Japanese and modern Western concepts of "high," the architect Arata Isozaki believes the Western eye fails to see the ethical possibilities of this dimension:

> The raised wooden floor is a clean, artificially created surface isolated from the earth, a surface on which people can sit without concern. Unlike the Japanese wooden floor, the upper stories that have not been part of Western homes from early times are not a surface in a completely different phase. Although these upper-story rooms are far removed from the surface of the earth, shoes are worn in them; and chairs, tables, shelves, beds and so on are essential because the floor is "unclean."[20]

His image of Western notions of height as agelessly different from the Japanese is not quite right. The religious height of the medieval city

---

[20] Arata Isozaki, "Floors and Internal Spaces in Japanese Vernacular Architecture," *Res* 11 (Spring 1986), p. 65.

was sacred because it pointed up to the kingdom of God; it was both physical and spiritual orientation. Were a medieval builder transported in a time machine to a modern skyscraper, he would find it profoundly, disturbingly profane, the sanctity of the vertical dimension contaminated simply by becoming instantly accessible. But the articulations of modern height are not of unclean values, as the Japanese architect fears, nor of the worldly clamor of the street brought within a church, as a medieval builder would. Instead, "up" means "neutral." Skyscraper height lacks the symbolic value either of the Japanese house or the medieval church.

Gridded space does more than create a blank canvas for development. It subdues those who must live in the space, but disorienting their ability to see and to evaluate relationships. In that sense, the planning of neutral space is an act of dominating and subduing others. But the visual designer will do so, not with a sense of Machievellian cunning, but in a more self-conflicted way.

For instance, by the time homes for families were built in vertical grids, their makers felt that something was wrong. In New York, moreover, the apartment house aroused echoes from a peculiar past, the use families made in the nineteenth century of hotels as semi-permanent residences. Such families wandered from hotel to hotel, the children only occasionally allowed to run in the corridors, the families dining in the same large rooms with commercial travelers and foreigners and unknowable women. But, more generally, planners had come to believe that vertical structures were inherently neutral, and so "inhumane," forms that provided shelter in its full meaning. An editorial in the New York *Independent* newspaper argued in 1902 what was coming to be felt by the garden city planning movement in England, and by socialist planners under the sway of face-to-face community ideals in France and Germany, namely, that large apartment houses destroy "neighborhood feeling, helpful friendships, church connections and those homely common interests which are the foundations of civic pride and duty." In New York this view was codified in the Multiple Dwelling House Act of 1911, which treated all apartment buildings as similar in social function to hotels; the "lack of fundamentals on which a home was founded" could be perceived, as late as 1929 in one of the first books on apartment house architecture, to derive from "a building of six, nine, or fifteen stories, where the plan of one floor is repeated exactly throughout the entire building; individuality is practically non-existent."[21] A skyscraper is no place for Ruskin's dream.

The commonsense view of an evil is that when people become conscious of it they react against it. A more realistic account is that people act out the evils they discover. They know what they are doing is wrong and yet they move closer and closer to making it happen, in order to see if what they think or perceive is real. Certainly this is true in our time among those who have built vertical grids for families. It was with a fear in their minds of the loss of family values in neutral, impersonal spaces that many architects and planners in the 1930s built the great housing projects that would eventually realize these very fears. In the same way, housing projects meant for the poor, like those along Park Avenue in Harlem in New York, have been designed according to the principles of the unbounded, amorphous grid. Everything is graded flat; there are few trees. Little patches of lawn are protected by metal fences. The Park Avenue projects are relatively free of crime but, according to the complaints of the residents, are a hostile environment for the conduct of family life. That hostility is built into their very functionality; they deny one is living in a place of any value. The massive building of workers' suburbs in Europe has deployed the same visual vocabulary of neutrality. There are, as I say, no devils in this story; the housing project is a reformist dream dating back to nineteenth-century efforts to build healthy homes en masse for workers. Only, the visual vocabulary of building betrays another set of values, one which converts old ideas about unbounded space into new forms of repression.

The very practice of neutrality permits this divorce between intention and act. The Puritan knew a version of this divorce: he lived in the world but not of it. In secular society, power can make use of it: "I wasn't really involved in what I was doing, therefore I wasn't responsible for it; it was not me." The result, for housing planners at least, was that the visual technology of power alienated them, too, from their own work. Weber observed that treating the world

[21] Quotations from John Hancock, "The Apartment House in Urban America," in Anthony D. King, ed., *Building and Society* (London: Routledge and Kegan Paul, 1980), p. 181.

neutrally ultimately made the person doing so feel empty as well. This refraction of power is as true of modern architects as it was of early capitalists who sought to take control of the world through detachment.

Neutrality, as a space of social control, seems in this way to explain a great divide between nineteenth-century European planning and those more modern practices that first took shape horizontally in nineteenth-century America and are now more universally, vertically deployed. Baron Haussmann was engaged in remaking Paris during the era in which Central Park was created. Haussmann confronted a congested city a thousand years old whose twisted streets were a breeding ground for, in his mind, the unholy trinity of disease, crime, and revolution. He imagined a traditional means of repression in face of these dangers. The cutting of straight streets through a congested Paris was to make it easier for people to breathe, for police, and if necessary, troops to move. The new streets of northeastern Paris were to be lined with apartments over elegant shops, in order to attract the bourgeoisie into previously working-class districts; he imagined a kind of internal class colonization of the city. At the same time that he opened the city mass transport to the swift flow of traffic, he also hoped the working classes were to become more locally de-pendant upon a new urban gentry; the Boulevard Richard Lenoir was built as such a street. Haussmann sought to create a Paris of steady if demanding customers, of concierge-spies, and a thousand little services.

American urbanism during its great flowering has proceeded by another path of power, one which repressed the overt definition of significant space in which domination and dependence were to occur. There is no building form like the Haussmannian apartment house with its service web. Instead, both horizontal and vertical develop-ment proceeded among us as a more modern, more abstract opera-tion of extension. In the making of the grid cities "new" Americans proceeded as in their encounters with native Americans by erasure of the presence of an alien Other rather than by colonization. Instead of establishing the significance of place, control operated through con-sciousness of place as neutral.

The Spiritual
Quest Is No
Longer a Heroic
Struggle

Words like "power" and "control" suggest a solid grip upon the
world. In the case of neutralizing control this is wrong. Max Weber
sought to evoke the qualities of grid power in his famous image of
modern life lived in an "iron cage;" the image makes sense only if
it implies that the trainer is shut in the same cage as his beasts. For
instance, such consequences of neutrality appear in a short story by
Henry James called "The Beast in the Jungle." His tale concerns a
man, John Marcher, who is able to live peaceably a life of conti-
nuities. But behind this social facade, he apprehends a terrible disaster within himself, poised to destroy him: "Something or other
lay in wait for him, amid the twists and turns of the months and the
years, like a crouching Beast in the Jungle."[22] By chance, Marcher
meets a woman in England, May Bartram, to whom he confided
this fear many years before, during a visit to Italy. Miss Bartram has
remembered his secret, and taken it seriously. The two now become friends; his inner dread becomes a bond between them, the
promise of a deeper connection between them than that of proper
spinster and bachelor. But the beast in the jungle also keeps them
apart; since Marcher is haunted, he thinks he must grapple with the
beast before he can live. They grow old together thus, intimate at
a distance. Miss Bartram falls ill of a blood disease; just before she
dies she struggles to tell him what the beast is but her strength
fails.

James intended "The Beast in the Jungle" to be a parable; it was to
be of "the man of his time, *the* man, to whom nothing on earth was

---

[22] Henry James, "The Beast in the Jungle," in Willard Trask, ed., *The Stories of Henry James*
(New York: Signet, 1962), p. 417.

to have happened."[23] This representative man has failed to live, in living a life of inner anguish: "It wouldn't have been failure to be bankrupt, dishonored, pilloried, hanged; it was failure not to be anything."[24] In mourning he discovers why the seeming inner drama of his life has been no life at all. In the cemetery where he makes regular visits to Miss Bartram's grave, he one day notices a man wrecked with grief over another woman's tomb. At first he is puzzled, and then horror-struck. In observing this woebegone man, Marcher realizes he had "seen *outside* of his life, not learned it within, the way a woman was mourned when she had been loved for herself."[25] He had failed to love Miss Bartram apart from her connection to his secret—and now in the graveyard the beast has sprung. There was a terrible shallowness in his obsession with his inner demons, the beast has bitten his consciousness, his knowledge that he can never regain time delayed. The beast was Marcher's waiting to live.

In one way, this is a parable simply of a modern fear. One has to wait so long to be in a position to be ready, to know what one is doing, to be strong enough to "really live." But James's parable even more suggests something about the consequences of gaining control through acting neutrally.

When no information is conveyed from the neutral exterior of difference, the eye looking inward "sees" not a corresponding emptiness but rather confronts a secret. It is a secret of time that no clock can tell, the secret of what one will become. In the neutral space of the grid, differences are classifications and names that are static in meaning. The interior, by contrast, is the time of process-as-value. Marcher's entire life was such a process he treasured, this secret he carried within that could not be seen, classified, let alone verified. In the world of grid differences, when feelings, desires, or beliefs are stated outside, they become subject to the threat of neutralization. The best defense against the things that one cares about being treated neutrally is never to be too emphatic about them, too exposed.

The self thus remains in process, a process ever more stranger to its own needs. The process of intimating, reflecting, hoping, and

[23] Ibid., pp. 449–50.
[24] Ibid., p. 428.
[25] Ibid., p. 449.

feeling becomes the search for a catharsis that never comes, an end-lessly delayed gratification. All his life Marcher kept faith with his beast, until too much denial turned on him. And, at the end, he had become a vacuous man.

In his American travel notes, Tocqueville records how much one place looked like another, how little variation the local economy, climate, and even topography seemed to matter in constructing a town. This homogeneity in building a city Tocqueville had at first explained as the result of unbridled commercial exploitation. In his later years he added a further explanation, resonating to James's story. The famous American "individual," rather than being an adventurer, is in reality most often a man or woman whose circle of reality is drawn no larger than family and friends. The individual has little interest, indeed, little energy, outside that circle. The American in-dividual is a passive person, and monotonous space is what a society of passive individuals builds for itself. A bland environment assures people that nothing disturbing or demanding is happening "out there." You build neutrality in order to legitimate withdrawal:

> The reproach I address to the principle of equality is not that it leads men away in the pursuit of forbidden enjoyments, but that it absorbs them wholly in quest of those which are allowed. By these means a kind of virtuous materialism may ultimately be established in the world, which would corrupt, but enervate, the soul and noiselessly unbend its springs of action.[26]

And then the beast springs; in emptiness things come apart.

"Taking control" as we know it in this modern form is thus really about losing control. The duality is evident to the eye now in the bars of New York. There are bars everywhere in the city, bars devoted to heavy drinking and bars that are a mere afterthought, like the bar in the Museum of Modern Art; there are bars in discos, bank buildings, brothels, as well as improvised in housing projects. Spiritual struggle in its form as Protestant ethic denies the outside a reality in itself;

---

[26] Alexis de Tocqueville, *Democracy in America*, trans. Edward Reeve (New York: Vintage, 1963), vol. 2, p. 141.

denies the value of being present in the world. It is therefore disconcerting to hear "presence" asserted in the bars on the edge of a
Harlem project like the one along upper Park Avenue. (There are no
places to drink in public within the forest of towers itself.) It is strange
because the language of sociability is so broken into fragments. I used
to think it was because I was there, but in these Park Avenue bars
after a while people forget about a stray, balding, familiar white.
These are family bars, cleaning women and janitors drinking beer;
more lively places nearby are for people living on the shadows of the
underworld. The family bars next to this project seldom have an
actual bar; they are just rooms where someone has put bottles on a
table. Here it is as though time has stopped; the day hangs in dust
roused by the commuter trains shuttling in and out of a tunnel next
to the buildings. The bar at night has a television turned on without
sound; there is the ebb and flow of police sirens, a fan in summer.
This is the space that talk filled, but I came to understand it was
enough: the drops of sound made for a consciousness of presence, of
living, if barely audible, *here*.

By contrast, a resolutely neutral bar of absence can be found in
places of power—for instance, in the bar of the Pierre Hotel on Fifth
Avenue just where Central Park begins. The physical contrast between this bar and the room up in Harlem with a table crowded with
bottles is so extreme as to be meaningless. The Pierre bar, with its
ample tables, flowers, and subdued lights, has always conveyed a
peculiar discretion; people come here who need to do business without being seen to be doing it. This is evident in little details: when
people recognize others here, they seldom table-hop; at most there
are brief nods of recognition. The drinks at the Pierre are mostly for
show. Two men will sit for an hour nursing the glasses in front of
them; the waiters are trained not to hover.

It is a nervous bar with so many people paying careful attention to
one another. The Pierre bar is neutral in the way a chessboard is. And
yet in this power center, among these men in their quiet, expensive
clothes, sunk deep into their leather chairs, the atmosphere seems
more charged by fear than entrepreneurial zeal. The men are afraid
of giving away too much. *Control* is a meaningless word uptown; here
it is a synonym for anxiety. If you don't pay careful attention, things
will come apart.

The visitor intent upon seeing men like Marcher in the modern city might do well, though, to avoid either extreme, the bars either of the Harlem housing project or the Pierre Hotel. The signs of his spiritual quest are most likely to be found in certain bars in the afternoon, like the Lion's Head in Greenwich Village, or the little bars at the front of French restaurants in the Fifties, after people have finished lunch. These compose a scene of truants—a scene of men who should be back at the office but are having a drink instead, not necessarily alcoholic, merely delaying, and of men, and now also of women, who have nowhere particular to go in the afternoon, perhaps unemployed, or engaged in the myriad of jobs in New York— agenting, publicity, graphic design—that do not require the full-time attention of those who aren't at the top.

The bars in which people pass their afternoons in New York are unlike Parisian cafés, the *cafés des amis*. The bartenders don't want these customers; the bowls heaped with salty, thirst-inducing nuts placed on the counters before lunch are withdrawn after it, the bartenders themselves are less responsive to requests for drinks, even though they have more time; some of the truants do drink until they drop, but others are more likely to want to talk, and they expect the men behind the bar, like a captive audience, to listen. In the old working-class bars, Irish in Hell's Kitchen, Polish on the Lower East Side, the windows blacked out and a radio and television blaring at the same time from different stations, afternoons pass in this desultory way, plumbers and carpenters dropping in for a shot and gossip between jobs; on the front stools of the French restaurants those at leisure are not at rest, their talk is tinged with an undertow of urgency, which is perhaps why the barmen are uncomfortable having them there, even though people are well, often very carefully, dressed, as if this indeed were the afternoon's appointment.

The urgencies are about something important that is about to happen, a deal shaping up or a love affair, deals that turn out to be a chance remark dropped by a prominent, distant acquaintance and affairs that begin mentally after the first date. Or there are stories about where people grew up, stories that come easily to the speakers because they have been polished through use, one man occasionally interjecting a comment or exclamation to show another he is listening, before he takes up a later point in his own tale. The most curious thing about the stories is how the tellers sit as they talk, usually directly facing the counter in front on them, on which they lean their elbows and behind which the barman bends over his sink polishing a glass, men talking to one another by looking at their reflections in the mirror behind the bar.

Here was "material," I first thought when I entered this sea. And then, after a few years, it was clear there was no writer's "material" here, for these stories seldom made sense. Something was always left out in the account of the important deal that would explain why it might work, or a woman's "problems" would be alluded to, heavily but without specifics, as a man explained why he was alone most nights. The men in the bars lacked craft. And if indeterminate and illogical, these stories were also curiously neutral, the speaker seldom moved by his tale, at least audibly, the voices recounting problems with women or big deals equally, perhaps with the poise that polished repetition does give and also perhaps like Marcher driven by the compulsion to tell it once more in order that, by chance, the telling might suddenly reveal the hidden meaning of the tale. In the bars there is a place and a time for each man to recount his fragments as though they are just about to become wholes.

After listening to these year after year, however, I have begun to realize that here, in the stream of bland voices and unfocused words, as the light fades outside the front windows, we are truly within the city's grid. These are emblematic New Yorkers, men and women whose lives are endlessly pregnant with meaning and yet to whom, like Marcher, nothing ever happens. Their lives are afflicted with that peculiar lack of concreteness, that endless becoming, which marks the space of the city.

The cross within the circle is a peculiarly modern as well as ancient Egyptian sign. It represents two ways in which the human subject lives walled in from the world. The circle confines his or her experiences of compassion and mutual regard within the walls of authority; the grid is a geometry of power on which inner life remains shapeless.

The
Eye
Searches
for
Unity

chapter 3

The Open Window of the Eighteenth Century

The Haw-Haw

IN A LETTER to Messrs. Rutledge and Shippen, two fellow Americans traveling to Europe in 1788, Thomas Jefferson recommends they pay more attention to architecture than court life because, "As we double our numbers every twenty years, we must double our houses. Besides, we build of such perishable materials, that one half of our houses must be rebuilt in every space of twenty years. . . ." This prospect disturbed Jefferson not one bit. The most casual walk in the woods would convince anyone there was more than enough to go around.[1]

It was a very different attitude toward abundance from that of a century before. In the course of John Bunyan's *Pilgrim's Progress*, the pilgrim, Christian, encounters Madame Bubble, a wellborn lady whose physical charms are overflowing, whose manner is pleasant, who enjoys company and food. She is a witch who tempts Christian sorely. What makes her dangerous is her very outpouring of sensual life:

She makes variance betwixt rulers and subjects, betwixt parents and children, 'twixt neighbour and neighbour, 'twixt a man

---

[1] Thomas Jefferson, *Writings*, ed. Merrill D. Peterson (New York: Library of America, 1984), p. 660.

and his wife, 'twixt a man and himself, 'twixt the flesh and the heart.[2]

The Puritan's "errand in the wilderness" was a work of introspection in a world of scarcity. Whereas "gardens [are] peculiarly worth the attention of an American. . . . We have only to cut out the superabundant plants," Jefferson counseled.[3] In devising the six-by-six-mile land divisions that were to map all land in the continent in a grid system, Jefferson believed this to be merely a beneficent ordering of a teeming and welcoming world. The profusion of nature invites man's use of his own powers of rational design.

It is often the plight of believers in the organic to confront what one might call unfair diseases. Unfair diseases refuse to go away when the sufferer is treated with pure air, proper diet, and plenty of exercise. The Enlightenment's remedy of Nature for spiritual malaise supposed no such cure, only the possibility of moments of relief. The solitary walker who appears in Rousseau's *Reveries of a Solitary Walker*, composed in the autumn of 1776, spoke for his contemporaries in declaring

> [During] my solitary walks and the reveries that occupy them
> . . . I give free rein to my thoughts and let my ideas follow their
> natural course, unrestricted and unconfined. These hours of sol-
> itude and meditation are the only ones in the day when I am
> completely myself and my own master, with nothing to distract
> or hinder me, the only ones when I can truly say that I am what
> nature meant me to be.[4]

Rousseau evokes the providential qualities of this easy, meandering freedom again and again in his *Reveries*, which is a hymn to wholeness written by a man who knows he is complicated to excess. The sense of feeling whole, all the parts of oneself finally able to coexist, the *Sturm und Drang* of life finally calmed as one crosses

[2] John Bunyan, *The Pilgrim's Progress from This World to That Which Is to Come*, ed. Roger Sharrock (Oxford: Oxford University Press, 1960), pp. 302–03.
[3] Jefferson, *Writings*, p. 660.
[4] Jean-Jacques Rousseau, *Reveries of a Solitary Walker*, trans. Peter France, under the title *Reveries of the Solitary Walker* (New York: Penguin, 1979), p. 35.

a field or takes shelter from rain under a tree—this wholeness gives one enough peace that reason can do its work of balancing the mind. A man feels himself, as a result of his immersion in the plenitude of the natural world, to be one creature among many; his hopes and troubles and defeats finally are set in their proper context of a world that flourishes no matter what his story, which teems and goes on, no matter that he has, like Rousseau, spent most of his life in difficulty.

The cross within a circle we have seen to be a peculiarly modern, rather than ancient Egyptian, sign. It represents two ways in which the human subject lives walled in from the world. The circle confines his or her experiences of compassion and mutual regard within the walls of authority; the grid is a geometry of power on which inner life remains shapeless. The eighteenth century had a different design for the relation of self to environment; the Enlightenment conceived a person's inner life opened up to the environment as though one had flung a window wide open to fresh air. Natural abundance made this open window give upon an inviting scene.

Pastoral writers since Vergil have evoked the peace the natural world could bring to those disgusted with the struggle for power or the machinations of ordinary social life. The open relation between human nature and the physical environment, as conceived in the eighteenth century, is special in that these Enlightened souls believed in no necessary conflict between the natural and the artificial. What men and women make is as natural as what they find—or almost.

Even Adam Smith, in *The Wealth of Nations,* believes in this open window between inner life and physical space, though Nature's raw provisions seemed to him scant indeed:

> So miserably poor that, from mere want, [people] are frequently reduced, or at least think themselves reduced, to the necessity sometimes of directly destroying, and sometimes of abandoning their infants, their old people, and those afflicted with lingering diseases, to perish with hunger, or to be devoured by wild beasts.[5]

[5] Adam Smith, *The Wealth of Nations,* 1776 edition, books 1–3, ed. Andrew Skinner (London: Penguin Classics, 1986), pp. 104–05.

Human beings can rectify this terrible scarcity, if only they will use their natural powers of invention. Smith believed the division of labor was the key to this increase; his celebrated example was of a pin-maker who laboring alone could make, at best, 20 pins a day, while laboring in concert with others could work on 4,800 daily. Smith's contemporaries thought this a discovery of genius.

The hopes for material abundance aroused by the division of labor were to be frustrated in the course of the Industrial Revolution, as in the home this principle of division of labor was to create an environ-ment of emotional isolation. Yet though the eighteenth century is often faulted in retrospect for having placed so much faith in the abundance made possible by new forms of production, Smith's idea scarcely does justice to the breadth of invention of his age. It was indeed in those inventions which aimed to unify, rather than those which aimed to divide, that the Enlightenment showed true genius.

This genius marked the Enlightenment's planning of the physical environment, indeed shaped the very conception of the "outside." For instance, the Enlightenment gardener sought to aid Nature in provisioning the pleasures of walking. *Flâner* means in French "to stroll along, observing," a *flâneur* one who delights in doing so. The stroll, as designed by the 1760s, was not quite as passive a surrender to nature as it might at first seem. The planners of the English Garden of the eighteenth century designed clever devices to simulate an illusion of the lack of restraint in nature.

The haw-haw was one of these. It was a channel dug into the ground along the edge of fields; along the bottom of the channel a fence was laid. From the ground, at some distance, one might thus see cattle and horses roaming in the field and think the animals were free to wander; miraculously, they never strayed or escaped. The haw-haw is a device adapted from the paved ditches dug around medieval *bastides*—of the kind built at Cordes—wall and ditch con-ceived as one defensive unit. In the seventeenth century French gardeners began to use both paved and earthen ditches without walls to define the edges of formal gardens; the fence in the trough was to keep out people as well as animals. Early in the eighteenth century English garden designers then began to play with making the device both more irregular, following the serpentine shifts of the ground, and more nearly invisible, by building up both sides. The historian David Watkin thinks Vanbrugh was the key figure in making this change (Vanbrugh and Bridgeman's haw-haws of 1709 can still be seen on the grounds of Blenheim Palace), which is certainly right, but the taste for this illusion was widespread among people without much visual training as well as among the emerging class of professional improvers and landscape designers. Moreover, the illusion in the *jardin anglais* of free-roaming animals, mixing with strolling human beings soon caught on in continental Europe and provincial America as well. Decades later Horace Walpole, in explaining the origin of the name *haw-haw*, revealed the nature of the enthusiasm for this invention uniting man and nature:

> But the capital stroke, the leading step to all that has followed, was . . . the destruction of walls for boundaries, and the invention of *fosses* [ditches used alone]—an attempt then deemed so astonishing, that the common people called them Ha! Ha's! to express their surprise at finding a sudden and unperceived check to their walk. . . . I call a sunk fence the leading step for these reasons. . . . The contiguous ground of the park without the sunk fence was to be harmonized with the lawn within; and the garden in its turn was to be set free from its prim regularity, that it might assort with the wilder country without.[6]

"Set free from its prim regularity, that it might assort with the wilder country without." Certainly, but if what delighted people about this artifice was the illusion that on the grounds of an estate or farm it was possible for people and animals to live without restraint, no one looking from a terrace toward a field of grazing sheep was in the least deceived. One's pleasure in looking through the open window was indeed increased by the knowledge one had a hand in contriving the view.

As it was with lack of barriers, so it was with the production of the

---

[6] Horace Walpole, *Anecdotes of Painting in England*, vol. 4, pp. 263–64; in this punctuation and spelling quoted in David Watkin, *The English Vision* (New York: Harper & Row, 1982), pp. 8–9, to whose gardening eye I am much indebted.

sense of abundance of bloom. In the beds of the English Garden, profusion and carefully calculated disorder were created by mixing species of flowers from different parts of the world, the flowers of different blooming periods and the foliage contrasting; this planting technique expressed the same desire to create an environment of seemingly untamed, ever productive free growth—among which it was, however, also possible to stroll even if one was wearing a wide pannier skirt; by chance Nature had also provided a winding alley of crushed stone to walk upon. The landscape designers of the Enlightenment felt no contradiction between illusion and freedom in all the styles of estate and garden design that span the age—from William Kent's early efforts in Kensington Gardens to create informality in nature (surely an odd conjunction in theory), to the taste for chinoiserie or for Gothic ruins (the construction of the new, safe ruin posed an exciting engineering challenge), down to Humphrey Repton's "red books," which contain his recipes for moving large bodies of earth and heavy rocks in order to arouse picturesque visions of untamed nature. Through devices like the haw-haw or the careful interplanting of different flowering species in the same spot the age literally cultivated the sense of freedom in nature.

In the house late-eighteenth-century designers delighted in the same sort of invention. Beds were set on springs so that they could be hidden in closets—revealed, lowered, raised, and hidden all by a gentle pull on a silken cord. Elaborate dumbwaiters were fitted out with coal braziers and ice buckets. Bookcases turned on hidden pivots to reveal suddenly that a library gave upon a little bedroom, fitted out for those times when the Quest for Knowledge culminates in the urgent need for a snooze.

These devices were the opposite in principle and in practice to the division of labor in the later Victorian houses. Jefferson at Monticello, for instance, was a master at devising such machines. Jefferson's machines surmounted the room barriers in a house; they served as inner windows. In a similar spirit painters of the age sought to overcome the barriers between painting and viewer, the painters making their subjects seem as if directly, immediately fixing the gaze of the viewer. This presence that came from surmounting distances, this pleasure of presence aided by artifice, this was the gift unity made to the eye.

In the *Encyclopédie,* Diderot defined the machine as "the extension of the hand." To use Jean Starobinski's word for one struggle in Rousseau's life, the Enlightenment machine, when applied to the environment, sought "transparency": the illusion was transparent and the boundaries were no longer opaque. Consciousness that one is viewing an illusion is a heightened state of subjective self-awareness, and yet this was for the Enlightenment no barrier to looking outward. Instead of his self-awareness leading to tortured self-absorption, a man of this time, pleased with his perceptions, preferred to stroll.

The land planner of the Jeffersonian persuasion, for instance, considered grids as imaginative constructs helping him to stroll through nature on a grand scale. Jefferson did not want them to become blueprints for country roads—which is one reason why he yielded so readily to L'Enfant's criticism of his Washington plan; the creator of Monticello himself resisted doing in the Virginia countryside what he proposed for a town. The Enlightenment map is often the furthest expression of those powers of artifice and improvement expressed on an estate. Topographic impossibilities are drawn very precisely; boundaries are seen in the mind in order to think about what is contained within each unit: Cartesian logic aids in organizing teeming matter.

The cornucopia is not quite, however, a sufficient image of Enlightenment plenty, these possibilities of nature. When Rousseau wrote in *The Nouvelle Héloïse* of Nature as a teacher of enthusiasm, he meant that awareness of Nature would tame Héloïse and set the context of her spontaneous outbursts. It makes no difference to the succession of the seasons that she loves or suffers. One might derive from these rhythms, as did the elderly Rousseau, even some peace of mind: storms come and go, storms in the countryside and storms in the soul. Nature is full, but in the rhythm of the day or of seasons she does not come to grief, because she does not overflow. Similarly, those sudden precipices and surging waterfalls that Repton delighted in contriving never put the *flâneur* at risk; they were meant to be stimulating rather than overwhelming.

This was the Enlightenment antidote to inward-turning subjectivity, inner distress. What one saw from one's open window was an exemplary scene, a scene full of life but of life given shape; the viewer had aided the landscape to be more of itself. Those who preferred such engaging views became true sons and daughters of Nature: worldly creatures, purposeful, graceful, and modest animals. Our forebears were more comfortable outside than we are. Their ideas of wholeness made them so. They had a distinct sense of exposure— exposure to a natural world that goes on and on, no matter how sad or complicated or unfulfilled its inhabitants are inside themselves.

It is easy but misleading to see the past as an accumulating history. The naturalists of the eighteenth century who believed in the unifying power of the eye were radically out of line with the theological doctrines taught by their elders. In contrast to the Christian emphasis on sanctuary, they sought union; in contrast to the Christian conviction that worldly sensations are illusions, they found physical stimulation to be of positive moral value. In looking at how they built houses, gardens, and lives based upon these principles, it seems we could only envy them.

And yet, I believe, this admirable organicism can be no remedy for our difficulties: wholeness is no remedy for inwardness. The reason has to do with how the "outside" of urban culture is structured as a distinctive realm. It is a place where different ages, races, classes, ways of life, abilities can all crowd together on streets or in large buildings; the city is the natural home of difference. The figures of the Enlightenment, when faced with differences, felt an impulse to overcome them, to invent something like the haw-haw that surmounts the danger to both animals and people of being in fact mixed together. Their belief in wholeness evaded the sheer fact of difference. Though these pre-industrial designers never meant to be prophets, their difficulties in coping with the phenomenon of difference are instructive. The difficulty attends, I think, any attempt to lift the Christian burden through an organic ideal.

Civilization or Culture

The tension between wholeness and difference preyed on the minds of Enlightened people when they began using the word *culture* in opposition to the word *civilization*. Culture represented for them the forces of wholeness in society, while civilization represented a certain kind of acceptance of difference.

The word *civilization* was first applied in the middle decades of the eighteenth century to everyday life, rather than to legal affairs. An older usage in French and English spoke of civilization as the institution of a "civil" suit in court. The common usage of the word *civility* derives from the manual of instruction for children written by Erasmus in 1530, *De civilitate morum puerilium*. Erasmus's book, which was the source of "Sit up straight!," "Don't chew with your mouth open!," and other by now familiar childhood oppressions, in its opening sentences indicated the gap between an education in civility taught to children and the quite different ideal of civilization adopted two centuries after Erasmus by a generation of adults:

> If a child's natural goodness is to reveal itself everywhere (and it shines forth most in the face), his gaze should be sweet, respectful, and decent. Wild eyes are a sign of violence; a fixed stare is a sign of impudence; wandering, distracted eyes are a sign of madness. The glance should not be sidelong, which is a sign of cunning. . . . To lower and blink the eyelids is a sign of frivolity. . . . It is important that the eyes signify a calm and respectfully affectionate spirit.[7]

Here, civility means bodily behavior that forthrightly represents inner character. Civilization, in the later age of wigs, was about the virtues of a certain kind of disguise.

These virtues in the 1740s to the 1760s were a response to a nearer oppression. Civilized behavior contrasted to the elaborate and stiff court etiquette, especially the regulation two generations earlier, in the last years of Louis XIV, of every minute of the day in terms of whom to attend, the proper words to say, how long to grow one's fingernails given one's rank, the proper moment to put one's snuffbox into one's pocket after dining with a marquess as opposed to the

---

[7] Erasmus, *De civilitate morum puerilium libellus* (1530) (Basel: Froben, 1922), p. 1.

correct moment in the presence of a prince of the blood. (A marquis may see you take snuff, a prince of the blood must not.) Among the grandchildren of the age of the Sun King, in the 1760s civilized referred to the way a broader population began enacting ideas of kindness to strangers. This code of politeness ran the gamut from paying attention to the comfort of others in one's house no matter what their rank, to expressing sorrow to an acquaintance upon learning the news of the death of a loved one without feeling it necessary to enquire into the legal condition of the lovers. People began to treat one another without reference, as we would say, to their identity. From reading classic Renaissance, civic-minded books of court behavior like Baldassare Castiglione's *Book of the Courtier*, this generation had moved to consulting guides for an easier, everyday etiquette like the *Galateo*. *Civilized* described manners that could be applied anywhere to anyone—which made for a more relaxed exchange. Those swayed by these lighter, more impersonal manners lived in a gilt and powder-blue society, lightly tinctured with malice. Their city was a city of visits, chinoiserie, and coffeehouse disputes, their countryside was populated by hired ornamental hermits and carefully constructed ruins.

The ability to read indirection was the cardinal virtue of a civilized conscience, conscience both in the sense of awareness of others and of concern for them: A guest looks through the window of a country house and remarks how beautiful the orchards are this year, whereupon his host leads him outside to offer the peach the guest has in this way asked for. In the *Encyclopédie*, Jaucourt's essay on friendship lists the following categories of friend: the friend

1. "With whom one has nothing in common but simple literary amusements."
2. "Whom one may have cultivated for the pleasure and charm of his conversation."
3. "The friend of good counsel" who has a right to "the confidence that one bestows upon friends who are also family and kin."[8]

---

[8] Quoted in Roger Chartier, et al., *A History of Private Life*, vol. 3, trans. Arthur Goldhammer (Cambridge, Mass.: Harvard University Press, 1989), pp. 449–50.

What is important about such a list is that it is not a hierarchy from inferior to superior friendship; each of these friendships has its own value. The friend who simply offers conversation perhaps makes a gift of relief and sheer pleasure of talk that cannot be offered by the intimate who knows everything, with whom everything has been said. A year after the French Revolution had begun, Goethe was still declaring to his friend Knebel, "It is always better to enchant friends a little with the results of our existence than to sadden or to worry them with confessions of how we feel."[9] Politeness does not make declarations of "what I want" and can be offered to strangers; society had found in this a means to be comfortable with the sorrows, both early and late, of intimate life.

In a way, this ethos of civilization is the spreading to a more bourgeois society of the ideal of nonchalance, of *sprezzatura*, which a century before was taken up by nobles who had set themselves against slavish royal submission. For large numbers of people, negligent informality defined civilized behavior, while art came to be appreciated for its ease in an age weary of grandeur and capable of intense pleasure in decor.

Civilization, as people so moved understood it, is not an ideal of the organic. Instead it is one vision of how to encompass social and personal differences, especially when these might make for invidious comparisons. The civilized man or woman sets a value on impersonality, and finds a language of impersonality that avoids reference to the identities of the speakers. The codes of civilization were one way to infuse value into the outside; they were one release from obsessive interiority.

The advocates of Enlightenment detested this civilized release. The organic ideal was to be an alternative release, a better solution, because the overtones the first modern critics of civilization heard were tinklings, sounds that these writers found jangling. It offends our senses still to think of as "moral" those behaviors and beliefs that would make the burdens of life lighter, but such was the civilized conception of the age of wigs. Nor does gracefulness seem the artistic credo for a lifetime, but in lightness the painters and musicians of the

---

[9] Johann Wolfgang von Goethe to Karl Knebel, 23 April 1790, *Werke, Briefe und Gesprache*, ed. Ernst Beutler (Zurich: Artemis Verlag, 1948–53), p. 306.

age of wigs thought they would discover the secret of a sure touch. As a consequence, the attack on civilized values mounted in the middle of the eighteenth century was an affirmation of the weightiness, the sheer seriousness of culture.

In Kant's *Ideas on a Universal History from the Point of View of a Citizen of the World*, written in 1784, the philosopher declares, "Cultivated to a high degree by art and science, we are civilized to the point where we are overburdened with all sorts of social propriety and decency." Kant uses the word *cultivation* in the sense of that awareness of the slightest vibration, the slightest nuance of need in one's surroundings. "The idea of morality is a part of culture. But the application of this idea, which results in the similitude of morality in the love of honor and in outward decency, amounts only to civilizing."[10] And as a consequence, those forms of expression that diverted people from recognizing and stating the truths of social life were destructive of seriousness, though virtues according to the dictates of civilization. Echoing Erasmus, Kant wanted people to represent in their outer behavior what they are inside.

The "mask of virtue" was the symbol to the Enlightened of the evil of civilization, and perhaps the most inflamed attack on the well-mannered, considerate, and self-effacing considered as a mask came in the writings of the elder Mirabeau. In the 1760s Mirabeau *père* wrote,

> I marvel to see how our learned views, false on all points, are wrong on what we take to be civilization. If they were asked what civilization is, most people would answer: softening of manners, urbanity, politeness, and a dissemination of knowledge such that propriety is established in place of laws of detail: all that only presents me with the mask of virtue and not its face, and civilization does nothing for society if it does not give it both the form and the substance of virtue.[11]

Instead of the ideal of the civilized man, Mirabeau and others who were Enlightened therefore gave new meaning to an old ideal, that of the *honnête homme*.

[10] Immanuel Kant, quoted in Norbert Elias, *The Civilizing Process*, vol. 1. trans. by Edmund Jephcott (New York: Urizen Books, 1978), p. 8.
[11] Quoted in Elias, *Civilizing Process*, p. 38.

Long before the Enlightenment, the *honnête homme* was the late Renaissance ideal of a gentleman, a person whose elegance found form in quiet speech, modest drinking and eating, clean clothes: assurance was expressed through self-restraint. This *honnêteté* partook of the lightness and nonchalance that marked the nobility who kept themselves aloof from the court. In the eighteenth century it came instead to suggest directness, solidity, forthrightness; these qualities had been democratized. Their clearest statement, I think, is not in words but in the paintings of Chardin, whose canvases evoke the immediate, direct life of bottles, jugs, and fruit. *Honnêteté* is expressed in the manner of the painting, which leads the eye directly to consider the things represented. Chardin's solidity was the reality the critics of politeness sought.

Of course, contempt for "masks of virtue" had a meaning beyond what the Enlightened could see. Here is, from a children's instructional manual of Year III of the French Revolution, the same difference between the civilized and the *honnête homme* as was first envisaged in the age of wigs:

> In the days when men judged themselves and were judged according to their birth, their rank, and their wealth, much study was required to learn all the nuances of consideration and politeness to be observed in society. Today there is but one rule to follow in life's commerce, and that is to be free, modest, frank, and honest with everyone.[12]

Those who unmasked themselves were to find in the French Revolution that this medicine for superficiality could literally prove fatal; turned upon by his fellow revolutionaries, the child of Nature was asked to justify himself and save his life by proving what he really believed and who he really was. Those impure traces from his civilized past, traces of diffidence, courtesy, and irony could become his death sentence.

But to the earlier writers of the Enlightenment, as in the paintings of Chardin, vulnerable nakedness did not characterize the condition opposite to the masks of civilization. The opposition which told in

[12] Quoted in Chartier, *History of Private Life*, pp. 204–05.

Enlightened minds was not simply that between the face and the mask, the forthright man and the ornamental hermit. Those who preached the virtues of organic unity imagined a more profound contrast. It was between civilization and culture, *Zivilisation* versus *Kultur*.[13]

We know the distinction between culture and civilization in English when we speak of someone as a *cultured* person, and the French know it in praising a person as *cultivé*, the Spanish as *cultivado*. To be cultured means much more than to have nice manners. (The phrase I have just written seems just good common sense to a modern bourgeois; an aristocrat of the old regime might smile, very faintly, upon encountering the "much more." Given the darkness and wickedness of life, courtesy might be achievement enough.) To be cultivated means one has absorbed the art, literature, and thinking of past and present, that one has seen something of the world, yet the hint of husbandry in the word suggests its further meaning: a stronger self, more deep-reaching beliefs, have been achieved by virtue of work upon the raw human material at hand. To be honest is not to be simple. Rather, the idea of culture reflects the same assumptions that produced the haw-haw: the aim is to strengthen one's nature by contrivance.

In the Enlightenment, civilization consisted of ritual that reaffirmed the existing social order. The elder Mirabeau attacked the artifices of polite civilization not because they were artificial but rather because politeness was a stale form of invention. Paying compliments is a matter of repeating formulas; politeness conceived as a finer regard for the feelings of others deploys mostly strategic silences, salving evasions, and white lies. There is no real human engagement; maintaining the barriers between people indeed becomes an end in itself. The paying of compliments adds nothing to the world, nor increases its store of knowledge.

Cultivation, on the contrary, promised that the natural materials spread throughout the human species could be put to more radical use. From its origins, Diderot, Kant, and other Enlightenment writ-

[13] A contrary view to the paragraphs that follow can be found in Lucien Febvre, "Civilisation, évolution d'un mot et d'un groupe d'idées," in *Civilisation: le mot et l'idee* (Paris: C.I.S., 1929), pp. 1–55.

ers imagined the formation of a cultured person to involve a reciprocal process of personal judgment and social participation. The more a
person surveys the world in an open, uninhibited spirit, the more he
or she becomes involved in it as a critic and actor. The organic ideal
as a living ideal appeals today, as in the past, not just to the fact of
unity, but to personal and social change: One of the meanings of
"cultivation" is to grow what did not exist before in a wild state. For
the Enlightenment social writers, the great example of this was the
world of work. These observers "discovered" work as a dignified
activity; previously, manual labor had been treated as akin to the
efforts of domesticated beasts; the bureaucratic, clerical jobs expanding within the central monarchies had been viewed with little more
respect. By contrast, the men and women who wrote the entries in
the *Encyclopédie* on cooking, sewing, bread-making, and calculating
(accountancy) believed that by rationally cultivating and shaping even
these menial forms of labor the worker might become a deeper, more
complex human being. Once consciousness was aroused a cultivated
worker might abhor the world on view—for instance, how his work
was controlled by employers. His self-cultivation would lead him to
behave very differently than he had been schooled in the equilibrating rituals of civility that produced a polite, deferential employee.
But such a radical response would be truly an engagement with society, the Enlightened reformers thought. Social involvement and
individual self-formation would be inseparable. This is perhaps the
less charming view to be had from an open window than that of a
landowner surveying his estate, but the social principle is the same as
the visual principle: everything inside is engaged with everything
outside. It is radial wholeness.

When German educators sought a name for this engagement they
used the word *Bildung*. The *Bildung* could be imagined as deriving
from a process akin to painting, though it creates an odd sort of
picture. The more formed a person is, the more coherent as a per-
sonality, the more interwoven is he or she with others as a social
being. Thus the *Bildung* is a group portrait; as the artist—society—
paints in each of the individual faces more distinctly, the picture
becomes ever more clear in its overall design. Whatever challenges
adults make to the existing social order they will make not in a spirit

of alienation and rejection but rather in the name of life that "makes sense"—these two simple words that ask for so much.

The psychoanalyst Erik Erikson is the most forceful modern exponent of the Enlightenment ideal of organic connnection. In his essay "The Problem of Ego Identity," he begins by defining identity as follows:

> It is this identity of something in the individual's core with an essential aspect of a group's inner coherence which is under consideration here: for the young individual must learn to be most himself where he means most to others—those others, to be sure, who have come to mean most to him. The term identity expressed such a mutual relation in that it connotes both a persistent sameness within oneself (self-sameness) and a persistent sharing of some kind of essential character with others.[14]

"Persistent sameness within oneself . . . persistent sharing of some kind of essential character with others": psychology would now phrase the Enlightened ideal of culture as coherence between the intra- and the intersubjective. Forming a sense of one's place in the world, in this scheme of Enlightenment, does not affirm incoherent time, the puzzle of our separateness, or permanent unease. It may recognize these shadows, as any adult understanding must, but it seeks to emancipate people from an undeveloped existence. Today we put a premium on youth as the prime age of development. Writers like Erikson reflect an Enlightenment emphasis on growth within adulthood. An adult has the power to unify, to make experience cohere, to cultivate his or her existence. The use of imagery of light is apt to describe this process: light is to flood in upon the interior, the illuminated soul is to look outward; thus, its existence will become more connected to others, more whole.

It might be thought that here, surely, an ideal dedicated to wholeness *must* embrace difference: if one takes life seriously, one wants to open out, to expand rather than to stand still: to grow, surely human beings need to experiment, they need diversity. This is logically what

[14] Erik Erikson, "The Problem of Ego Identity," *Psychological Issues* 1, no. 1 (1959): 102.

Enlightened cultivation suggests. For instance, in his *Art as Experience*, the American philosopher John Dewey maintained that engaging the rough grain of differences in things is the great moment of truth in art. Instead of talking about grand intentions and meanings, the artist must pay attention to the materials which will give intentions concrete life. The philosopher thought the encounter with resisting rocks or difficult clauses would make the artist grow; he or she would learn how to cultivate his or her powers of expression. This is the Enlightened ideal brought to bear on difference. If it makes sense in art, surely it makes sense in life? Surely the experience of diversity in a city will make a more developed human being?

There is, today, a disturbing sign that the organic, enlightened attitudes we have traced do not lead to embracing complexity. We find this in the very fact that many modern planners who subscribe to the organic ideal in cultural terms have given up on visual planning. These planners perceive that architects are absorbed in making signature buildings like designer clothes; they detest modern architects who often put more emphasis on stunning forms than flexible forms adapted to human uses. These planners point out that parts of New York are beginning to look like a fashion parade of styles in glass shirts, brick shoes, and steel hats. In the same way making megaplans for mega-buildings seems antisocial, this tyranny of definition (whose roots go back to the medieval city) involved in planning on a grand scale. Therefore these planners focus on "communication."

The substitution of verbal communication for visual definition echoes with an eighteenth-century ideal of unity. The planners who focus on making people talk about goals, mutual difficulties, and everyday frustrations seek to create communal solidarity. Their hope is that a sense of unity and common resolve will appear among people who have undergone endless nights of talk in rooms furnished with plastic furniture and lit with strong fluorescent light, the participants having drunk too much watery coffee out of papers cups and struggled to keep awake when it is not their turn to talk. Few planners who have pursued this path in the last generation would want to argue that "the people" best know their own needs; whether or not that is true, it is beside the point. In a society threatened by passivity and withdrawal, to encourage ordinary citizens to talk about social realities is to make the speakers care about one another, or so it is hoped. The old educators would have recognized in this new attitude to "communication" their values of cultivation and *Bildung*. The point of this verbally-oriented planning is also organic: to achieve solidarity through talk.

The wholeness the Enlightened man looked for he too sought to hear; he believed in the beneficent powers of freely flowing discourse; his coffeehouse (these places were only for men) was where he sought to hear unity. There was a reason for this talk. People came to find out what was happening in the city; a Londoner or Parisian in search of news went in search of coffee. Any stranger had the right to sit and join in the talk, the room awash in tobacco smoke but not in alcohol fumes, as "libations" were thought to slow the tongue rather than loosen it. The coffeehouses of the Enlightenment were the places where political parties met; these chatting rooms were the original seats of insurance companies like Lloyds of London, whose members needed to know everything to calculate their risks. Planners of "communication" are in search of some kind of modern replacement for the coffeehouse.

But the coffeehouse was not a place for unbridgeable differences of class or belief to be expressed. Similarly, modern "communication planning" founders on difference. We want to assume that give-and-take grows tissues between people, but between rich and poor, black and white, exchange may not bind. The reason these tissues do not grow is suggested, I think, in the very avoidance of design by people who want to create unity. For the visual designer who addresses the exterior physical fabric of city is constantly dealing with parts which cannot, and should not, be bound together into a whole. Put schematically, the world of things—made by different hands at different times—is a revelation of otherness, of discontinuity, rather than of secret, elective affinities waiting to be joined.

How is the believer in unity to cope with things that are discontinuous? This question dogged the Enlightenment urban planner who addressed himself to the city. He too believed in the values of open communication as embodied in the coffeehouse. Yet he had great difficulty in applying his own gifts to an urban environment because of the intractable otherness of physical objects and urban spaces.

They defeated the designer's powers of inventing openness. And yet this defeat was, and is, unacceptable. The city is not only a *civitas*—a place of communication. It is also on *urbs*, as St. Isidore discovered; if its physical ports cannot be merged into a unified whole, still they must be connected to one another. How should those connections be designed?

The Square
of Nature

In the Enlightenment, the flooding in of light, so that one was drawn to look through an open window, did not usually give upon urban street scenes in part for the most prosaic of reasons. Those who walked in cities were forced to wade through horse dung and slops from houses on streets that were usually unpaved or poorly laid. The biology of disease, the offense to the senses of rotting vegetable, fish, and flesh—all these less-pleasing emanations of nature were on pungent display in concentrated form.

Moreover, Rousseau's Paris and Hogarth's London seemed to moralists of the time places in which people were robbed of inner life by illusions quite different and less beneficent than those aroused by the haw-haw. The urbanite, constantly comparing on the street his own condition to that of others, became convinced that he "needed" much more than he had; the simplest laborer in London was more in danger of succumbing to the Rake's Progress than his country bumpkin cousin. In the countryside nature stimulated people in a different way: "These hours of solitude and meditation are the only one in the day when I am completely myself and my own master, with nothing to distract me. . . ."[15] Rurality, revery, solitude induced a sense of being whole rather than of lacking amusement.

Adam Smith was an interesting case of these convictions. He saw the city as a place of enervation, but the prejudices of his age do not sit entirely easily with the principles declared in *The Wealth of Na-*

[15] Rousseau, *Reveries,* p. 35.

tions. For Smith, like the modern urbanist Jane Jacobs, believed that the division of labor began in the center of towns and spread outward to the countryside. Towns generate the wealth of nations and yet, he thought, the taste of towns is for luxuries, for "vanities," for things passing through the prism of envy and display. It might be said of this age that it was both urbane and antiurban. Jefferson despaired of what would happen to Enlightenment were cities to grow; he despaired that citizens of his own country could practice political virtue in them. Put broadly, cities were thought places more fit for civilization than for culture. Their social relations discouraged the development of a solid, *honnête* character. They were morally as well as physically unhealthy places.

It was given these antiurban prejudices that the Enlightened planner set about to remedy the defects of the city through creating unities. The logical urban form to use in creating unity was the town square, the site in the city that concentrates crowds for business and pleasure. In the Christian conception of the city, these profane squares were allowed the play of the random and the uncontrolled. In the Enlightened square, concentration was used as the social foundation of visual unification.

Though I propose to illustrate how difficult it was to design unity in squares, it would be a distortion to say the Enlightenment simply failed in the effort to create some squares of great complexity. For instance, the series of town squares built by Stanislas Leszczynski, king of Poland, during his exile in the French city of Nancy are perhaps the most philosophically resonant urban constructions of the mid-eighteenth century. They are a sustained study in the interpenetration of nature with severely regular forms. These simple buildings are in turn adorned with ornaments plastered everywhere, on their tops, their sides, their gates. The exiled Pole carried ornament to magnificent excess. The squares formed by these structures are an enduring monument to the power of human will to build, but they are dynamic rather than woodenly monumental for in the midst of so much construction, when one's eye searches constantly for the relief of the trees, the exiled king's designers also carefully provided it. Nancy's achievement is about the human being—as a generic creature—experiencing unity between a series of urban squares and the seeming overflowing of trees and shrubs into the building picture. These plants are like a crowd populating the city. But the king's design does not address the real people in the squares, or what these people are doing.

Enlightenment planners sought to address human complexities and discontinuities by using two strategies, one treating the city as a special domain of its own, the other seeking to link this socially unified square within the city to larger unities, those of city and country, mankind and nature. Conventionally, the history of city planning assigns the first effort to French and the second to English designers, which like all conventions is more convenient than precise. But it is certainly true of the greatest designer of French squares, Jacques-Ange Gabriel, who conceived of the city square as unifying a special domain.

Gabriel's chief creation in Paris is the currently named Place de la Concorde, the vast rectangle in the center of the city into which principal roads of Paris debouch. Since today this square is populated only by angry motorists, it requires an effort of will to see it as Parisians did (the Place de la Concorde was begun in 1755 and finished in 1792; Gabriel worked on it from 1763 to 1772). On one of its sides was a principal quay of the Seine; Gabriel articulated, through a set of stone inclines, the means by which carts could go down to the water's edge to off-load the river boats. Before the ramps workers had depended on ropes and pulleys to move goods up; cargo was frequently lost in the mud. Similarly, Gabriel rationalized the relation of the Louvre palace to this frantic commercial scene by creating a parterre on the east face of the square; the royal world could stroll out to, and could look down upon, everyday life, but from the palace needn't see it. Most of all he sought to articulate motion through Paris occurring here by adapting the haw-haw to urban ends. Around the loop of roads in the center of the square he excavated four deep ditches, and filled them with dirt and covered the dirt with grass, which was a most un-French material at the time, and not thought quite fit to walk upon. These four grass ditches served to keep pedestrians and carriages apart, even as they were mixed together in the same space, just as Vanbrugh's haw-haw mixed while keeping apart humans and animals.

There is a painting by Piet Mondrian entitled *Place de la Concorde* (1938–1943) which the urbanist Paul Zucker misunderstands, I think, in a significant way. Writing of Mondrian's canvas, which looks like a map of the center of Paris rendered in the abstract—a square of white defined by a series of bordering lines, themselves criss-crossing—

Zucker comments in disappointment that "although the regularity of the layout is somewhat reflected in the painter's geometric image, the vitality of the square's three-dimensional reality is by no means conveyed."[16] But Mondrian has represented not the map but rather the difficulty of this great square. In his painting the edges where the lines meet the frame of the canvas are not defined; indeed, Mondrian has put in little irregular blocks along the edges to suggest that something else is beginning to happen, off the canvas and unseen, impossible to infer from the shape of the center. Mondrian has well understood in this way the problem of unity in Gabriel's design: the center did not in fact unify the city. This square was not like a key which, turned in the lock, opened up all around it. The "vitality" that Zucker perceives in the design was defeated in use. Gabriel sought to create order in the whole of the city by providing a rational center—yet soon the quays were choked again with fallen goods rotting in the mud; the king put up a temporary barrier of wood to shut out the noise of the people. The Enlightened mapmaker Patte drew a map of the Place de la Concorde showing how orderly a relation the new structure had to the gardens of the Tuileries, but no sooner was the place built than the concentration of whores in the Tuileries increased and men left standing in the square, stalling traffic, while they arranged for assignations in the bushes. Both illicit and licit traffic, traffic of both humans and animals on foot choked the place itself. This very effervescence of life succeeded in overcoming the Parisian dislike of grass, and Gabriel's greatest invention, the adaptation of the haw-haw to urban use, was literally trampled underfoot. This is what we see in Mondrian's painting: unity coming apart. It is a painting of otherness. The peculiar power of the city is to take apart the program of unity, such as Gabriel conceived for the walls, streets, and haw-haws in the Place de la Concorde.

In English urban planning we see designers of unity reaching for more, attempting to make use of artifice so as to create greater continuity between city and country in the process of creating an urban center. Squares like London's Bedford Square (1775) and Russell Square (1801) were constructed with an island of nature in the midst of new urban housing, and the emphasis was on "building" nature. Lever shovels with cast-iron claws were developed that could dig out

[16] Paul Zucker, *Town and Square* (New York: Columbia University Press, 1959), p. 187.

deep root balls around large trees; the root systems of these mature trees were then wrapped in burlap, and the trees taken from the countryside and established in their new site. The result was that the trees looked as if they had always been there, that the squares were enclosures of an ancient nature, and that the rows of houses had, as it were, been grafted on. What was a massive land-development scheme thus was made to look incremental, gentler, more in harmony with the established past. As with the haw-haw, the illusion was at once self-evident and satisfactory to inhabitants of the squares as well as to their developers.

It was at this time that the crescent form and the terrace house became staples of the English urban vocabulary, and these forms were thought, even more, as binding and unifying elements in the creation of a city. Unlike the Inns of Court in London or early squares like Leicester Square (1635), which were self-enclosed places devoted to specialized activities, the crescent and the terrace were conceived to be like the fingers of a hand, reaching out into new territory, connecting it to the body of the city.

How well this act of embodiment worked can best be seen in the Enlightened designs for the city of Bath. Bath derives its name from the springs that had soothed the Romans when the town was known as Aquae Sulis. In the Middle Ages it had been a center for making and trading cloth; its fortunes then had declined until Queen Anne visited the city in 1702 and 1703 for the waters (which taste like Evian water lightly perfumed with sulfur). Richard "Beau" Nash became its social arbiter a year later; he was a man whose strict dictates of fashion would have better suited an outpost of the court of Louis XIV than the realities of a more relaxed and socially mixed age. Late in the century Oliver Goldsmith described the heterogeneous stew of bodies in Bath's waters as

> clerks and factors from the East-Indies, loaded with the spoils of plundered provinces; planters; negro-drivers from our American Plantations; agents who have fattened in two successive wars; brokers and jobbers of every kind; men of low birth.[17]

---

[17] Quoted in Sigfried Giedion, *Space, Time and Architecture*, 5th ed. (Cambridge, Mass.: Harvard University Press, 1961), p. 147.

How should a city be built for this diverse crowd?

A father and son had to find answers for this question, the father by building in a civilized way, the son in an Enlightened way. John Wood the Elder began work in 1727 as master builder and architect for the town. Queen Square, his greatest project, is the very apotheosis of the Enlightenment ideal. The square is a garden designed to be like the courtyard fronting a great mansion, with appendages surrounding its three sides. In Queen Square this mansion is the entire north side of the square, an assemblage in fact of several houses put to differing uses; they are unified on the façade into a whole. Queen Square, both on its great north front and its lesser sides, gives no hint of the diversity hidden behind the façades.

That sounds a negative statement but is in fact the duality that John Wood the Elder had to encompass. Bath was not a royal court. It was a city for sufferers from gout and lovers of dancing—both the disease and the love drew all sorts of people. He had to find a way to bring them together that would be satisfying to all. Bath was a commercial resort; its life depended upon something like architectural politeness. And so he enclosed them doubly: behind the building façade and then also as a mass by designing promenades which concentrated people into them as a moving body, limping from disease or from too many quadrilles. The square and its principle radiating streets the elder Wood conceived as a crowd container. His solution is even more apparent in King's Circus he began to build just north of Queen Square in 1754. The modern viewer has to imagine Wood's circle of perfectly even buildings, both in height and façade, without the trees that have since grown up in the center. Originally, all the front windows in King's Circus gave upon their equal and opposite numbers; looking out the window of any one building the eye traveled around a pleasing circle of stone. Again, this established a polite fiction. Behind the regular façades King's Circus swarmed with people inhabiting everything from grand apartments to brothels; the space had no logic of use behind the façade. Whatever happened behind it was masked, yet the open space of the Circus thronged at all hours with people. This was the elder Wood's version of the duality of civilized life. Otherness is contained within a round wall.

King's Circus was completed by John Wood the Younger after his father died. John Wood the Younger began to build in a different way, according to Enlightened principles. His squares are not created by forms that mask human differences—his was not a civilized architecture as that word was now coming to be used. The younger Wood was a child of his times and of nature. In Bath he built a connecting street (Brock Street) out of his father's circus that led to a completely different urban ensemble. This was the Royal Crescent, completed in 1769, in which the thirty houses forming the crescent are as severely classical with their Ionic columns as anything his father built, but the son's work gives out, suddenly, on the English countryside. The younger Wood's solution to how to give form to the city was to thrust its architectural fingers out into nature. Thereafter the great building projects in Bath would follow suit, similarly reaching out of the town, like the Lansdowne Crescent of 1794, which is really a snaking line of buildings that follows the contours of its site rather than imposes upon it as did the constructions of the elder John Wood.

The younger Wood did not mean for the street to be a container at all; it was rather a conduit to get people out of the crowded condition that his father sought to orchestrate. The impulse of conducting the crowd out of the square, an impulse of dispersion, would appear again and again in urbanism seeking unity between landscape and city. The younger Wood's fingers of buildings became, in the hands of Daniel Burnham a century and a half later (1909), the principle by which the great planner conceived reorienting Chicago to its waterfront: the major roads lead to the waterfront which becomes a green park next to the inland sea; the vital edge of the city Burnham also conceived as the point of dispersion. Olmsted shut out the city; these plans dissipate it; the crowd is a force to be weakened by design.

It is one of the great ironies in the history of urban form that these structures meant to organize a crowd of people evolved so that the edge became their point of vital development, and the center became of ever less value. In that dispersion toward the empty edge, the design avoids the otherness concentrated at the center.

The Place de la Concorde and the squares and crescents of the younger John Wood embody profound dilemmas in urban design: How to encompass diversity in unity? How to make the social differences contained in crowds cohere in designs that aim at visual wholeness between people and nature? Gabriel's design was defeated in its form by the human differences it sought to relate. Wood's Enlightened ambitions of unity were even greater, but they led him out of the city; he dispersed the crowd. Indeed, in place of the diversities for which his father built a civilized mask, Wood sought to simplify the human material with which he worked; his houses, unlike those of his father, are meant for single (and wealthy) families. Nature has been gained, difference has been lost. And this difficulty too signifies more largely: the chastening, calming wisdom that speaks from Vergil's *Georgics* to Rousseau's *Reveries of a Solitary Walker* should not be knowledge of one's limited place in nature gained by knowing less about one's fellow human beings.

What invention could bind strangers together? What could make social diversity as abundant and instructive as was natural diversity? These were the urban difficulties of those who believed in wholeness, and they still are.

chapter 4

The Unexpected
Consequences
of Visual Unity

THE CHRISTIAN CITY put great value on the inside—on shelter within buildings as on inner experiences. The Enlightenment city sought to take people outside—but on to fields and forests rather than streets filled with jostling crowds. If the Christian pilgrim had difficulty relating his faith in God to the parade of human differences on a street, so the Enlightened planner found it difficult to reconcile his faith in nature with an urban crowd. The reason the polarities matter today is because of what lies in between. Our society is subject to enormously varied and complex stimuli in economic, political, and erotic life. Yet both the codes of inwardness and unity which have shaped our culture make it difficult to cope with the facts of diversity. We have trouble understanding the experience of difference as a positive human value.

This general difficulty is particularly urgent among those who are engaged in urban and architectural design. The planners who have devoted themselves to Enlightened forms of "communication" work are experts in *Gemeinschaft*. In the face of larger differences in the city they tend to withdraw to the local, intimate, communal scale. Those who work visually and at a larger scale find it as difficult to organize diverse urban scenes as did the younger John Wood. The modern planner lacks visual precepts for how races might be mixed in public places, or how to orchestrate the zoning and design of streets so that economically mixed uses work well. It is equally obscure how to design house projects and schools that mix races, classes, or ages. Human diversity seems something beyond the powers of human design.

The Enlightenment bequeathed a peculiar, indeed surprising legacy to the modern world which has compounded this difficulty. The Enlightened ideal of wholeness has passed into the modern definition of the integrity of well-made things. Thus a conflict has arisen between buildings and people: the value of a building as a form is at odds with the value of a building in use. This conflict appears in some simple ways. It seems wrong to alter or change an old building with an addition at the side or new windows, because these changes seem to destroy the "integrity" of the original object. Changing historical needs are seen as threats to the integrity of the original form, as though time were a source of impurity. Groups dedicated to urban preservation sometimes speak, indeed, of a city as though it ought to be a museum of buildings, rather than a site for the necessarily messy business of living.

The way buildings are constructed now contributes to this conflict. Buildings now are much less flexible in form than the rows, crescents, and blocks of the past. The life span of a modern skyscraper is meant to be forty or fifty years, though steel skeletons could stand much longer; service stacks, wiring, and plumbing are planned so that a building is serviceable only in terms of what it was originally intended for. It is much harder to convert a modern office tower to mixed uses of offices and apartments than it is to convert a nineteenth-century factory or eighteenth-century row-block to these uses. In this shortened time frame, the "integrity of form" acquires a special meaning. The original program for a building controls its brief lifetime of use. The physical urban fabric has thus become more rigid and brittle.

Our eighteenth-century ancestors never meant to bring a world of brittle buildings into being; nor, in the making of buildings, as in the making of constitutions, did they believe there is anything sacred about original intentions and first forms. They wanted, instead, the open window to arouse the public's enthusiasm. But in time the enthusiasm aroused by experiences of unity between inside and outside subsided; "unity" came to refer to what objects were *in them-selves*. The Enlightenment bequeathed to us the anti-social building, its visual values expected uses and changing needs. This is the unexpected consequence of the search for organic unity of form.

Sympathy and
the Sublime

This anti-social denouement of the organic quest is particularly surprising, since the younger John Wood, no less than his father or Gabriel, considered himself a choreographer of human movement in the city, and his eye to be thus a sociable organ. As part of their understanding of social life, writers of the Enlightenment had a quite practical idea of what happened to people when they acknowledged the existence of strangers. One human being could enter, if only for a few moments, into the thoughts, needs, and desires of another human being, no matter how different that person was, through an act of the imagination the Enlightened writers called "sympathy."

Perhaps the clearest statement of sympathy is the declaration Adam Smith made at the very opening of his *Theory of Moral Sentiments*:

> As we have no immediate experience of what other men feel, we can form no idea of the manner in which they are affected but by conceiving what we ourselves should feel in the like situation. Though our brother is upon the rack, as long as we ourselves are at our ease, our senses will never inform us of what he suffers. . . . It is by the imagination only that we can form any conception of what are his sensations. . . . It is the impressions of our own senses only, not those of his, which our imaginations copy. By the imagination we place ourselves in his situation, we conceive ourselves enduring all the same torments we enter as it were into his body.[1]

---

[1] Adam Smith, *The Theory of Moral Sentiments* (Oxford: Oxford University Press, 1976), p. 9.

To say "I put myself in his place" means I don't account his difference from myself; for a moment, I try to imagine his suffering, his need, by translating it into terms already familiar to me. Adam Smith is quite clear about this: "It is the impressions of our own sense only, not those of his, which our imaginations copy." So sympathy as a mental operation isn't something wild, or even exploratory; it is rather the conquest of the unlike by making it seem familiar. Smith was a practical man; he thought people were prepared to go only so far mentally to reach out emotionally.

This sane idea of sympathy might seem mere complacency, which, in the Enlightenment, it was not. For the writers who believed in the powers of sympathy, its effect was to draw people during the imaginary moment of sympathy out of themselves. When Rousseau asks, in his *Essay on the Origin of Languages*, which way people might find it possible to pity others, he replies, "in transporting ourselves out of ourselves: by identifying with the person who suffers."[2] If the mental tools of sympathy take the difference out of other people, the moral effect is one of displacement of oneself. Benjamin Constant appreciated as well the ego-transcending virtues of sympathetic enthusiasm ("The first condition for enthusiasm is not to observe oneself shrewdly"), yet Constant sounds the same cautionary note as does Adam Smith about the human capacity to live for long based on what one experiences during the burst: "We moderns have lost in imagination what we have gained in knowledge; we are incapable, because of that knowledge, of durable exaltation."[3]

The burst of sympathy was one way our ancestors experienced unity with others. It was a passionate union, but on adult terms: intense but not forever. Moreover, sympathy did not suppose that in caring about you I understand you. Just for a moment, I feel as though I were you.

It was, paradoxically, in the ideal of a momentary, sympathetic flush that our ancestors laid the cornerstone for the modern concept

[2] Jean-Jacques Rousseau, *Essai sur l'origine des langues*, in *Oeuvres Complètes* (Paris: Gallimard, 1959), p. 614. (my translation).
[3] Benjamin Constant, "De L'esprit de conquête et de l'usurpation," in *Oeuvres Complètes* (Paris: Gallimard, 1957), p. 1013 (my translation).

of an anti-social architecture. This occurred when visual designers sought to realize the ideal of sympathy in a certain kind of space.

Bursts of enthusiasm were, they thought, most likely to occur in "picturesque" places. In his *Essay on the Picturesque* a disciple of Repton's, William Gilpin, declared that "*roughness* forms the most essential point of difference between the beautiful and the picturesque." And in turn a disciple of Gilpin's, the Herefordshire landowner Uvedale Price, elaborated the idea in his own *Essay on the Picturesque*: "the two opposite qualities of roughness, and of sudden variation, joined to that of irregularity, are the most efficient causes of the picturesque."[4] These formulas produced a whole genre of paintings in which tempests are a favored theme and twisted trees necessary natural furniture. In literature the imagery of the picturesque was put to greater use by such writers as Emily and Charlotte Bronte. *Wuthering Heights* is a novel in which "roughness," "sudden variation," and "irregularity" provide the setting of the plot and characterize the plot itself.

Lurking behind the effects of the picturesque was a theory, that of Edmund Burke's *A Philosophical Enquiry into the Origin of Our Ideas of the Sublime and the Beautiful* (1756). Burke famously defined the emotions of the sublime as arising from experiences of terror, obscurity, and the infinite; beauty, on the contrary, is produced by "small, smoothness, gradual variation and delicacy of form."[5] Sympathy is aroused by sublime terror, which in turn can be designed, designed by picturesque techniques. Here is how an unlikely candidate for the picturesque, the Chinese pagoda favored in the 1740s as a haunt of the family's ornamental hermit, was seen by one of its partisans later as a source of sublime terror, if the original were properly understood:

> Bats, owls, vultures and every kind of bird of prey flutters in the groves; wolves, tigers and jackals howl in the forest; half-famished animals wander upon the plains; gibbets, wheels and the whole apparatus of torture are seen from the roads; and in

[4] Both cited in David Jacques, *Georgian Gardens* (Portland: Timber Press, 1984), p. 145.
[5] Edmund Burke, *On the Sublime* (London: Mallard, 1907), p. 62.

the most dismal recess of the woods . . . are temples dedicated to the king of vengeance.[6]

In this scene of horror as painted in words by William Chambers, we are suddenly aroused by the "pathetic descriptions of tragical events" inscribed on the pagoda's "pillars of stone."[7] We are engaged in imagination as we might not be by "smallness . . . smoothness" and the other effects of the merely beautiful. It was in picturesque scenes that sympathy was aroused. Inspired by terror, all our senses go on alert. The contriver of an eighteenth-century estate hoped similarly to shock the *flâneurs* on an estate into heightened awareness of their surroundings by placing a waterfall strategically in the woods, this torrent of water also inspiring awe and fear.

Any modern reader must smile at Chambers's description of the sublime power of the Chinese pagoda. In a way, however, the link between the sympathetic and the sublime tells a simple home truth: when things are going smoothly people do not pay much attention to each other. And of course the theatricality in this notion of the terrifying ruin was self-conscious, just as the haw-haw was. Our Enlightened ancestors were perfectly clear, finally, that they would flush with awe only for a moment. The storm of feeling would pass, the impulse of sympathic connection subside.

The sublime building, as understood in the eighteenth century, was unlike a church. In a church you were making connection with God; the building is a medium between you and the divine. Whereas the sublime building was thought to be an experience unto itself. Terror, sudden awareness, electricity were generated by its very form. It had this life all of its own. The idea of the integrity of the object derived from the experience of magic which the Enlightened man of reason permitted himself, the magic power of things, if they are made in a certain way, to transport him out of the ordinary. Mozart's opera *The Magic Flute* is a work of the sublime in this sense, its emotional decor much like that of Chambers's Chinese pagoda. The modern cult of the object is about what is left when the artist no

[6] Sir William Chambers, quoted in Watkin, *English Vision*, p. 73.
[7] Ibid.

longer strives to arouse that momentary sympathetic union between people and their environment. He or she seeks only for the sublime effect—the seizure, the shock in itself, for itself. At that moment, anti-social art is born. And for the architect in particular, there is something unexpected in this birth, as I say, since the effect of the sublime came originally from a hunger for unity, between person and object, person and nature, person and person.

The Technology of Unity

Sigfried Giedion's classic manifesto *Space, Time and Architecture* is a modern expression of the cult of the object. His manifesto is doubly interesting because it justifies this worship of objects by appealing explicitly to an ideal of natural unity. To be sure, Giedion's Nature is not Thomas Jefferson's. The modern architect believes that we have discovered a principle of unity in Nature wholly unsuspected before Einstein. This principle is the unity of space and time. Giedion's charge to his colleagues is that modern architecture must make use of this modern knowledge of the physical world. Indeed, he believes, modern artists are beginning to do so, while the makers of streets and houses have yet to catch up with Einstein:

> Space in modern physics is conceived of as relative to a moving point of reference, not as the absolute and static entity of the baroque system of Newton. And in modern art, for the first time since the Renaissance, a new conception of time leads to a self-conscious enlargement of our ways of perceiving space.[8]

That is, what Einstein calculated, Picasso painted. A cubist portrait may show simultaneously the side and the front of a face. Viewers

[8] Sigfried Giedion, *Space, Time and Architecture*, 5th ed. (Cambridge, Mass.: Harvard University Press, 1982), p. 436.

have the sense of their own point of view simultaneously in two places rather than of the face turning. Rightly or wrongly, Giedion thought that being in two different places simultaneously was what modern physics revealed about Nature. Moreover, Giedion believed modern architecture is a particularly favored modern art because it can use new building materials and technology to make simultaneous time and space palpable in houses and factories.

These are not quite as abstruse assertions as they seem: Take a building like the one Walter Gropius and Adolf Meyer built in Cologne in 1914, the Administrative Office-Building of the Werkbund exhibition. Gropius declared that "the outward forms of the New Architecture differs fundamentally in an organic sense from those of the old," because in this building you are simultaneously inside and outside.[9] In front the entrance is flanked by two spiral staircases sheathed in glass, jutting out from the façade. From the outside you can see people moving up and down between floors. In the back the main floor is entirely sheathed in glass, so that everyone is visible inside. You can see through walls, your eyes move inside to outside, outside to inside. The confines of the interior have lost their meaning. Moreover, at street level Gropius and Meyer have used glass in and around the doors so that you can literally look through the building to people entering from the other side. This is wholeness, but of a more radical sort than Jefferson or the younger John Wood conceived. Inner and outer become apparent at once, like the front and side of a cubist portrait.

No big thing reveals itself at a glance. However, here you can find no overall image into which the parts resolve themselves, though everything is so open. Each space seemingly has its own logic; to understand how the stairs feel you have to walk them; the door, so oddly not a barrier, invites you to enter. And this invitation to move makes again a more complicated picture than the open window of the past. Time has appeared in the picture, movement-time. By guiding the inhabitant's movements, this office building seems to tell a story as complex as a modern novel. Gropius, Mies van der Rohe, and Marcel Breuer sought that. They wanted to make spaces that create a special kind of coherence due to the sequence of movement, move-

[9] Walter Gropius, *The New Architecture and the Bauhaus*, trans. P. Morton Shand (Cambridge, Mass.: MIT Press, 1965), p. 20.

ment through space binding person to building. All the inventions that opened up the interior of Enlightenment houses like Monticello seem to culminate in these modern structures. Inside and outside, room and room, are unified—a unity we start to experience the moment our bodies begin to move.

Modern architecture has sought to satisfy an Enlightenment craving: to live in a physically unifiable world. Certain architecture of the late Renaissance and early baroque period lay the groundwork for satisfying this craving. The undulating walls of Francesco Borromini's buildings make the eye travel across the wall plane slowly; it is hard to look at a wall plane all at once in a Borromini building like the church of S. Ivo in Rome (1642–1660). The flexible ground plans of the Turinese architect Guarino Guarini—as in the church of S. Lorenzo, 1668–1687—created mysterious spaces of great drama and no obvious purpose, to be fathomed only as one moved through them. These structures radically defy the modern minimalist maxim crystallized by the art critic Michael Fried: "at every moment the work itself is wholly manifest."[10]

For Giedion's near contemporary Geoffrey Scott, bodily movement was the secret in defining human scale in the environment, a secret he thought the Renaissance understood and modern planners do not. "We project ourselves into [the spaces in which we stand], fill them ideally with our movement."[11] When the body feels engulfed, because the shape of a street or square or interior has no relation in its immensity to any particular movement within it, then the form is out of scale; if a sidewalk is too narrow for the body to feel at ease in walking, the street is as out of scale as a ceiling that is too low. The Renaissance architect, in Scott's view, struggled with heavy materials and structural constraints to achieve the human scale that the Renaissance painter brought to life on canvas. The modern architect need not.

Yet here, in purely visual terms, is the germ of the idea of an object's integrity. Freedom of movement and of scale through and about the building and the space around it has given the modern

[10] Michael Fried, "Art and Objecthood" (1967), reprinted in Gregory Battcock, ed., Minimal Art: A Critical Anthology (New York: Dutton, 1968), p. 145.
[11] Geoffrey Scott, The Architecture of Humanism: A Study in the History of Taste (1914; reprint, New York: W. W. Norton, 1974), pp. 169, 170.

architectural structure a life of its own, different from the life of buildings in the past. Coherence in design is now freed of the engineering obstacles that imposed upon earlier buildings. The technologies of modern construction (glass walls, steel framing, electric lighting) make this new kind of free movement possible. They remove the old logic of necessary distinctions, of interior location of windows and bearing walls, as well as divisions between inside and outside. This makes it possible to build at last the Enlightenment ideal of the open form; in principle, barriers in a building have ceased to be as significant as they were in eras when engineering constraints more tightly dictated form. A building that can be made simply for the sake of its expressive form is a modern ideal of architectural integrity.

An old material has been put to new use in the service of this ideal. This material is glass. The walls in large buildings are now most often built with it in large plates, the plate glass set in steel frames opening up the entire world outside to the person working or living high up in the sky. In 1914 the engineer Paul Scheerbart declared that glass could dissolve the barriers of experience between inside and outside, in terms that would have been recognizable to an educator or a gardener in the 1770s:

> We mostly inhabit closed spaces. These form the milieu from which our culture develops. . . . If we wish to raise our culture to a higher plane, so must we willy-nilly change our architecture. And this will be possible only when we remove the sense of enclosure from the spaces where we live. And this we will only achieve by introducing Glass Architecture.[12]

This new technology of unity reveals how the architectural form has become socially aloof.

Manufactured glass is at least four thousand years old, but not until the Christian era did people learn how to make it transparent; they discovered transparency through experiments in heating and cooling the mixture of soda and lime that is simple glass. Not until

---

[12] Quoted in Reyner Banham, *The Architecture of the Well-Tempered Environment,* 2nd ed. (Chicago: The University of Chicago Press, 1984), p. 126.

1674 was it known how to alter the properties of glass by changing the very materials of which it could be made. In that year the British chemist George Ravenscroft replaced the soda lime mixture by a lead alkali one. This glass, which we use still for fine crystal objects, had far greater transparency and strength than soda-and-lime glass, but it was much too expensive for windows. The older glass cost little to make but broke easily when cast in large panes. Toward the end of the eighteenth century, the technology was perfected by reliably producing sheet glass, thanks to the use of cast-iron rollers for smoothing. Windows in all kinds of structures could now be made larger, but in the nineteenth century truly radical glass architecture appeared in two special building forms, the greenhouse and the arcade.

Greenhouses like those Joseph Paxton built for the duke of Devonshire at Chatsworth, which we know only from drawings and photographs, or Kew Gardens, or the Jardin des Plantes, are extraordinary buildings. The dappling play of light and shadow in these enormous glass halls, as clouds pass, as time passes, make space into action. The rooms constantly change their form, just as a stage is transformed through lighting, but here there is no sense of artifice; the sunlight alone does the work. Or rather, there is an artifice that does not register on our senses as a stage set because all the actors here are plants: the nineteenth-century greenhouse abolished the distinction between inside and outside in terms of light, while radically controlling this barrier in terms of heat and the penetration of smoke. The plants therefore flourished and the people walking among them experienced the sensation of being outside and inside simultaneously. This organic artifice under glass remains as magical to us as it was to the Victorians.

Moreover, glass created a more obvious drama, a drama of scale. A building sheathed in iron-framed glass radically reduced the cost of building big and also cut the time necessary for construction. Kew Gardens outside London and the Jardin des Plantes in Paris rose in a fraction of the time required to build St. Paul's or Notre-Dame. Glass was the material that overcame men's sense of great space as difficult to enclose. Until quite recently, then, the visual experience of joining inside and outside was a matter either of direct exposure, through an open window, or of looking through an often ripply material cut into small pieces and framed in wood or metal. Fully apprehending the outside form within, yet feeling neither cold nor wind nor moisture, is a modern sensation, a modern sensation of protected openness in very big buildings.

In the nineteenth century it is true, glass was used somewhat tentatively in dwellings for human beings. This ambivalence appeared in the building of arcades. With the prominent exception of the Galerie d'Orléans in the Palais Royal, most of the early nineteenth-century arcades are ordinary stone or brick buildings shoved close together, the space between them roofed over by glass. The later exhibition structures completely sheathed in glass, like the Crystal Palace in London, or the Palais de l'Exposition in Paris, were designed as temporary structures. To live entirely exposed to the outside seemed akin to walking around naked, which was not an appealing condition to our Victorian forebears. This was why they used glass less freely than their technology permitted, even in factories or offices. And indeed there is an inherent Victorian logic to the deferred construction of glass buildings until the elevator, the steel skeleton, and in our century air-conditioning, ensured that exposure would take place far above the ground, up in the sky, where no one could see you.

The peculiar physical sensation aroused by plate is complete visibility without exposure of the other senses. It is the physical sensation on which is founded the modern sense of isolation in a building. And, in this, the history of glass is inseparable from the history of lighting. The open gas lamp of the mid-nineteenth century was succeeded by the "Ricket's globes" that enclosed the flame and prevented gas fumes from permeating a room; this made it possible to use sheets of glass as permanent seals in windows, opening only for light. In a model house built in Liverpool in 1872, designed to illustrate an early version of combined central heating and ventilation,

the windows were not openable. Fresh air was fed in from the basement, warmed in a furnace, and distributed via a central lobby on each floor and through a perforated cornice into the room. Over each gasolier was an outlet grille that led to a duct.[13]

13 Witold Rybczynski, *Home: A Short History of an Idea* (New York: Viking, 1986), p. 146.

This model house is a primitive version of the technology that would operate in the skyscraper interior to isolate the interior from the outside, even though everything outside was visible. The combination of visibility and isolation then grew stronger with the development of air conditioning and the thermal glass wall (in which two panes of sheet glass are held within a metal frame, creating a thermal barrier) a half-century later. Corbusier's Cité de Refuge, constructed in Paris in 1932, brings this combination to fruition: it has a curtain wall facing south of thermal glass, and air circulation like that in the Liverpool house but as expanded by the French architect Gustave Lyon for the Salle Pleyel in Paris—a completely sealed structure. (The Cité de Refuge turned out to be a technological disaster because of the stifling heat trapped by the glass, and Corbusier was shortly to face it with a *brise-soleil*.) Despite its thermal problems, the principle of the sealed box of complete visibility has become the environmental model on which glass is today employed in most tall buildings.

The difficulties of the glass box, however, go much deeper than the temperature of the skin. In them we see modern technology used to make coherent structure, as the Enlightenment would have conceived of physical coherence—all the rooms flowing into one another, the building and its surroundings visually interwoven. Yet these structures also betray strong powers of isolation; they are "integrated" objects that can be sealed. Though technology has heightened visibility through plate glass, the world made visible through this window has been devalued in its reality. This is true of sensate reality: a man sees from his office window a tree blowing in the wind but cannot hear the wind blowing. It is true of social reality: in Detroit's Renaissance Center, which is a very bad pastiche of a wavy glass tower Mies van der Rohe conceived for Berlin decades earlier, deals unfold during the day insulated from the wail of police sirens in the streets below, the police beacons glinting and glancing off the wavy glass walls like quick sunrises and sunsets. The barrier of transparency in a plate-glass shop window ensures that an object for sale cannot be touched. The division of the physical senses that began in the Victorian greenhouse, and is so arousing there, has become now more deadening: sight is more routinely insulated from sound, and touch and other human beings.

The combination of visibility and isolation marks today the way buildings relate streets at ground level. Great sheaths of plate glass are routinely used as ground-level walls; there are usually just a few, restricted entrances. Thus the building is more isolated from the street than older buildings with smaller windows that open even though there is, to use Giedion's phrase, visual "penetration" between the inside and the outside. On parts of Park Avenue in New York, block after block of unbroken street-wall is made of plate glass sheathing banks, office supply showrooms, luxury car dealers, and expensive clothes shops, each ground-level business with a single, policed entrance. One might also experience a similar sense of disconnection if the tightly controlled entrances were set in brick walls, but not in quite the same way: seeing what you cannot hear, touch, or feel increases the sense that what is inside, is inaccessible.

To be sure, the first great modernist architects wanted anything but this to happen. They were socialists, they were Enlightened, they saw the practice of architecture literally building a more unified, coherent society; Erik Erikson's credo of identity could have easily served the makers of the Werkbund office building in Cologne as a motto. The way the modern materials at their disposal came to be used meant, however, that their art created isolation rather than connection.

These curious powers of isolation revealed in a visually open, free architecture explain in part how the built environment has become at odds with the social life of the city. One could explain these uses of glass simply in terms of economics or power. For instance, plate glass so deployed is the perfect building material for a neutral city, since it devalues the tactile reality of what one sees. But culture adds to power the problem of legitimation. "Integrity" is a moral category. The form of the object has acquired, as it were, rights against being tampered with. Architecture forms a special case in relation to the ideal of integrity, for it comes into being in ways paintings, sculptures, and poems do not. The making of a piece of urban architecture is a messy process, involving an army of specialist designers and technicians at war with opposing armies of government officials, bankers, and clients. To assert that the buildings which result have the single-minded imprint and pristine integrity which earns them the

right not to be touched subsequently is in one way, therefore, ludi-
crous. But modern architects do assert that right.

An Architect of the Sublime

The grounds for asserting this right appear most graphically in the
work of perhaps the greatest of modern architects. Mies van der Rohe
was the architect who did more than anyone else to make plate glass
the physical stuff through which our century sees. It was Mies who in
1921 conceived an office building for the Friedrichstrasse in Berlin
entirely sheathed in glass, Mies who a year later unveiled a model of
a glass tower with walls of billowing curves and folds, thus converting
the metaphor of a curtain wall into a literal if ideal vision of curtains
of glass rising forty stories into the air. It was Mies who, exiled to
Chicago in 1937, began to build these ideal visions of glass in that city
where the early skyscrapers with inner glass atriums had already
suggested that the transparency of a window might be extended to
the transparency of an entire wall, from which it was only a logical
next step to an entire tower that might become transparent. It was
Mies who built in New York in 1956–1958 the city's greatest glass
tower, the Seagram Building on Park Avenue, a work of extraordinary
elegance. And of course it is Mies, archon of modernism, who is now
accused of fathering a soulless environment of glass towers in which
men and women are as cut off from one another as from the outside:
Mies, the father of visual solitude.

In one way this could simply mean that Mies in his Berlin days did
not imagine that towers manufactured by machines entirely of man-
made materials would thicken and reproduce themselves in cities,
crowding close together, just as Raymond Hood, the genius presiding
over Rockefeller Center, sought to prevent the manufacture of modernity from creating a mountain of metal and glass. Mies usually
drew his earlier towers as single structures alone on the horizon,
where one saw them freely from all sides.

The glass world imposes solitude upon its inhabitants: if I put the matter thus, I write as though the material dictates the meaning. Instead, glass has to be used in a certain way to arouse a sense of lonely space. The difference appears in the contrast between the glass houses built by Philip Johnson (his own in New Canaan, Connecticut, or an earlier glass house in Cambridge, Massachusetts) and the Farnsworth House Mies built after the Second World War in Plano, Illinois. Johnson's glass house in Cambridge sits directly on the ground, the floor and the ground being virtually at the same grade. The Cambridge house forms one side of a rectangular courtyard, the other three sides are enclosed by a high fence, the court is paved, its edges are planted; the inside of the house achieves a real unity with this protected exterior space. In Johnson's New Canaan house, the trees and shrubs seem as much a part of the decor as the lamps and paintings. In these glass boxes there is a comfortable feeling of unity with nature; gentlemen of the eighteenth century would feel at home in them.

Yet in the Farnsworth House of Mies, the space arouses quite different emotions. It is a rectangle of glass walls sheathed in white-painted steel; the box floats on eight steel stilts four feet above the ground; a rectangular terrace, also on stilts, lies along one side of it and slightly lower. There is a functional reason for the stilts, since the land is the floodplain of the nearby Fox River, but form has not followed function here. As the irate first owner was later to complain, there were far more efficient ways to design a floodproof house. A house on stilts, indeed, proclaims that this is a threatened dwelling; when you look at the Farnsworth House, especially up from the ground as you approach by foot, you sense it. Though the present owners have sought to create an English groundsward around the house, I'm told the ground is usually as soft and squishy on this floodplain as it was the day I visited—beautiful land but uncomfortable. Among other things, there are snakes. The Farnsworth House, with its base at chest level, its terrace at waist level, seems to hover, floating like a spaceship, and you hurry forward to hoist yourself up to this refuge.

The house, however, does not offer sanctuary. The threat of nature that urged you toward it is reinforced once you reach the terrace;

there is no refuge for you or for any other living thing here. The use of huge sealed sheets of glass for every exterior vertical surface means you cannot go in where you see safety. Nor is the sight of people within reassuring; they look as if they don't belong there, as if no one belongs inside. Mies achieves this effect in part by the unusual height of the glass walls, in part by the heaviness of the wood pedestal that contains the kitchen and bathrooms, which sits in the center of the glass box. The pedestal is perfectly balanced weight against the wall planes, the furniture precisely and elegantly defined within the interplay of central mass and outer boundaries. But the intrusion of someone dozing in a chair (though it's hard to nap in a Mies Barcelona Chair), someone else reading a magazine while munching potato chips—all these normal signs of domesticity become obscene. Instead, this is a space in which we experience the terror of nature sharpened by a building offering no promise of refuge. It is a modern expression of the sublime.

In principle the glass panel should be the most "friendly" of building elements, in the sense of most flexible and adaptive to various human needs and design programs. This was the lesson of Paxton's Crystal Palace and the other exhibition halls of its type. Again, nothing in form could seem farther from Mies than Buckminster Fuller's geodesic domes, especially as the domes were articulated by François Dallegret to cover both a building and the area just around it so that inner and outer space become absolutely one. Dallegret's was a reasonable version of Fuller's own dream to cover all of Manhattan with a dome. (In fact, the hemispherical shape creates serious practical problems of air stratification and heating; it is also hard to accommodate the workings of windows and doors to a curved integument.) But Fuller domes don't combine easily with structures that aren't domes. Geodesic domes betray the same logic as do the glass towers of Mies, as structures in and of and for themselves. Fuller believes that glass might be a "unifying" material in the Enlightenment sense. In practice unity means to him what it meant to Mies: visibility combined with isolation. The domes work best when set by themselves alone in a forest.

Why should the pursuit of unity between interior and exterior through glass have ended this way? In the case of Mies, who was a much greater artist than others who have sought to make use of the possibilities of glass, there is an uncomfortable explanation for his use of modern technologies of visibility toward isolating ends.

The Religion
of Art

The Christian belief in clarity and precision as divine has reappeared in secular form, as the cult of the perfect object. The design of the sublime in the eighteenth century was of open nature, of ruins, or of follies like the Chinese Pagoda; these were sites for the hot, enthused connection to an awe-inspiring scene. Whereas in the unities established in the buildings of Mies van der Rohe—unification through glass of precisely determined orders of space—the sublime instead rejects this hot arousal. They are aloof, cool buildings, majestically calm. In this solitude the object is possessed of its integrity. In the minds of the medieval Christian builders, the church was to be protected by a zone of immunity from the chaos of the world. In the modern form of the sublime, the beautiful work of art is to be protected from the soiled hands of the user.

This aesthetic first was explored by romantic writers. A glass house on steel stilts, as a work of art set in hostile nature, a work in its very perfection inhospitable to human beings—this would have been perfectly comprehensible to writers like Sénancour, the author of a novel of ideas, *Obermann*. When a person shuns society, gives himself or herself over to solitude, he or she does not find the natural world to be a sanctuary; this was, Sénancour declared, the sheer sentimentality of Rousseau and the eighteenth century. Through solitude we instead apprehend the utter cruelty of the physical world to human beings. Géricault's image of nature's cruelty in the *Raft of the Medusa*, or Delacroix's drawings of storms and of the desert were pictures of the brutality of nature which prompted romantic writers to understand the word used so easily today to describe modern architecture, the word *cold*. These writers tried to understand this word as

naming complex processes occurring within the human psyche react-
ing against nature. Why, for instance, did Mies build the Farnsworth
House on stilts? Sénancour might have answered for the architect
as he defended his own prose: Only when the artist creates a cold
space, only then can he realize in pure, still form a contrast to the
viciousness of the world. Cold withdrawal testifies to the artist's
will, his refusal to be either a victim of nature or a servant of others
in society. This defense might indeed have served Mies well; the
Farnsworth House is an object made in a hostile natural setting
that is in turn hostile to human use and mess. The Philip Johnson
houses are by contrast friendlier to plants, animals, and people, and
less challenging.

In wholeness, isolation; in coherence, withdrawal. These were the
mutations the romantics discovered in their fathers' worship of unity.
The mutation was identified in an equation, an equation in art par-
alleling the individualism that took form in nineteenth-century economic behavior: self-sufficiency equals integrity. But whereas in the
economic sphere this equation was a license to act, to challenge, to
exploit the world, the equation of individualism had another effect in
art. To make something complete and self-sufficient unto itself as
expression is to create an object that transcends mere vulgar, worldly
measures of practical use, or delight in habitation. The integrity of an
object is not about its reception. This formula in the present draws on
the rejections of the past. The psychological aristocrats of the romantic era who made the *émigration intérieure* thought they had to withdraw themselves from the polluted mire that was everyday existence.
Mere scorn was not enough, however, to orient their lives. The artists
among them were more fortunate; the romantic artists emigrated
within by making poems, buildings, and paintings thought to have a
self-sufficing integrity. Mies is a romantic architect in this sense.

The modern sublime arose from this romantic malaise and its resolution in art. To understand why Mies is a sublime artist in glass,
while the young Philip Johnson is a skilled craftsman, I think of how
Sénancour made an imaginative leap in *Obermann* when the protagonist became depressed by the people around him. This man hard-
ened by the world has come to feel absolutely empty inside. He
decides to go for a walking tour by himself in the Alps. High in the

mountains there is not a living plant to be seen; he spies a hawk for an instant and then this single sign of animal life disappears into a valley. The air is cold and dry, piercing his lungs every time he takes a breath. He who on the ground believed in nothing now finds that the nothingness of the Alps begins to fill him with its own power; he experiences a wave of awe, as though he were in a church. It is a moment of the sublime—not of the sudden, hot sort—rather felt as awe of the eternal ice, of enduring absence. Thus could the romantic artist name the architectural power of Mies's buildings: here too timeless absence acquires a sacred character. This is what the phrase *the religion of art* means.

In art the consequences of creating a self-sufficing, unified object is that it seems untouchable. This romantic permutation of the sublime has become incorporated into the modern belief that works of architecture in a city should be protected, that their form should be inviolable—the very word *inviolable* suggesting that these human creations have a magic which subsequently renders them untouchable by men and women. It is as though using a building were like playing a Beethoven sonata, in which the player has no right to change any of the notes of Beethoven's score. It would be sacrilege to do so.

The interiors of Mies van der Rohe's rooms are charged with this transcending self-referential power. The grace and harmony of a Mies room depend on finely calculated balances, on the exact placement of furniture (his own, naturally), the presence or absence of paintings, the textures and colors of rugs. Frank Lloyd Wright, who also designed his own furniture as an integral part of his architecture, was no less a dictator by temper, but Wright's dictation is very different. It is possible to move the furniture around in a Wright interior without radically affecting the sense of the room's volume. In a Mies room the least change of the position of a chair alters how big the room feels. Mies's architecture makes the whole depend on one man's absolute control of the parts. This change of consciousness is what the romantics first sought to plumb by understanding the conditions in which a man-made thing acquires, as it were, rights against human beings. The work of art is treated with reverence. This reverence bespeaks the withdrawal of objects from the world of human beings, an authenticity in which the objects are invested with their own mana. In spaces conveying this power in modern New York, like the entrances to Mies's Seagram Building or Breuer's Whitney Museum, we do feel awed, awed by space alien to us, space drawn into itself. This is how the romantics understood the sublime; solitude was transmuted into things that will resist the depredations of nature or other people. Such an art aspires to the qualities of a sacred object. An art, that is, that should not be touched, not be used.

The architecture that Sigfried Giedion celebrated is embedded in a tragic irony. The pursuit of the whole has revived the religious break between the spiritual and the worldly. The art of Mies van der Rohe is an art marking this divorce, and it is great art, greater certainly than the work of architects who have made a more conscious effort to reckon with their surroundings. It is forged from the architect's power to see coherence, to create unities, but these powers have passed across the fatal divide in our culture in which the whole becomes the self-sufficient, in which it achieves its integrity through becoming a thing unto itself. They arouse in others an intimate of absence, of untouchableness. This is our experience of the sublime.

This religion of art is a faith fatal to those who design environments. For the consequence of this faith is an even greater indifference to the everyday needs of people using buildings, an indifference to use equal to the negligence of Christian otherworldliness. The integrity of an object conflicts with the needs of generation after generation who must somehow contrive to live in it. The story the work of Mies van der Rohe tells, at its most troubling, is that what makes for great art no longer makes for conscience. *Unity* has lost its moral meaning.

The
Humane
City

chapter 5

Exposure

In the Presence
of Difference

A P O E T of nineteenth-century Paris first tried to imagine how cities could give birth to a new form of subjective life. In Charles Baudelaire's essay on his friend Constantin Guys, first drafted in 1845, the poet praised the painter as a man for whom "no aspect of life has become *stale*."[1] The essay in which this praise occurs has a somewhat equivocal title—"The Painter of Modern Life"—because to Baudelaire much of modern life had indeed gone stale, especially life in Paris. The Parisians of his day seemed bored by themselves as much as by one another; *ennui*, inner indifference coupled with constant dissatisfaction, irritation and restlessness without cause or goal, the fear one was merely existing rather than living—these were the diseases which attacked them. The concrete details of daily life bored them, but equally their lives lacked the nobility of faith in something great. *Daring* was a word they applied most often to investments.

Unlike his near contemporary Søren Kierkegaard, the poet saw another remedy for this inner weariness than renewed faith in God. Baudelaire instead found a remedy for the spiritual difficulties of his contemporaries in one kind of bad art.

The sketches of Constantin Guys which Baudelaire admired are

[1] Charles Baudelaire, "The Painter of Modern Life," in *The Painter of Modern Life and Other Essays,* trans. Jonathan Mayne (New York: Da Capo, 1986), p. 8.

simple, crisp evocations of everyday life on the streets; they show
people taking walks or riding in the Bois de Boulogne or laughing in
a café. They are sketches of pleasant encounters far removed from the
darkness of the romantics or the pained strokes of Baudelaire's own
verse; Parisians conjured by Guys's brush have turned outward and
seem to care about one another. The symbol was perhaps what Baudelaire most liked about these drawings. Guys had drawn, Baudelaire
thought, at least a salving possibility of modern life: relief from one's
inner, subjective demons in a city of passing encounters, fragmentary
exchanges, and large crowds—remission from the subjective in that
space. These sketches showed people in the presence of otherness—
all the difference of age, taste, background, and belief that are concentrated in a city—and aroused by the diversity around them.

Ironically, it takes a second-rate society artist like Guys—who
Baudelaire likened in point of technique and visual sophistication to
a savage—to show us this, because we see the outside as the space of
the superficial. A crowd of strangers on the street walking, talking,
shopping, going to or from work, appears caught together in a web of
routine; this life in common is inferior to the real life happening
inside each person in the crowd. Such an opposition betrays the
soul-sickness of boredom, Baudelaire thought: nothing out there is
worthy of me.

In one way the poet himself lived the opposition he criticized, from
the early 1840s on. In his poetry the crowd appears as a terrible force,
suffocating or disorienting the poet; in his daily round the poet swam
in the crowd with pleasure. Baudelaire the dandy dressed in ruin-
ously expensive waistcoats, parading and observing on the streets. As
a young man he became an inhabitant of the famous Hôtel Pimodan
on the Île St-Louis, one of the places of self-conscious Bohemia in
Paris creating its own mythology of art, liberty, and revolt; its deni-
zens appeared frequently in print to explain how they lived, often
even before they had unpacked their belongings. It was this same
Baudelaire who late at night shut his door on the third floor of the
all-too-picturesque dwelling and made the art which earlier in the day
he had merely represented as a way of life.

The stones of Paris are insubstantial to this, the city's greatest poet;
unlike Ruskin in his *Stones of Venice*, had Baudelaire undertaken a

guide to his own city he would have recommended the flea markets, the whorehouses, and the cafés as the most important places, from a spiritual point of view—which was the view of a person suffering from an oppressive inner life. In a crowd he lost himself—and the loss was precious to him.

Baudelaire saw in the modern city the possibility for transcending the cultural forces we have depicted. The modern city can turn people outward, not inward; rather than wholeness, the city can give them experiences of otherness. The power of the city to reorient people in this way lies in its diversity; in the presence of difference people have at least the possibility to step outside themselves.

Baudelaire's faith in the powers of diversity offers one way to assay the experience of otherness on streets today.

Since I've lived in New York I've liked walking, avoiding subways or taxis whenever I can. These days I usually walk from my apartment in Greenwich Village up to midtown on the East Side to eat, an amble of about three miles. There are plenty of restaurants in the Village but none quite like those just above the United Nations, in the side streets of the Fifties. They are French, but not fashionable; food is still prepared with butter and lard and cream, the patrons are bulky and comfortable, the menu seldom changes. The restaurants are in the ground floors of townhouses, and most are done up alike: a bar in front leading to a long room lined with banquettes of red plush or red leather; Sunday-painter oil paintings of provincial France hang in gold frames on the walls above the banquettes; a kitchen is tucked in the back. People say New York is an unfriendly city, and I suppose any one of these restaurants could be cited in evidence. The waiters, Italians or Frenchmen in late middle age, lack that air of reassuring familiarity tourists like. But the restaurants are filled with people seemingly quite content to be left alone, many regular, solitary clients as well as couples speaking quietly.

To reach the French restaurants I have to pass from my house through a drug preserve just to the east of Washington Square. Ten years ago junkie used to sell to junkie in the square and these blocks east to Third Avenue. In the morning stoned men lay on park benches, or in doorways; they slept immobile under the influence of the drugs, sometimes having spread newspapers out on the pavements as mattresses. It was then the sort of scene that might have attracted Baudelaire's spleen: in a prose poem of 1851 the poet wrote of a poisoned group of workers:

> This languishing and pining population . . . who feel a purple and impetuous blood coursing through their veins, and who cast a long, sorrow-laden look at the sunlight and shadows of the great parks . . .[2]

The dulled heroin addicts now are gone, replaced by addict-dealers in cocaine. The cocaine dealers are never still, their arms are jerky, they pace and pace; in their electric nervousness, they radiate more danger than the old stoned men.

In Baudelaire's Paris misery and wealth were inextricable; everywhere he walked he encountered aggressive beggars and spontaneous fights, his lapels were grabbed by men selling watches while his pockets were picked by men stealing them. These disorders stimulated his muse. The civilized man must, somehow, take into account pain he can do nothing about. But now that accounting does not occur. Baudelaire's inflamed poetic voice no longer conjures an observer's impression of the woe of drugs, for the sight of these human beings whose bodies are short-circuiting on cocaine, while disturbing, is not too disturbing, if I also keep moving.

Along Third Avenue, abruptly above Fourteenth Street, there appear six blocks or so of white brick apartment houses built in the 1950s and 1960s on the edges of the Gramercy Park area; the people who live here are buyers for department stores, women who began in New York as secretaries and may or may not have become something more but kept at their jobs. Until very recently, seldom would one see in an American city, drinking casually in bars alone or dining quietly with one another, these women of a certain age, women who do not attempt to disguise the crowsfeet at the edge of the eyes; for generations the blocks here have been their shelter. It is a neighborhood also of single bald men, in commerce and sales, not at the top

---

[2] Charles Baudelaire, *Spleen de Paris*, trans. Harry Zohn, in Walter Benjamin, *Charles Baudelaire, A Lyric Poet in the Era of High Capitalism* (London: Verso, 1983), p. 74.

but walking confidently enough to the delis and tobacco stands lining Third Avenue. All the food sold in shops here is sold in small cans and single portions; it is possible in the Korean groceries to buy half a lettuce.

"By 'modernity,' " Baudelaire wrote, "I mean the ephemeral, the fugitive, the contingent, the half of art whose other half is the eternal and the immutable."[3] Gramercy Park is a community of refugees, like so many other places in New York, but here there are refugees from the family. These are ephemeral lives, one might say, their daily round consisting of little bits of business, of shopping after work, of watering plants and feeding cats in the evening. Most of the imagery of anomie, isolation, and estrangement of the nineteenth century assumed that solitude was an urban affliction. The image of a mass of solitary, middle-aged people living in characterless apartment buildings still might conjure a pathetic picture. Yet there are lots of people on the street in this swath of Third Avenue at all hours; though hardly fashionable, these blocks skirting Gramercy Park are in the companionable spirit of Constantin Guys. There is nothing sublime in this solitude; it seems to enhance the ordinary business of life.

Unfortunately, in a few minutes of walking this scene too has disappeared, and now my walk takes an unexpected turn. The middle Twenties between Third and Lexington is the equestrian center of New York, where several stores sell saddles and Western apparel. The clientele is varied: polo players from the lusher suburbs, Argentines, people who ride in Central Park, and then another group, more delicate connoisseurs of harnesses, crops, and saddles. The middle Twenties play host as well to a group of bars that cater to these leather fetishists, bars in run-down townhouses with no signs and blacked-out windows. What makes the middle Twenties distinct is that all the customers in the leather shops are served alike—rudely. Saddles and whips are sold by harassed salesmen, wrapped by clerks ostentatiously bored. Nor do the horsey matrons seem to care much where the men with careful eyes take their purchases, no curiosity about the blacked-out windows from behind which ooze the smells of beer, leather, and urine. A city of differences and of fragments of life that do not connect: in such a city the obsessed are set free.

[3] Baudelaire, "Painter of Modern Life," p. 13.

My walk takes me along a diverse street, but its differences evoke something other than the vivid scenes in which Baudelaire's *flâneur* becomes profoundly engaged.

The first modern school of urbanists was established in the United States at the University of Chicago around the time of the First World War. These Chicago urbanists, most notably Robert Park (originally a journalist whose visual impressions of the city came from investigating crimes, accidents, fires, and political demonstrations), sought to understand the relation between the city as a "place on the map" and as a "moral order," their version of *urbs* and *civitas*. They came to be experts in this lighter involvement.

The teacher of the Chicago urbanists, the Berlin sociologist Georg Simmel, had begun to influence them through a famous lecture given in 1909 about defenses against the outside. Its title was "Die Grossstadt und das Geistesleben," which translates as "The Great City and Mental Life." These men who were bred on reporting crime in the Chicago stockyards found writing about the mental life of cities slightly uncomfortable, at least in the abstract manner their teacher conceived of it—Individual Spirit struggling with Impersonal Collective Form. They sought for a way to translate the mental life of the city into concrete facts. For them, as for Baudelaire, the culture of the city was a matter of experiencing differences—differences of class, age, race, and taste outside the familiar territory of oneself, in a street. And as for the poet, urban differences seemed to Park and Louis Wirth provocations of otherness, surprise, and stimulation. Yet these sociologists had a brilliant, counter-intuitive insight; provocation occurs in the very loosening of strong connections between people in a city.

People who were outsiders, the Chicago urbanists first thought, are likely to benefit from the outside conditions of urban life; "Neither the criminal, the defective, nor the genius has the same opportunity to develop his innate disposition in a small town that he invariably finds in a great city."[4] Deviance is the freedom made possible in a crowded

---

[4] Robert Park, "The City: Suggestions for the Investigation of Behavior in the Urban Environment" (1916), reprinted in Richard Sennett, ed., *Classic Essays on the Culture of Cities* (New York: Prentice-Hall, 1969), p. 126.

city of lightly engaged people. But a community of single, middle-aged women also deviates from the "normal" connection between family and community; immigrants who barely speak the language of natives deviate; so do political radicals, so do Asians and Hispanics. Were one to add up all the "deviant" populations in many big cities, the deviants would form the majority. Thus Park in his later writings, like his younger colleague Wirth, moved away from conceiving of the city as a place that permits differences, and toward understanding the city as a place that encourages the concentration of difference. Its "moral order" is the lack of a moral order that exercises hegemony over the city as a whole. And indeed, these fragments enter into the life of every urbanite so that he acts out, in Wirth's phrase, a number of "segmented roles." The city dweller passes from place to place, activity to activity, taking on the coloring of each scene, as easily as a chameleon changes colors in various surroundings:

> By virtue of his different interests arising out of different aspects of social life, the individual acquires membership in widely divergent groups, each of which function only with reference to a certain segment of his personality.[5]

The Chicago sociologists were the first writers on cities to champion the virtues of a fragmented self. A woman who thinks male/female, a businessman who thinks rich/poor, a Jamaican who thinks black/white, experience low levels of stimulation from the outside, Wirth thought. A fragmented self is more responsive. Thus Enlightenment unity and coherence are not, in this urban vision, the means to self-development—an ever more complex, fragmented experience is.

The Chicago urbanists felt density to be the secret of the city's powers of stimulation. In crowding human differences together, a city's thick impasto of experience should break down the boundaries of the self by sheer pressure of numbers. The Chicago urbanists did not therefore imagine people in a crowd could define the complexity they lived: these differences produced disordered reactions rather than the clear perceptions that occur in simpler, more controlled environ-

---

[5] Worth, "Urbanism as a Way of Life," in Sennett, *Classic Essays*, p. 156.

ments. Nor did the Chicago urbanists equate a crowd and a community: if stimulation occurs as individuals move between communities and scenes, gradually people lose an inner life, they become their skins, their "segmented roles." This was how the Chicago urbanists came to celebrate the outside, the exposure of humans to one other.

The smell of urine is perfumed if only I keep walking. In the upper Twenties along Lexington Avenue bags of spices lie in ranks within the shops run by Indians and Pakistanis; when the doors are open in spring and fall, the combined scents waft out to the street, but like most of the ethnic enclaves in New York these sensuous sights and smells are not beacons to the outside world. In the Indian shops few of the bags of spices are identified by labels. This brilliantly simple expedient discourages all but the most intrepid of tourists who, upon asking for an explanation of the mysterious bags, will be smilingly informed by perfectly polite shopkeepers that one is "hot spice" or another an "imported ingredient." The shop owners stand in their doorways in summer, making jokes or comments—could it possibly be about us?—which are met by their neighbors with the faintest parting of the lips, the slight smile that acknowledges more, and perhaps condemns more, than a loud laugh.

New York should be the ideal city of exposure to the outside. It grasps the imagination because it is a city of differences par excellence, a city collecting its population from all over the world. Yet it is here that the passion of the Parisian poet—that desire for enhancement of stimulation and release from self—seems contravened. By walking in the middle of New York one is immersed in the differences of this most diverse of cities, but precisely because the scenes are disengaged they seem unlikely to offer themselves as significant encounters in the sense of a vivid stimulus, a telling moment of talking or touching or connection. The leather fetishist and spice merchant are protected by disengagement; the admirable women who have made lives for themselves near Gramercy Park are also disengaged, not those needy sort of Americans who feel they must tell you the entire story of their lives in the next five minutes; the junkies doing business are seldom in a mood to chat. All the more is this true—more largely—of the races, who live segregated lives close together, and of social classes, who mix but do not socialize.

Nor are the chameleon virtues of the Chicago urbanists much in evidence: people do not take on the colors of their surroundings, the light-hued colors of otherness. A walk in New York reveals instead that difference from and indifference to others are a related, unhappy pair. The eye sees differences to which it reacts with indifference. I, too, feel no curiosity to know what is problematic in the life of a drug dealer; I am too polite to intrude upon the solitude of a middle-aged woman, or to violate the privacy of another man's sexual obsessions. When I do reach out, harmlessly, the spice merchant pushes me away with his irony.

This reaction of disengagement when immersed in difference is the result of the forces that have created a disjunction between inner and outer life. These forces have annihilated the humane value of complexity, even in a city where differences are an overwhelming sociological fact. Sheer exposure to difference is no corrective to the Christian ills of inwardness. There is withdrawal and fear of exposure, as though all differences are potentially as explosive as those between a drug dealer and an ordinary citizen. There is neutralization: if something begins to disturb or touch me, I need only keep walking to stop feeling. Moreover, I suffer from abundance, the promised remedy of the Enlightenment. My senses are flooded by images, but the difference in value between one image and another becomes as fleeting as my own movement; difference becomes a mere parade of variety. This display of difference on the street obeys the same visual logic, moreover, that ruled the construction of the first modern interiors. These scenes are sequential and linear displays of differences, like the rooms in a railroad flat. Linear, sequential distinctions are no more arousing outside than they were inside. A New York street resembles the studio of a painter who has assembled in it all the paints, books of other artists, and sketches he will need for a grand triptych that will crown his career; then the painter has unaccountably left town.

Which brings us again to power. The last lap of my walk passes through Murray Hill. The townhouses here are dirty limestone or brownstone; the apartment buildings have no imposing entrance lobbies. There is a uniform of unfashion in Murray Hill: elderly women in black silk dresses and equally elderly men sporting pencil-thin mustaches and malacca canes, their clothes visibly decades old. This is a quarter of the old elite in New York.

The quarter likes to depict itself as a dying neighborhood—aristocracy buried by the loud men, civility crushed in the hands of people who have the temerity of their vigor. In one way the manners of Murray Hill simply mirror those of the spice merchants five blocks south—the same self-effacement and strategic discretion; a dealer in turmeric and the senior vice president of a bank are at least brothers in silence. But old money/power reveals a further dimension of indifference.

The center of Murray Hill is the Morgan Library, housed in the mansion at Thirty-sixth and Madison of the capitalist whose vigor appalled old New York at the turn of the century. The talk at black-tie dinners here is dull; the Morgan does not glitter. Some few of the men at Morgan Library dinners will go to the Century Association nearby for that sort of exercise, or even farther afield to the Grolier Club. The Century has chamber music concerts and art exhibits and evening lectures; at the Grolier there is bibliophile chat; the dinners at the Morgan evoke the aura of civilized discourse without a taxing expenditure of thought. At the tables set under the library's dark oak beams, dwarfed in the architectural volume of J. P. Morgan's swagger, people speak cozily of children and of their friends' divorces.

Near the Morgan Library is B. Altman's, an enormous store recently closed which was regularly open in the evenings so that people could shop after a day of work. Often one saw women, of the sort who live nearby in Gramercy Park, shopping for sheets there; the sheet-shoppers had clipped the advertisement for a white sale out of the newspaper and still carried it in their unscuffed calf handbags; they were hardworking, thrifty. I have, as I say, often seen them stop after a round of shopping to contemplate these other women in their unfashionable dresses and jewels in old settings, the men in their worn dinner jackets, entering the portals of the Morgan Library, the doors opening and closing by the aid of flunkies within so that those about to dine need not push. There was a moment of hostility on the street, perhaps clouded in the shopper's eyes by her surprise at how shabby are the permanently rich, and then a shrug—her slight shrug of the shoulders.

In one way the negligence of the diners at the Morgan to their circumstances was thus mirrored at its entrance, in this lifting of shoulders, as though between circumstance, place, and person there were only a neutral connection. The shopper shrugged, accepted, and, like me, moved on; life will go on. This oil of the mechanism of indifference is not the machine of power itself. Instead, the display of indifference is how the eye sees power at work in space. In walking the streets where people go about their own business, we are constantly witnessing scenes of submission in which the actors think they are simply keeping to themselves, numbed to the fact that true indifference requires a privileged place in society. Submission passes through power's magic lantern so that the image illuminated on the city's streets does not irritate the eye. Submission appears on the streets as detachment. If what one sees hurts, one can always keep walking.

Now I've sighted the restaurant. The east Forties between Lexington and First avenues is the most neutral area of Manhattan, a forest of tall, dull apartment buildings in and out of which junior diplomats at the United Nations move their children and their chattel as governments at home rise and fall. Office towers each month encroach upon residential towers, a marriage of towers in the sky that blot out the sun on the streets. On the periphery of the city, one can see literally miles of burned-out or abandoned ruins, the buildings often with bricked-up windows or windows covered in sheets of metal behind which, at night, one spies gleams of light. This permissible belt of desolation in so rich a city is like a boast of civic indifference. Near my restaurant in the very center, the buildings, especially at night, have their own derelict, homeless air, the remaining townhouses more like provisional structures than dwellings a hundred years old, as they are so obviously slated for the wrecker's ball.

The essence of developing as a human being is developing the capacity for ever more complex experience. If the experience of complexity is losing its value in the environment, we are therefore threatened "spiritually," though the spiritual life of a modern person must unfold in an exactly opposite direction from the path taken by the early

Christian who sought to become a "child of God." Since the images I
have described are of a place built with money and governed by
politicians, one way to think about how to restore complexity to the
environment is obviously to consider the remaking of these material
forces. One would ask how the political economy of the city must
change, in order to change what Park called its "moral order." Wise
and realistic as this approach would be, I will not pursue it.

Usually what is left out of discussions that resolve culture to money
and power is the cultural dimension of culture itself. The anthropol-
ogist Clifford Geertz has sought to bring the "powers of interpretation" into the circle of forces that organize human affairs. These
"powers of interpretation" could hardly be autonomous from money
and power, but again, they are not mere reflections or representations. In particular, the power of words or of the eye serve a critical
faculty. I want, in the second half of this essay, to understand how the
experience of complexity might be gained in the urban environment
through the powers of visual interpretation with which people are
armed. Isidore's "conscience of the eye" sought to apply declared
beliefs and overt morals to vision. His problem was how to represent
his values. My walk is about the more modern problem. It concerns
the difficulty of arousing conscience through visual experience rather
than representing faith in stones.

An Exile's
Knowledge

E. M. Forster's injunction "Only connect!" takes a surprising turn
when we seek to connect to strangers rather than to those we know
intimately or at last familiarly. The surprising turn is suggested in
even so routine an experience as my restaurant walk. Along the way
I took little photographs: the Drug Addict, the Professional Woman,
the Spice Merchant. My street vision was like Kevin Lynch's desire
for legible images of places in the city—a clarity that deadens. Would
I have been more aroused by what I saw if these pictures of strangers

were more puzzling, less immediately recognizable? That is, if instead of right away recognizing their identities, I had to study the people I encountered—would this uncertainty make greater demands upon my attention? What on the street would make the little snapshots of identity less interesting to me than finding what was concealed beneath this overt clarity?

No one was more animated by these possibilities than Hannah Arendt, the political philosopher exiled in America from Nazi Germany. Her politics came to be about transcending particular identities, a politics prompted by her experiences of exile in New York. And while her writing seldom touches directly on visual problems, her concerns are directly relevant to the critical powers of the eye.

The Need for Roots, the title of a book Simone Weil wrote as the wave of exiles began to flee Europe, might seem to describe well Arendt's youthful beliefs. Throughout the 1930s Arendt worked ardently as a Zionist. Even in this period she did not imagine Jews could or should find a "home" in Palestine, "home" in the national sense; rather she imagined that Jews would put down roots as one group amongst the myriad peoples already established in Palestine. In a place so charged with history that it could belong to no one, Jews would create a space of freedom—no longer schlemiels, pariahs, victims of not belonging; they would do so living in a place of differences, the land shared. This nuanced Zionist dream faded for her, in part because the other Zionists insisted on establishing a nation, which seemed to her wrong because it was just more of the European national error, and it also faded in part because Arendt wanted the European Jews to mobilize an army to fight Hitler; this army became to the young philosopher a more pressing dream as she waited in Paris and then fled to the south of France. But no one organized an army. By the time she arrived in America, she thought history had finally taught her its lesson, she who, as she so often said, had so little taste for "politicking." Uprooting was at the very heart of politics.

The middle-European Jewish exile world she found in New York seemed condemned to memory. The entire city was filled with generations clinging to the past. Arendt's contemporaries were divided in their memories between horrors or deprivations that had impelled them to move and longing for a vanished home. Other immigrants, even if not politically persecuted, were similarly turned backward in time; the city was packed with little enclaves where the old language was spoken, where even the foods of the past fueled nostalgia. These exiles wanted nothing to do with the outside and the present. But Arendt knew that, in the foreign place to which he or she has come, eventually the exile must travel beyond the realities summoned through memory in terror and in regret; an exile must go forward in time, if only because his or her children will do so without the same sense of loss. This was more than anything the emotional center of Hannah Arendt's politics: the exile obliged to transcend dreams of home, *Gemeinschaft*, or religious destiny. The problem of politics was how people who could count on nothing, who could not *inherit*, might therefore invent the conditions of their own and their common lives. No identity can be recovered; therefore, turn outward.

In Arendt's writing she calls creating an alternative to identity a process of "natality." "Natality," Hannah Arendt writes in *The Human Condition*, "may be the central category of political . . . thought."[6] What she meant by "natality" is not one's birth as a Jew, a peasant, or a Frenchman. These origins are not one's fate; she means "natality" more as the birth of will to make oneself over again as an adult: "The new beginning inherent in birth can make itself felt in the world only because the newcomer possesses the capacity of beginning something new."[7] Political action is to her a process of giving birth, of initiatives taken in a world that cannot be lived as it was inherited.

A friend of ours was once in the toils of a profound depression, unable to eat, a thirty-year-old moving with the gait of an aged man, tempted each day by suicide. This friend was also being smothered in advice, all of which ended in the injunction, "You must see a psychiatrist!" Arendt alone counseled against the chorus; she thought it would "trap him forever within the prison of himself." And it was this attitude, I think, that caused her to feel the reverberations of exile in the everyday lives of people who had never been menaced by dictators. They, too, needed to experience something like the rites of passage of exile from the past in order to release themselves from the

---

[6] Hannah Arendt, *The Human Condition* (New York: Anchor, 1969), p. 9.
[7] Ibid.

prison of subjectivity. Her near contemporaries Simone Weil and Samuel Beckett thought of exile as a symbol of the affliction of modern man. Arendt thought of it more as the emblem of that journey human beings need to take to become adults, to be free of memory's chains, to live *now*.

In this her writing connects to the city. Her philosophical colleague and fellow exile Leo Strauss believed that the truths known to the philosopher had to be kept secret from the masses, who were incapable of making use of knowledge. By contrast, Arendt celebrated the Greek *polis* as a form of urban life in which speech was open and full. She particularly appreciated the remark which Aristotle made in passing, that an urban space of assembly should be only as large as a shouting human voice can make itself heard in. (On level ground, and given the heights of Greek buildings, such a space would be quite small; it isn't clear whether the Greeks themselves sought to observe this rule of speech in constructing their *agorai,* or town squares. The amphitheater as a form more suited this rule.) Self-determination was very much associated in her mind with the idea of the city. And she credited that act of self-determination: through argument and debate people create the conditions of their own freedom; the polity has rights against the predetermined, rights against the past.

Her view could be applied to urban forms other than those of the Greeks. The medieval city was conceived by its burghers as a place in which people could write their own *secular* laws, exert their political will, rather than be bound by inherited obligations of manor or village. These laws were as irregular and varied as the streets of the towns, often self-contradictory or unclear, enacted with little sense of anxiety about form, made for what suited the moment. Clarity belonged in the realm of the divine. To express this freedom to will their own secular lives, the medieval burghers carved over the gates of several Hanseatic cities the motto, *Stadt Luft macht frei,* "city air makes men and women free."

In the same way, Arendt's work provides a way to interpret what the modern fear of exposure in cities is about, particularly exposure through debate or simply talk to one's fellow citizens. In her view the fear of making contact is a lack of the will to live in the world. Immersion in subjective life that accompanies the search for shelter also expresses a lack of will. Arendt's enemy is a kind of social depression. She seeks to understand, beyond the physical sensation of stimulation, what is at stake in the experience of exposure.

The exile's voyage to citizenship from his or her past to engagement in the present might be described as the "disappearance of the subject," which means that each person's "I," by a painful and indeed unwilling passage, ought to become less and less important. In conceiving this journey that establishes a difference from the past so great as to be a rebirth, Arendt was obliged to reconsider the very nature of the human being asked to make such a long and traumatic voyage. The Enlightenment scientist Johann Lavater had declared, in Goethe's paraphrase, "that without help from many external means, one had enough substance and content in oneself, so that everything depends solely on unfolding this properly."[8] One's inner nature was full. Lavater's image of human nature was of an unfolding in time; as a plant unfolds its leaves and flowers, the human animal also reveals its possibilities in stages.

For Hannah Arendt there was no inside to unfold; or rather, this inside belonged to that human animal, slave to its own instincts and emotions, trainable like a pigeon and in essence no different in eating, excreting, procreating, and dying. Arendt contrasted this to the human *being,* our nature expressed as an active verb; in being human, men and women find ways to detach themselves from slavery to their bodies. Her writing could be seen as laying the ground for the feminist declaration that "biology is not destiny." There is no destiny. There is no truly human nature, as Lavater understood it. Instead, there is only struggle for freedom in the present, a radical struggle for freedom, outside.

Her work is important for an understanding of the form of cities for two reasons. First, hers is an attempt to understand the prime condition of the city—impersonality—as a positive value. The exile is an emblematic urbanite because he or she must deal with others who can never understand what it was like in the place abandoned. The exile must find grounds for a common life with these others who do not, who cannot, understand. Lacking a shared story, one therefore

[8] Johann Wolfgang von Goethe, *Dichtung und Wahrheit* (Mainz: Beuter Verlag, n.d.), p. 664.

has to make a life on more impersonal terms. In discussing justice, one has to appeal to principles of justice, for instance, rather than invoking the folkways of a particular ethnic group. Principle rather than shared custom becomes the focus. The idea of impersonality she applied more generally. To her, the poor man empowers himself by refusing to disclose the particularities of his suffering to the authorities as a needy man—"you hurt me, now you help me" is no recipe for power. She believed blacks could struggle most effectively for justice in demanding what is due human beings rather than what is particularly due blacks; justice has no color.

Transcending identity should make us look at others on the street in a new way. Simply put, who is on the street matters less than what they are doing. The point of Arendt's writing was to focus her readers on actions they could take together, or discuss, actions with meaning no matter who performed them. Her love of the impersonality of New York daily life came from this; she was truly color-blind, as she became in a way blind to religion and to social class.

Yet it was just here that something went wrong. She could not connect. Her difficulties were parallel to those of Mies van der Rohe; she excluded sympathy from her compass. In the case of Mies we have seen how this exclusion made the building into a shrine, its intregrity at odds with the city. In the case of Arendt, the exclusion of sympathy meant the work of mutual arousal failed.

Arendt and Jean-Paul Sartre were among the first to describe themselves as "anti-humanists," by which they turned against the pieties of place and compromise made by bourgeois culture. For the urbanist, this anti-humanism, when underlined by a contempt for the softness of sympathic feelings creates its own dilemma: strangers can't communicate.

One sign of Arendt's own difficulties was the way her understanding constantly misfired when brought to bear on concrete events. At the end of Arendt's life, her friend Mary McCarthy challenged her about the adequacy of excluding social custom and circumstances from her vision of an engaged society:

I would like to ask a question that I have had in my mind a long, long time. It is about the very sharp distinction that Hannah

Arendt makes between the political and the social. . . . Now I have always asked myself: "What is somebody supposed to do on the public stage, in the public space, if he does not concern himself with the social? That is, what's left?"[9]

The need to talk does not tell us what is important to talk about. Again, Arendt managed to offend many blacks in a celebrated essay whose purpose was to uphold their rights. She caused immense anguish among her fellow Jews by her writings on the Nazi concentration-camp officer Adolf Eichmann. She wrote cogently and simply; anyone could understand her who took the trouble, yet somehow she failed to connect—failed to make herself understood which, more than anything, puzzled her. The reason for this, I believe, is that her "anti-humanism" made it difficult for the critical faculties to become expressive and provoking, rather than abstractly assertive. She paid no attention to the problem of how people in cities express themselves to one another. Her writing is a cautionary tale because it ignores what we might call the art of exposure.

The difficulty of her own relation to New York once made this clear to me. I am thinking of a small moment on the kind of steamy day that used to bring old people out of their apartments on the Upper West Side, some seeking relief on the benches in the traffic islands on Broadway, the cars, taxis, and trucks whizzing past at least creating a breeze, others sitting on little folding camp stools in front of their apartment houses, clumps of three or four together, women in black dresses, men in shirt-sleeves, rumpled suit-pants, and braces, the heat forcing these old people to expose domesticities to the street.

At this time the Upper West Side was peopled by young Puerto Rican families, young conservatory musicians, and these elderly exiles from Central Europe, who came mostly from Hungary, Austria, and Germany on the run from Hitler. The exiles had troubles with the Puerto Ricans, not so much because these neighbors were poor as because they were Latin: the noise and exuberance of late-night family life on the street seemed no way to raise proper children, especially on streets stained with dog shit and perfumed with gasoline

[9] Quoted in Melvyn Hill, ed., *Hannah Arendt: The Recovery of the Public World* (New York: St. Martin's Press, 1979), p. 315.

exhaust. The Puerto Ricans spoke a foreign language not English, which was foreign enough. Moreover, many of the Puerto Ricans were devout Catholics, peasant-devout, frequently crossing themselves, a gesture that aroused in the Jews who had escaped the gas chambers emotions so complicated as to be very hard to put in words, and certainly not in Spanish ones.

The exiles had trouble with the young conservatory students, who could have been their own grandchildren. The old might have found relief from the noise of their young neighbors if they could have relieved themselves by reliving to these young people their own stories, passing these on to those who could hear well and so could bear witness. With the peculiar time-claustrophobia of the young, however, the musicians said to one another, "You can't live in the past." Also, the exiles had trouble with one another, whom they knew too well.

Arendt and I were walking on this hot, exposed day from West End toward Broadway, threading our way between clumps of men and women who squatted on camp-stools, sipped iced tea from plastic cups, and nibbled on little cakes, when suddenly she was recognized. Her picture had appeared frequently in the Jewish press since she had published her book *Eichmann in Jerusalem* a while before, and the person who called out to her must have known her in this way, for it didn't sound a friendly "Hannah Arendt?" nor was he smiling as he spoke to her briefly and then turned away back to his own group of camp-stools. They, not knowing her name, were obviously surprised that he should have done something so sudden, so Latin a thing perhaps, as round on the street upon a gray-haired woman who was wearing, just as she should have been, a black dress. I asked Hannah what he had said, "He asked me, was I ashamed of being Jewish?"

There had been several months of vicious controversy over her book, in which she had portrayed the evil of the Nazi mass-murderer as a kind of absentmindedness and implicated certain Jewish leaders in the destruction of the Jewish people. Hannah was no sweet old grandmother, and she was disposed to keep her sufferings to herself. Still, she stopped and turned to look up and down the street of sweating old people, her glance falling for a while on the back of the man who had accosted her and sat now, far away in time and place, in silence sipping tea from his plastic cup. She lingered among her fellow exiles, and then shrugged at his back.

Arendt's writings equate the impersonal with the tough, the strong, the resolute, as opposite to the weaknesses of a self-involved and sheltered subjectivity. She dismissed the powers of sympathy. Because Arendt was at the opposite, but equal, pole from those who believed that mutual concern required the sharing of identity, she denied all the *Gemeinschaft* emotions associated with sharing an identity with others: warmth, speaking silences, communion. She was opposed to considering "soft" emotions because they seemed to give little of the strength needed to break with the past and gain the present. Baudelaire's belief in a warm impersonality seemed to her a nonsensical association of words. Her silence came out of that hardness.

Of course, "natality" might suggest there is an analogy between the natural, animal functions of the human body and the activities of politics; moreover, "natality" might suggest love to play as strong a role in social relations as in parenting. Hannah Arendt resisted both these suggestions: she asserted without hesitation that, in the political domain, freedom has nothing to do with love. In a famous passage from *On Revolution,* Arendt contrasts pity to solidarity, the adult solidarity gained through free political discourse. "Compared with the sentiment of pity," she declares,

> solidarity may appear cold and abstract, for it remains committed to "ideas"—to greatness, or honor, or dignity—rather to any "love" of men.[10]

Why are those two words in quotes? Because "ideas" are suspicious to most people, and "love," at least in politics and beginning with "love of the Fatherland," is suspicious to Arendt. Pity, compassion, and empathy belong to the human animal, are the marks of animal pain and neediness. Similarly "the birth of the political" means something quite opposite the birth of a baby: it means the creation of an almost super-adult, who deals with others without proclaiming his or her neediness, personal state, or inner condition.

[10] Hannah Arendt, *On Revolution* (New York: Viking Compass Books, 1965), p. 84.

When writers talk about the disappearance of the subject, about writing "degree zero," they mean a kind of flint-hard prose, in its very coldness an assertion of its strength. This prose is less interesting to read than to write. "Degree zero" can make for this loss of arousal in social life as in literature. Moreover, Arendt rendered incomprehensible to herself the lives of those who had not achieved her own resolution, who remained needy, confused, and physical. Arendt's writing sets out the intellectual dimensions of the modern "outside." But her shrug in silence poses a question for the critical eye: how, outside, is sympathy among strangers to be aroused? The formulas of the eighteenth century will not serve. What will?

The Stranger's Knowledge

In 1962, a year before Arendt published the work on Eichmann that brought down upon her the fire of her fellow exiles, the American writer James Baldwin published an essay in the *New Yorker* magazine called "The Fire Next Time." This essay—part autobiography, part reportage on the Black Muslim movement, part homily—revealed to the liberal and affluent reader of that magazine something of the rage of black Americans that would break out during the next decade. Nothing could be further in style and spirit than the discourse Arendt imagined to give birth to "the political." Baldwin's text embodies the rage it explained. The tone moves rapidly from that of distant observation to ringing denunciation, then back again to detached description, the prose lapping forward on these waves as if Baldwin were exhausted, then revived and driven forward by outrage at what he has to tell. However, in the artful mutations of passion that occur in "The Fire Next Time," this essay might have suggested to Arendt how engagement is aroused among strangers.

There's nothing lurid, particularly, in the scenes of Harlem evoked in "The Fire Next Time." The shock of it when published was that this essay challenged the liberal belief that blacks would become another ethnic group in America, one which, once granted civil rights, would climb the American ladder. Indeed, in the early 1960s, liberal circles imagined blacks were gratified at the civil liberties at last coming to them. Gratified and grateful share a common root in language; this language conveys that one man bestows freedom upon another as if making a gift, as if whites had decided the time had come to accept blacks as full human beings and now the blacks would thank them. What Baldwin's essay brought home to his readers was the moral disgust blacks felt for those who saw themselves as benefactors.

Baldwin's essay could be read as a document of doubt that the words "I understand how much you must have suffered" could ever make much sense. Old-fashioned sympathy makes for frail language in a country so obsessed by race. "The Fire Next Time" suggests quite another way to think about race. Blacks and whites who can never understand one another, who are permanent strangers, can still live together. They need not be cut off in mutual indifference. At the outset of his essay, however, Baldwin gives no warning any of this will happen. We seem to have embarked instead on a familiar guilt trip.

Baldwin starts "The Fire Next Time" with a letter to his nephew, ostensibly to let this young man know how to deal with whites, in fact to slip some bitter pills to those reading over his nephew's shoulders. Baldwin is perfectly aware of us snooping:

> I hear the chorus of the innocents screaming, "No! This is not true! How *bitter* you are!"—but I am writing this letter to you to try to tell you how to handle *them,* for most of them do not yet really know that you exist.[11]

The familiar device of the reader-over-the-shoulder Baldwin puts to a peculiar rhetorical use: an inversion of racial stereotypes. The racists of his youth considered blacks to be innocent, sweet-tempered if subject to kind discipline but irrationally vicious if left to their own devices. These attitudes toward blacks Baldwin inverts as attitudes his nephew ought to adopt toward whites: treat whites as innocent and vicious unless properly guided. This inversion allows him to

[11] James Baldwin, *The Price of the Ticket: Collected Nonfiction 1948–1985* (New York: St. Martin's Press, 1985), p. 334.

make a surprise attack on the sort of readers who might be attending him in the pages of the *New Yorker*. Instead of enlightened benefactors they are the children in need of help.

We seem headed for an accusatory orgy, but suddenly Baldwin changes the subject. Abruptly, he launches the body of the essay by describing his loss of faith in himself as a child preacher. The young Baldwin evidently became an inspiring orator during his early adolescence in Harlem but gradually realized that, "Being in the pulpit was like being in the theater; I was behind the scenes and knew how the illusion was worked."[12] Baldwin tells how he became more and more disgusted with his own powers of rhetoric, his own capacity to make a church audience "rock" until . . . until what? Now the narrative breaks off again; instead of telling when and where he lost religion, he begins to reflect suddenly on the relations of Christianity and race. These are cogent reflections, to be sure, on how the Christian doctrines of love are so easily perverted to love only of one's own kind, whereas the young Baldwin in his naïveté thought Christian love was the love of anyone for anyone else. That Christianity might in practice be a weak language is a gravely important idea—but it is placed in the middle of a memoir to substitute for the outcome of an arresting story.

Baldwin's critics have noted something odd in the prose, in the logic, for instance, of this story of the child preacher, an account that ends in a personal question mark; the question mark dissatisfies them. "The transfiguring power of the Holy Ghost," Baldwin writes,

> ended when the service ended, and salvation stopped at the church door. When we were told to love everybody, I had thought that meant *everybody*. But no. It applied only to those who believed as we did, and it did not apply to white people at all.[13]

The impersonal transition concludes as Baldwin balances this criticism of the black church to the separate but equal appropriation of Christianity by white missionaries for white purposes. His critics wanted him to represent himself, to define himself, as a black writer

[12] Ibid., p. 347.
[13] Ibid., p. 348.

being black by writing the personal geography of his blackness, which contains it in a package. You handle such a package delicately, but you can pick it up and move it around.

In the hands of a lesser writer like Imamu Amiri Baraka (Le Roi Jones), anger at whites becomes a judicial process; the story of the injuries is given as clearly as possible, and the black protagonists are charged by their author with drawing the right moral. It is a literature of witness. The stories Baldwin tells do not bear witness in this usual sense. The disappearing author engages us in his politics for an answer to the question of where he is, what happened to him. The terrain of impersonality here is at the opposite pole from Arendt's austere temper, and yet, in this personal disappearance, we begin to pay attention to what he is saying, pay attention to race in exchange, as it were, for James Baldwin's identity.

Baldwin makes more of this in the second half of "The Fire Next Time." We move ahead twenty years; the scene changes from New York to America, where Elijah Muhammad's Black Muslims have their headquarters. The Black Muslims proclaim explicitly what Baldwin had heard implied in the churches of Harlem: "God is black." From this theological vision comes a social vision of total separation; the Black Muslims believe integration to be a slave's dream fostered by those who want to continue to be masters, masters without guilt. Baldwin sees in the Black Muslims a convincing version of black power and self-respect—and something more. The movement regulates everyday life down to the minutest details according to Black Muslim principles. In this severe, chaste, aloof house of daily life, the Black Muslims define what it is to be human; for blacks, any other dwelling is a way of delusion or weakness, while there can be no entrance here for anyone who is white. The white man is a devil. After appearing on a television program with Malcolm X, Elijah Muhammad's lieutenant, Baldwin says,

In the hall, as I was waiting for the elevator, someone shook my hand and said, "Goodbye, Mr. James Baldwin. We'll soon be addressing you as Mr. James X." And I thought, for an awful moment, My God, if this goes on much longer, you probably will.[14]

[14] Ibid., p. 358.

Finally he might disappear for good.

Baldwin is invited and decides to dine with Elijah Muhammad. He is impressed by the discipline and good humor of Elijah Muhammad's followers, the monastic purity of their life. The leader himself impresses Baldwin by his softness. But Baldwin is also appalled. "I began to see that Elijah's power came from his single-mindedness."[15] They begin to talk about Christianity, of Allah allowing this infidel religion only as a testing and tempering of black men; they speak of religious commitment, which leads Elijah Muhammad to ask Baldwin about his own. Here is Baldwin's reply:

> "I? Now? Nothing." This was not enough. "I'm a writer. I like doing things alone." I heard myself saying this. Elijah smiled at me. "I don't, anyway," I said, finally, "think about it a great deal."[16]

Carefully, stroke upon stroke, Baldwin has told us a story of what he might do to escape the enslaving, the fearful and the blind Other, the white. Only a word and he can surrender, become Mr. James X, and in these radical terms solve the problem of race as his identity. Now, even more than in Harlem twenty years ago, we have arrived at a denouement. With the single-mindedness Baldwin first remarked, Elijah challenges him—you should think about this all the time. What now happens?

Almost nothing. The scene fizzles out. Baldwin begins to explain the Black Muslims a little more, indicating how they might see his weakness, but this en passant; as a first-person narrative, what now happens is that dinner politely ends, and a Black Muslim driver conducts Baldwin to another part of Chicago, where he has an appointment with some white friends. But by now this narrative violation has made the reader all the more attentive to the general reflections on race rolling into the text in ever larger waves: now the outcome of this dramatic confrontation is contained in them. Indeed, at this point in the text of "The Fire Next Time," something crucial does happen to the language. Baldwin addressed the reader less and less as "you"; more and more he employs "we."

[15] Ibid., p. 361.
[16] Ibid., p. 363.

This is his answer to Elijah Muhammad. Baldwin's readers find out nothing more about the outcome of the turning point in his life; the man's story is more elusive than ever before, save that he has changed pronouns. The anger still reverberates in the prose but now it is anger outside the bond of that "we," that bond between an unknowable writer and his readers, readers whom he is no longer rejecting, as in the preface addressed to his nephew. The language the writer uses contains all the pain, confusion, and rage of his past, but he has found a way to speak of his life in such a way that he transcends it. Instead of a guilt trip, the journey the writer makes is one in the rhetorical evolution of his own voice; at the end of this journey he makes contact with those whose lives are ineradicably unlike his own.

Jacob Burckhardt once praised Machiavelli as follows: "He was at least capable of forgetting about himself while delving into things."[17] It is one version of the disappearing subject, praise for a man's cool capacity to judge the world. Hannah Arendt approved it. The change Baldwin recounts in his life is something quite different, for himself and for his reader. He disappears, our narrative expectations are thwarted, and we attend to disquisitions on race without doubting, without thinking "this is all rhetoric," even though the waves of Baldwin's rage rise ever higher. Now we believe that voice at once personal and impersonal; now, too, the reader is ready to be angry. Thus, the essay earns its last two sentences:

> If we—and now I mean the relatively conscious whites and the relatively conscious blacks, who must, like lovers, insist on, or create, the consciousness of the other—do not falter in our duty now, we may be able, handful that we are, to end the racial nightmare, and achieve our country, and change the history of the world. If we do not now dare everything, the fulfillment of that prophecy, recreated from the Bible in song by a slave, is upon us: "God gave Noah the rainbow sign, No more water, the fire next time!"[18]

---

[17] Jacob Burckhardt, *Die Kultur der Renaissance in Italien* (Vienna: Phaidon, n.d.), p. 51.
[18] Baldwin, *Price of the Ticket*, p. 379.

Baldwin's essay suggests the emotional experience that lies beyond identity; it is experience that incorporates incompleteness and doubt rather than aims at assertion. In this essay we are told the story of someone whose confusion turns him outward rather than plunges him ever more inward, looking for a resolution, for an answer. His language comes to include the enemy. Much more than the architecture of ideas Arendt constructed, here impersonality takes on a compelling value, impersonality in the sense of relating to others as unknowns, puzzles, presences rather than clearly labeled, fixed categories of "black" and "white."

What then does "we" mean? At one moment of my restaurant walk, the Indian merchant said to his twelve-year-old son who was filling a paper bag of turmeric for me and spilling the spice, "How many times do I have to tell you to go slowly?" In hearing this universal litany of fatherhood chanted again, suddenly I felt only the presence of a father and a son; perhaps the Indian, who had smiled at my questions and pushed me away by answering "imported ingredient," if now he noticed me noticing, might have been moved by my existence as well. It would have occurred when our eyes met after looking at bag and boy. At this moment one might seem to have spoken Baldwin's "we."

Were, however, I to announce to the Indian at this moment, "we are both fathers," I would perhaps earn another of his faint smiles or his son would perhaps earn another scowl; the family was losing face in the presence of a stranger. And similarly, were I to accost one of the leathermen, as his whip was being wrapped, to reassure him that though I didn't share his tastes I accepted them as just part of the human condition, he might wrest his eyes from the thongs nestling in tissue paper to glance at me in alarm: perhaps I was a cop trying a new form of entrapment in order to arrest him. If not, what right had I to name his desire? Differences do not exist to be overcome. The lady carrying a bag of sheets might lock eyes with the lady entering the Morgan Library. A recognition might pass between them, but the moment of truth would be no moment of sorority. This hostile arousal is also Baldwin's "we." Baldwin's voice is that of someone who has learned how to speak to strangers, not in the polite tones of eighteenth-century civility, but instead more directly and forcefully. It is about a harsher connection made out of arousal by the Other, made by feeling the presence of those who are different. In order to sense the Other, one must do the work of accepting oneself as incomplete.

The meaning of "sympathy" for us is about something other than friendliness or, as Arendt thought, pity. Instead sympathy is a condition of mutual concern aroused as one loses the power of self-definition. Cunning, art, design—as we shall see—are necessary to bring about this loss.

The eighteenth-century ideal of *Bildung* was an ideal in which the life of an individual became psychologically complete through the same acts that integrated the individual into society. "The Fire Next Time" has some of the characteristics of a *Bildungsroman,* but on more modern narrative terms. Baldwin explores the repressive world that shapes his history by precluding certain impulses to completion and wholeness in himself. On the one hand an incomplete self, a lack of catharsis; on the other hand, "we."

George Simmel, the teacher of the Chicago urbanists, wrote an essay, "The Stranger," to define the quintessential urbanite in terms of a segmented self. "The Fire Next Time" deepens Simmel's imagery. A man or woman can become in the course of a lifetime like a foreigner to him or herself, by doing things or entering into feelings that do not fit the familiar framework of identity, the seemingly social fixities of race, class, age, gender, or ethnicity. Moreover, this person is not someone who is reckoning the changes occurring in his or her life, as though toting up accounts; strangeness is not experienced by making such calculations, either of oneself or of others. Something unanticipated remains unexplained and unresolved within; one accepts the permanent puzzle and turns outward. But for this to happen something other than linear, sequential experience is necessary. Baldwin's story is an example of that other, non-sequential narrative, that non-linear experience of difference.

This non-linear experience of difference might be thought of as an *émigration extérieure.* One goes to the edge of oneself. But precisely at that edge, one cannot represent oneself to oneself. Instead one sees, talks, or thinks about what is outside, beyond the boundary—in Baldwin's case the other people he has included in his angry "we." To take this journey is the modern, secular quest which creates sympathy.

Hannah Arendt and James Baldwin represent two poles of response to indifference. At one pole the subjective world is shunted aside so that people can speak to each other directly, resolutely, politically. At the other pole subjective life undergoes a transformation so that a person turns outward, is aroused by the presence of strangers and arouses them. That transformation requires the mobilizing of certain artistic energies in everyday life.

chapter 6

Streets Full
of Life

Invention and
Discovery

H O W   C A N   S P A C E be endowed with the life of Baldwin's words?
The force of these words was to effect a discovery, the discovery of a
more problematic relation to whites. The question I have just posed
might therefore be rephrased: how can a street yield similar, puzzling
discoveries?

In 1661 the geographer Hickeringill described with a certain irony
the voyage Columbus made to the West Indies 150 years before.
About Columbus's belief that he had sighted India the geographer
wrote: "Columbus, to whose happy search the West Indies first discovered itself."[1] In this usage the voyager did not "make" a discovery;
the foreign scenes "discovered" themselves to him. Invention, as a
commonplace has it, is the mother of discovery. The voyage of Columbus might be considered an invention on a grand scale; even if he
found the wrong India, it was by the navigator's contriving a new sea
route that the surprising result occurred. This cliché is what Hickeringill's usage challenges. The important thing is not the voyager's
own designs but what reality joltingly disclosed to him, the reality
of something beyond his power to conceive—in this case an entire
continent.

[1] Cited in *Oxford English Dictionary of Words and Their Historical Sources* (Oxford: Oxford
University Press, 1971), p. 431.

The powers that mark a society as modern seem to have everything to do with people seizing control over the physical world through inventions. Hickeringill's near contemporary Francis Bacon was perhaps the first philosopher openly to justify manipulating the physical world in order to control it. Hickeringill's usage of *discovery*, however, also represents a modern value: the willingness to displace traditional ideas, to investigate, to take seriously facts or ideas that don't fit. This attitude is epitomized by a heroic moment on one of Columbus's voyages, though a moment that required no great physical courage from the navigator. It was when Columbus felt for the first time a twinge of doubt that he had sighted India. He accepted that the scene disclosed to him through the round window of his eyeglass was of unveiled women and hooded men who lacked Oriental eyes, of vegetation that looked nothing like what had appeared in books. But he kept the glass glued to his eye hour after hour, studying the strange scene rather than recalculating his course.

The modern urban analogue between invention and discovery might seem to appear in the contrast between carefully designed streets and streets with no one author—for instance, the streets in Paris built by Baron Haussmann in the nineteenth century, and the much older streets that give upon them. In the original Boulevard Richard Lenoir, which is one of Haussmann's great constructions, the center lane is reserved for fast moving traffic, shaded by trees; the center lane is flanked by two companion lanes for slower traffic, again flanked by trees; the sidewalks are reserved for walking and sitting at cafés. The design makes clear exactly where to do what, a clarity new for Parisians of the time; the Boulevard Richard Lenoir was greeted as a great planning innovation. Feeding the Boulevard Richard Lenoir are older streets which were and remain more self-effacing. It isn't clear what is happening on them, who lives on them, and how to use them—at least not before spending some time on these byways and becoming involved in their secrets. In these streets people make discoveries as prosaic as an unexpected shop, an odd votive offering lodged in the cracks between two buildings, or a house of the deaf. The power of discovering something unexpected to the eye gives them their value.

Such streets are prized, we commonly say, as being full of life, in a way that traffic arteries, for all their rushing vehicular motion, are not. "Street life" is a symbol of urban provocation and arousal, provocation that comes in large part from experiences of the unexpected. But, considered more closely, the problematic qualities of the side streets feeding into the Boulevard Richard Lenoir can't really be declared more possessed of life than the grand boulevard itself. There is a principled reason why "life" cannot simply be equated with blind "process." Intention is the genesis of every made thing; the sheer difficulty of bringing a poem or a law or a plan into being can only be satisfied when the process results in a form. Like vivid prose, street life needs to find a structure. There are a class of clarities we want to avoid: Kevin Lynch's "legible" streetscapes, places that are all about fixed identities of race or class or usage. But no form made apparent on the street leads to the equal and opposite evil, the grid experience of neutrality. How then to invent a form which provokes discovery? How to link invention and discovery? James Baldwin's story could be taken as a literary model; its non-linear prose yields surprising results.

The people of the age demarcated from Columbus to Hickeringill knew they had to find some way to invent things which in turn yielded surprising discoveries. And they did succeed in this—by inventing a new visual meaning for *linear* as well, linear streets purposely possessed of a puzzling, problematic life.

The Obelisks of Sixtus V

In the work of late Renaissance and early baroque city planning, it seemed self-evident that men and women could design ways to "see outside themselves," a metaphor these planners took literally. It was made evident in certain experiments in planning streets; these were based on the inventions of perspective in painting and drawing. Recourse to perspective as a model for urban design suggested to late-sixteenth- and early-seventeenth-century planners a new way to establish the meaning of a street line leading to a center—a meaning far different than the medieval sanctuary, though equally charged with importance. The centers created through perspective were places in which, it was thought, people would keep moving and look searchingly around them. In these centers discoveries would occur.

The most famous planner who created a city according to the art of perspective was Sixtus V, who began to transform Rome as soon as his pontificate began, in 1585. It was late in his life; his reign would last but five years, until he died in 1590. As though aware of the shortness of time for his task, the plan for Rome long mediated as a cardinal he immediately promulgated as pope and set his workmen to their tasks in a fury.

Pisanello, in a famous drawing of arches, suggests how perspective would later come to preoccupy Sixtus in remaking Rome. In Pisanello's drawing of these arches, no more than the merest sketch of ovals, the arches shrink in size as they move back toward a vanishing point: there are only five arches in his drawing, but the eye moves beyond them, as though there were a tunnel of space stretching all the way back to the horizon. And in this drawing *moves* is the operative word; in Pisanello's drawing, figures are lined up along one wall of the arches, figures turned in various poses, but no matter which way they are facing they seem to be walking backward toward a vanishing point on the horizon.

The rationale behind Sixtus V's remaking of Rome was religious: to link the seven pilgrimage sites of the city. The means were secular. He wanted to connect these sites through straight streets that established tunnels of vision. The pilgrim would search his or her way along these tunnels of vision. To endow a tunnel of vision with the perceptual property of movement, as in the drawing of Pisanello, it was necessary to establish a horizon point; the big flat façades of the old churches would not serve. Sixtus therefore dug into Rome's pagan past for a marker and came upon the obelisk.

Obelisks are tapering, three- or four-sided columns set upon a boxy plinth, with the tip of the obelisk either sharpened to a point or capped with a small round ball. The sliver of stone would, at a distance, serve as an effective means for creating perspectival vision. The reason lay in the tip of the obelisk: it creates a point in space. The

eye from far away ends its travels in following the directions given by
the stone by looking at either that point defined by the ball or—
immaterial yet not invisible—the point just above the sharpened tip.
The obelisks hover in this terminal space, their very existence dramatized by the perception that above them things are just about to
disappear.

Earlier in the Renaissance, sculptures like Verrochio's *Colleoni* in
Venice were conceived as dependent elements of buildings. Mich-
elangelo's plan for the Campidoglio, the top of the Capitoline Hill of
Rome (initiated in 1538, completed more than a century later in
1664), detached a bronze statue of Marcus Aurelius from such dependent placement; it stands in the middle of this amazing square
upon an oval traced in the ground, flanked by three buildings whose
flat façades seem bent by the oval pattern of the stones. It was this
gesture giving independence to a public sculpture from its building
context that Sixtus would later put in the service of displacing the
vision of the pilgrim as he or she moved from place to place in the
city. The system of such displaced sculptures meant that in making a
pilgrimage, the eyes of the pilgrim lead him or her from marker to
marker rather than to the inside of a particular church.

"Like a man with a divining rod Sixtus placed his obelisks at points
where, during the coming centuries, the most important squares
would develop."[2] The divide from earlier planning was simple: the
builders of Catholic Lübeck determined by building high how people
would know where the churches were; Pope Sixtus V established how
to get there. It was not seeing the churches themselves that would
orient people, but rather these stone slivers would activate a process
of perception, a linear orientation in the eye rather than attraction of
the place, so that the pilgrims would be drawn to the shrines rather
as Pisanello's figures move, magnetized, toward the horizon. Yet
there was no rest in his city so conceived; the moment one arrives at
one obelisk, one spies another down another tunnel of vision.

Optically, perspective is created when the eye triangulates; it measures near or far, tall or short by imagining a triangle of which the eye

[2] Sigfried Giedion, "Sixtus V and the Planning of Baroque Rome," *Architectural Review* (April
1952), p. 36.

forms one point and the object lies somewhere on an opposite side. In three dimensions perspective establishes all the relations between a point and a plane. The "illusion" requires rigorous calculation. However, perspective is not a rational operation that leads to a single answer. The size of a thing can be optically manipulated, as Piero della Francesca, one of the earliest experimenters in perspective, did by moving the reference point along the line of the horizon, or redefining the exterior plane; in doing so he was able to make an object seem closer or farther away from the viewer's own point of vision, larger or smaller. All the things in a perspectival space can change their appearance by the draftsman's manipulation of points and planes external to them. Perspectival vision transforms an object into a consequence of how it is seen.

Conventional wisdom usually describes the cultural values motivating perspective as those of a Renaissance version of Hannah Arendt's politics. The human eye, as a reference point, gives perspective its value; the eye, by changing perspective, can change how the world looks. The Renaissance theorist of perspective Leon Battista Alberti most succinctly defined the act of projection itself as follows: "The eye measures these quantities [of space] with visual rays as if with a pair of compasses."[3] And in a book of mathematical games written in the early 1450s, Alberti devised ways the designer could calculate vanishing points, the height of towers, and the size of other objects simply by reckoning his own position in relation to them, or could change how everything looks by deciding to change position. These games of invention order the visual world. The world can be made to cohere because of how one looks at it.

An apt instance of the viewer elevated to a perspectival master occurs in Brunelleschi's church of S. Lorenzo in Florence. In S. Lorenzo Brunelleschi designed the walls, floor, and roof so that one sees best by standing just inside to the left or right of the main doors. As one then looks down the church, it seems to diminish, the columns seem to get smaller as they recede from the plane established by one's eyes, the vault overhead seems to narrow. The vanishing point is not the altar, however, none of the ritual or prayer places are emphasized by this recession. The vanishing point seems indeed not within the building at all; it is suggested by the very rhythmical regularity of the perspectival operation to lie somewhere invisible beyond S. Lorenzo's farthest wall. That invisible vanishing point reinforces the sense, within the church, of where one is standing. One becomes aware of oneself seeing in perspective.

This church is a sharp contrast to the ethos of placement in older medieval churches; in them, where one stood to pray, to confess, to receive the Sacrament mattered in so far as the rite had to be precisely observed in order for the grace of God to enter into the supplicant. In S. Lorenzo the position in which a person stands matters because it determines whether he or she can see the building well. Perspective privileges one's sight, not one's faith. If one stands in the right place, the eye senses its control of the space.

There is an undertone of possessive domination in perspective so conceived. Alberti likened seeing in perspective to opening a window upon the world, the perceiving subject organizing the world through the window. In a famous etching Dürer shows an artist rendering his model by looking through a window at her; on the glass of the window a grid has been etched. Looking through this grid-window, Dürer's artist creates on flat paper her ample flesh, her curved contours in perspective. It is a striking icon of how the artist takes control of the world, the icon of a proud Renaissance. Rather than a window, however, John Berger writes, the metaphor would better be of "a safe let into a wall, a safe in which the visible has been deposited."[4] The object is possessed through perspective.

It was not perspective in this possessive version that Sixtus used to rebuild Rome. He built using perspective as a form for seeing outside oneself; in this form, perspective came to serve discovery rather than mastery.

The art historian Svetlana Alpers distinguishes between perspectives that establish "I see the world" and perspectives that establish that "the world is being seen." A famous instance of "I see the world" is Titian's *Venus of Urbino,* in which everything is correctly sized in relation to the single point where the painter stood looking at these

[4] John Berger, *Ways of Seeing* (London: BBC, 1972), p. 109.

things, as in Brunelleschi's church. "The world is being seen" perspective is exemplified by Vermeer's *View of Delft*. This cityscape has coordinated distances, volumes rendered in perspective, "without," in Alpers's words, "taking the position of a viewer external to it into account."[5] Vermeer created a world seen that does not arouse a sense of the "positioned viewer," a world that is instead modeled by "light and shadow, the surface of objects, their colors and textures. . . ."[6]

All the experimenters in perspective began with the premise that objects float in no-man's land, vague and imprecise and inconsequent, until the painter arranges them. Even the most imperial of the Renaissance experimenters in perspective knew they were paying a price in truth by these devices, for instance in foreshortening. Equally, Vermeer's *View of Delft* emphasizes through its very precision of perspective that this is a view made rather than found. Yet the world seen is perception that makes a journey outside the possessive self. The creation of such journeys through perspective is what Sixtus V achieved during his five years of remaking Rome. Perhaps the greatest of these journeys began in the Piazza del Popolo.

The Piazza del Popolo is the hinge at the base of a fan of streets. It was begun in 1516 under Pope Leo X but began to achieve its unique form in the work of Sixtus V and his designers. Sixtus's architect Domenico Fontana placed a red granite obelisk there in 1589; the year before he had placed another farther up Rome's most elegant street at that time, the Via del Corso, which is the center rib in this fan. From the piazza looking left, Sixtus had already imagined a similar rib running all the way to S. Maria Maggiore, where he had commissioned an obelisk in 1587. The very idea of the eye causing the body to move frequently overwhelmed the religious rationale of all this point marking and street cutting; having conceived this rib from the point in the piazza to the bulk of S. Maria Maggiore, Sixtus realized that if he made another street to the east, the Via Panisperra, he could connect the church to a perspective point built long before

[5] Svetlana Alpers, "Interpretation without Representation, or, The Viewing of 'Las Meninas,' " in *Representations* 1 (February 1983): 37.
[6] Svetlana Alpers, *The Art of Describing: Dutch Art in the Seventeenth Century* (Chicago: University of Chicago Press, 1983), p. 44.

any churches had existed in the city; a perspective was in waiting there, as it were: Trajan's Column. After Sixtus died the piazza was completed according to the same laws of perceptual movement. Facing the obelisk on either side of the Corso are two identical churches built from 1662 to 1669 by a team of Rainaldi, Bernini, and Fontana. They were designed strictly as street ends, façades on the piazza which frame a view down the street. The great rib to S. Maria Maggiore that Sixtus imagined was realized as the Via del Babuino, which links the piazza to the base of the Spanish Steps.

When finally completed, the Piazza del Populo created an experience of perspective in space entirely contrary to the experience evoked by Brunelleschi's Florentine church. Here, in the city, there is no one best vantage point, no single point where the urbanite says to himself, "if I stand just *there* I will see it all." Instead, the eye is swept down one tunnel-like street and then swerves to another, as was the conceiver of this amazing space diverted from pilgrimage by the sudden, pagan eruption of an obelisk; in this entire quarter of Rome the motionary laws of perspective rule without a single point of view. Even the caps of the twin churches in the piazza itself do not bring the eye to rest. The charged experience of the Piazza del Populo comes from how perspective creates movement in the city, turning the person in its web of streets outside the sufficiencies of his or her own perception, searching for where to go next, aware that no single point of view gives a pilgrim the answer. It is common to cite the Piazza del Popolo as an example of "coherence" in urban design, but this coherence entails restless movement.

Nietzsche called such nonpossessive, exploratory perceptions "perspectivism." There is a sense of limits established on the powers of people to control what they see. In this, the late Renaissance streets laid the groundwork for that kind of street life in which people look around them, searching streets in which discoveries are made by the eye. Yet more than an act of individual perception occurs here in these streets. The Renaissance designers who saw in perspective this way had a much grander title for these spaces; the inventors conceived their designs, in the very revelation of the limits of human control, to be tragic spaces.

*   *   *

In a famous passage from his study *Renaissance and Baroque*, the art historian Heinrich Wölfflin many years ago proclaimed that the baroque

> wants to carry us away with the force of its impact, which is immediate and overwhelming. Its impact on us is also to be only momentary, while that of the Renaissance is slower and quieter, but more enduring. We want to linger for ever in its presence.[7]

He concluded that "This momentary impact of the baroque is powerful, but soon leaves us with a certain sense of desolation." Today a viewer would not perhaps separate the Renaissance and baroque so neatly as styles. Instead of *desolation*, one might be inclined to use words like *dislocation, incompleteness, restlessness*. The designs in these terms bear on very modern problems; they suggest how the experience of otherness, of disruptive difference, might become available to the designing eye. Sebastiano Serlio, a designer who linked the Renaissance and the Baroque, directly picked up on such suggestions in his work.

Serlio, like other architects of his time, and unlike most modern ones, frequently used the theater as a laboratory for building streets. He experimented with backcloths, stage sculpture, and even stage machinery; what worked on stage was often taken as a guide for how to organize moving bodies on a street. Either in 1546 or 1551 he made a famous set of engravings as designs for stage backcloths, among them being two city views, one called *The Comic Scene*, the other *The Tragic Scene*.

Serlio's *Comic Scene* depicts an urban square with a corridor street receding in perspective behind it. The genius of this drawing is that the corridor moves the eye forward rather than back: the profane, intensely human action that is comedy will happen close up. Serlio has drawn the wall and door of a church as the far wall of this corridor for comedy; nearer he has drawn more domestic structures. The street debouches into a square capped by two buildings at the end of the street; unlike the caps in the Piazza del Popolo, these buildings

[7] Heinrich Wölfflin, *Renaissance und Barock* (München: Bruckman, 1926), p. iv (my translation).

are full stops. Before them, focused in the square, the action will occur. Through the action of perspective, Serlio makes the near the mundane.

Serlio's *Tragic Scene* sends the eye farther and farther away, as do the streets Sixtus made. In *The Tragic Scene*, however, there are no evidences of Christianity. Down the end of the street is an imperial gate with a heroic figure carrying a spear at its summit; behind it a set of barely visible stairs leading, presumably, to more street on a different level. Above and behind and to one side of the heroic figure, Serlio has placed an obelisk.

The genius of this engraving lies in how Serlio has positioned the obelisk. It is off center from the vanishing point established by the receding tunnel of the street, the point marked by the warrior's head atop the gate; behind him, the ball of the obelisk, marking another vanishing point, contradicts all this regularity. The eye as it looks to the horizon is therefore disturbed, and this disturbance reflects on the massive, imperial street. Its solidity, too, is displaced by the play of perspective; the eye cannot relate the order of stone to the order of space, and so jumps from one dimension to the other—just as in the Piazzo del Popolo and its fan of streets the eye is restless—a perspectival space making the viewer experience any single point of view as inadequate. This is a space of displacement.

Serlio's design found a partial realization in the great, half-finished Olympic Theater (*Teatro Olimpico* in the Piazza Matteotti) which Andrea Palladio began in the city of Vicenza in 1580. The Olympic Theater is a sharply raked amphitheater facing a proscenium stage. Palladio designed the stage wall (the *scenae frons*) as though it were the wall of a house. The façade is richly ornamented with statues depicting the patrons of the Olympian Society of Vicenza in Roman dress, set in two tiers of niches; above these local luminaries bas reliefs depicting the life of Hercules adorn a third tier. What makes this proscenium wall so evocative are the openings Palladio designed for it: a great arched opening in the center flanked by two squared-off openings on either side. Through these we see street scenes of exactly the sort of receding tunnel Serlio designed. All that is known of Palladio's own intentions for the street scenes is a sketch he made in 1580 of the stage wall. Four years later the Olympic Society bought the building behind the theater and Palladio's sketch now could be built in the enlarged backstage area of the theater. The architect Vincenzo Scamozzi took up the work in 1584, building three streets receding in perspective, seemingly endlessly, in fact extending only forty-five meters.

Scamozzi's labors are a masterpiece of perspectival control through foreshortening. But this master of perspectival precision saw just as Serlio did. In the central receding street, obelisks are placed along the tops of the buildings lining the street so that the eye looking down the tunnel is disturbed. Something is happening out of control at the edge; the eye darts to the obelisks atop the buildings rather than moves down the regularly marching, endlessly regressing space between them. This was the setting Scamozzi thought appropriate for the first play presented by the Olympian Society, Sophocles' *Oedipus Rex*.

Serlio named his *Tragic Scene* well. The classical tragedies to be presented on the stage would tell the story of men and women who learn the limits of human comprehension, striving and understanding. Serlio, Palladio, and Scamozzi created a stage set that would tell that same story visually, through the action of perspective, the power of perspective to engage men and women beyond their perceptual control. Perhaps what Wölfflin long ago felt in the sweep of baroque movement was not so much desolation as this intimation of human limits.

"Anti-humanism," as used by Arendt, Sartre, and their heirs, is a word one would do well to ponder. For the humanists of the historical Renaissance set the example for a visual provocation lacking in much modern urban planning. They could conceive of these visual provocations as, literally, ethical vision. The eye which perceived limits, incompleteness, otherness was engaged in the ocular experience of tragedy.

Serlio's tragic scene of the city finds at least one reflection in a modern version of "the world is being seen." When Marcel Proust stood before Vermeer's *View of Delft* at an exposition in the Jeu de Paume in May 1921, this painting of distance perfectly orchestrating color suggested to Proust something about his own novel. Proust sends one of his fictional selves, Bergotte, to this exposition, which causes the sick painter to become terminally ill. He dies, Proust remarks, for a "little patch of yellow wall with a pent-roof," and yet

Proust speaks of Bergotte's sight as "redeemed" by this fatal view of Delft.[8] The incident recalls in one way the words of Henry James to describe John Marcher's vision in the graveyard, "at last he had seen outside himself." These words have a literal as well as metaphorical meaning.

Indeed, at the end of *Remembrance of Things Past*, Proust's narrator declares that

> not only does everyone have this feeling that we occupy a place in Time, but this "place" is something that the simplest among us measures in an approximate fashion, as he might measure with his eye the place which we occupy in space.[9]

To forget pain, wrong-doing, and hurting is all too easy; the most comfortable time for most people is the time of omission. The narrator resolves to tell from his sick bed a story that will confront these omissions. He will tell his story by making use of space, by evoking places so that people will see what memory has omitted:

> in the course of my narrative, at least I should not fail to portray man, in this universe, as endowed with the length not of his body but of his years and is obliged—a task more and more enormous and in the end too great for his strength—to drag them with him wherever he goes.[10]

Proust's narrator will show through the degradation of a street or the shifting locale for prostitution or in the alterations of the houses of his childhood the limitations upon making life cohere through memories. He will thus create in words the tragic scene to the same effect Serlio had drawn it.

The urbanism of Sixtus V shows how a concrete object like the obelisk can be used to create a restless, problematic space. It is a space of

[8] Marcel Proust, *À la recherche du temps perdu* (Paris: Pleida, 1954, et seq.), vol. 3, pp. 182–88.
[9] Marcel Proust, *Time Regained*, vol. 7 of *À la recherche du temps perdu*, trans. Terence Kilmartin (New York: Random House, 1981), p. 1104.
[10] Ibid.

discovery, of exploration. Serlio's *Tragic Scene* is an admonition deduced from that space, an invention of perspectival space in which perspective passes beyond easy control. How does this humane, tragic vision in the past speak to our present?

Fourteenth Street

Fourteenth Street cuts across Manhattan from the East River to the Hudson River. The street, part of Manhattan's grid, is perfectly straight and very long, and punctuated in the center by a large park called Union Square. The recent history of this square and its buildings is an attempt to draw directly on the visual heritage of Sixtus V and his Rome. The designers working on the square and its surroundings have sought to draw people from the street into the square by the same sort of magnetic movement, a worthy effort to attract people by use of beacons and markers so that the poor and the rich will mix together. Yet these visual means have failed to realize their social intentions.

The park of Union Square itself was recently redesigned. The interior of the old park was opened up, bushes on its perimeter cut, so that drug dealing did not take place in shelter, hidden from surveillance. An attempt has been made to organize it in perspective from its Fourteenth Street side. Standing on Fourteenth Street in front of what used to be Mays Department Store looking into the park, the eye is taken up a set of rounded platforms rising to the level of the park grade, which is four feet above road level; paths are cut through the park to reveal a colonnade at the back, and here, in this piece of quasi-sculpture attached to nothing, the eye stops. The gesture of leading the eye up and back in perspective to a monument used in itself as a horizon can be traced back to the making of the Campidoglio. The formal invitation to the eye, however, cannot be acted upon by a New Yorker's body. Access to these sloping platforms is virtually impossible from across the road as car traffic cuts the steps off on Fourteenth Street as on the side streets of the square; to get into Union Square most people must use rather modest side entrances. Few people, in any event, accept the invitation; the park is thinly populated by day and empty by night.

Next to the renovated park, on its southeast side, an enormous new project has gone up. This is the Zeckendorf Towers, four towers of apartments set on a box of offices and shops fronting on Fourteenth Street as well as the park. The Zeckendorf development organization has given each of the towers the look of a giant obelisk by installing obelisk tips in metal on top of the brick towers (the commercial-office base is meant to serve as a common plinth). The obelisk as an invitation to approach is contravened, however, by the way the Zeckendorf Towers have been designed to be used. The residences are entered secretly, by a hidden entrance on Fifteenth Street. The building has an enormous supermarket hidden within it as well, so that residents can shop without inviting shoppers from the street. Fronting the square is a giant atrium lobby for the office plinth, faced in granite, with guards who evict people without business within.

Fourteenth Street is unusual in containing so many quotations from the late Renaissance and early baroque traditions of street planning. In one way, these references in both the square and the towers illustrate a simple point: you don't recover the spirit of the past by quoting its forms. But the Humanist lessons of the street are to be found here, in more modern forms.

At the eastern end of Fourteenth Street, there is a giant electricity plant, a place of desolation with its own austere beauty, the sun glinting in odd angles off the exposed, curving pipes ten stories high. There is a band of elderly regulars who haunt nearby coffee shops. These are men who used to work in the plant and now are tending it in memory and gossip. As one moves inward, on the south side of the street the Lower East Side of the immigrants begins. A generation ago this side of the street was lined with Polish butchers and Russian bakeries. On the opposite north side is Stuyvesant Town, a confection of artificial hills and valleys and apartments inserted into the city in the late 1940s, a talisman of what the good life looks like for those who could escape the slums. On Fourteenth Street this housing project raised a wall fourteen feet high to the Lower East Side, the few buildings of the "town" that touched the street offering no inviting entrance. The separation is reinforced by something quite rare in Manhattan—a parking strip; the lines of parked cars on both sides of it served as a further barrier between old and new life.

In time this border has crumbled. The Polish butchers and Russian bakeries have been partially replaced by bodegas and small chain stores that serve Hispanics who have moved into the housing project. The walls of Stuyvesant Town have been hollowed out—literally; they contain a hospital service facility beneath the knoll of grass that residents see from their windows. The parking strip is now choked at sunset in good weather by families who use it as a promenade, families from the tenements below Fourteenth Street and families of all ethnic and racial groups from the housing project. The street-border was not broken down by protest of the slum poor against the relatively privileged petit bourgeois. One year tough kids played between the parked cars, the next year little knots of family leaned against the cars, drinking beer and gossiping in the muggy summer evenings. The past crumbled into the present in little fragments of making do. No one willed the mixture to occur or now much discusses it; it is not a political event such as Arendt might have conceived, nor was it designed.

The street becomes more markedly mixed in this way as one moves toward the center. The remaining Eastern European stores sell to very elderly people still living in the nearby slums, but the Hispanic people, in shops that sell rolls of fabric for dresses and shirts, discount sheets, and used sewing-machines, have come here from all over the city; Fourteenth Street is a major stop on all subway lines. Puerto Rico, Colombia, and Haiti are bright young bodies among a gray Poland smelling of talc. And above these shops, in improvised little cubicles, are the offices of professionals, the doctors and lawyers who service the Hispanic community as well as the elderly Europeans.

At the point where Fourteenth Street intersects Third Avenue, one has a good glimpse of what makes this street so different from the street leading to the French restaurants in midtown. In a way, looking back to the power station, one sees less dramatic differences than one does looking up Third Avenue. There are simply varieties of poor people. But the differences along Third Avenue are segments on a

line; here, differences are overlaid in the same space. While few
Russians are consulting Spanish lawyers in the dingy upper reaches of
the buildings on Fourteenth Street, their own lawyers and doctors
share the same corridors of dust, Spanish and Russian mingling
through the thin partitions. The power of simultaneous perception is
aroused, rather than the linear perceptions of my restaurant walk.
This is a street of overlays.

Overlays of difference create the true human center of Fourteenth
Street, the blocks between Fourth and Sixth avenues. Here discount
and "gray market" electronics, luggage, jewelry, and clothes are sold
mostly to blacks, Hispanics, and poor whites. This part of the street
has a curious quirk. In New York it is legal for a merchant to extend
a display case eighteen inches out from the front of his store on to the
sidewalk. Some merchants rent the eighteen-inch strips to peddlers
whose goods are shaded from gray to black market. And again, on the
farther edge of the sidewalk, next to the street itself, peddlers pay to
spread down blankets on which there are "nearly new" goods, which
means, for instance, a radio smudged with the fingerprints of some
child to whom the radio was recently "mine."

The precariousness of Fourteenth Street may make for uncomfortable viewing: the clients for services above the shops are dying out,
or being pushed farther and farther away by the real-estate economics
of the city. The shops themselves remain lucrative only through cut-
throat competition, and, even so, commerce is constantly breaking
down in patches: the plate-glass fronts of the street are like bad teeth,
blackened windows gaping between fluorescent whiteness. Most attempts to provide the street with social amenities not related to consumption have failed; the several churches lining the street at either
end of Fourteenth Street have not successfully engaged the community. There is a military recruiting center, designed to attract young
kids off the street, but it has few takers. Because it is a center for
goods acquired by theft or "gray" trade (the peddlers acquire these
goods legally from wholesalers a little farther uptown who are silent
partners and specialize in merchandise smuggled through customs),
the street is filled with small-time hustlers who don't look tough
enough to deal in drugs.

Yet the very difficulty of surviving has prompted people to organize certain boundaries, boundaries that attach people to the street even though the sibyls of profit, usually brothers or nephews who have moved to the suburbs, may patiently explain to those left behind how to make more money in a less demanding environment. Competitors on the street are protective of each other in some ways; there is now a fairly well-organized effort to resist the demands both of the Mafia and of the police for protection money. A shoplifter running out of one store is likely to be chased on the street by other owners. After a while one sees how many children there are here, hidden from casual view—the children of shopkeepers or shoppers who have all sort of nooks and secret corners, who are playing between parked cars and trucks; a street of children who are constantly moving. The adjustments these children learn to make with their eyes is how to signal to others that they are friendly, and with their bodies to avoid kids who look like trouble. This can't be done by moving away, since they must stay in the vicinity of their parents; it has to be done by where one walks on the pavement, and how one manages one's arms. It is a street in which people are constantly adjusting their mutual limits—with their eyes and their bodies. Much of this life is possible only because it is not talked about, which is another overlay—the spoken and the unspoken. Moreover, the life on Fourteenth Street is not a matter of a single, equilibrating moment. It is constantly shifting, in who takes care of whom, in when people take advantage of others, as when the price of the eighteen inches of sidewalk illegally rented to a peddler is tripled when the peddler has a good day. These are the mundance signs of the kind of complexity suggested by the term "otherness." If one summons to mind the streets planned by the younger John Wood in Bath, the peculiar qualities of otherness on Fourteenth Street are immediately apparent. Instead of a dispersing crowd, here is an interacting crowd.

The otherness on Fourteenth Street recreates the value Serlio sought for in his *Tragic Scene*. The experience of the street establishes human limits. However, the humanism of Sixtus V, Serlio, Palladio, and Scamozzi was enacted by the design. The experience of overlays on Fourteenth Street has no designer. Moreover, the street is indubitably full of life, but it is life bent on survival; its exchanges, curbs, and negotiations occur without much reflection.

Despite this, there is a design principle at work on Fourteenth Street: it is the disruption of linear sequence. This street is what Baldwin's story looks like. The errors of invention such as appear in and around Union Square prompt in many observers the opposite conviction that "life" is synonymous with spontaneity, that street life cannot be planned. The fact that the civilities of a working-class street have no architect might seem to reinforce this conviction. Yet it is here that the ethical journey depicted in Baldwin's essay might be taken in space. Baldwin's journey was one in which the protagonist's impulses of assertion and definition were curbed; when they were curbed, a new consciousness of others came into being, a story very much like that depicted in Serlio's *Tragic Scene*. This journey is in its form much more than a neutral report of events; it is a highly crafted work of art, and the art, through the device of thwarted narrative catharsis, makes the journey an event the reader also experiences.

Today, the principle of disrupted linear sequence, the street of overlayed differences, is an elusive reality in urban design. It has proved elusive because of a second principle of design, again suggested by Baldwin's story. The invention which designers are seeking, in order to prompt the discovery of others on a street, has something to do with *time*. Sigfried Giedion argued the experience of time could be designed architecturally and urbanistically—this experience was to him about free and coherent movement. Baldwin's essay works because of the subversions of narrative coherence. If overlays of difference are the necessary condition for enacting a sense of connection between people on the street, is the subversion of coherent time a sufficient, complementary condition? And is it precisely this subversion of coherent time which a designer could draw? These may seem abstract questions, but there is something to be learned from the humanist past, again, about their present reality.

chapter 7

Places Full
of Time

Le Corbusier
and Léger
in New York

IN AN ACCOUNT of a journey he made to New York in 1935, *When the Cathedrals Were White*, Le Corbusier observes that Americans in general and New Yorkers in particular love machines more than one another, which he thinks is all to the good. American cities are machines, street-grid machines and skyscraper machines; in them we are clean, empty, and free. "The streets are at right angles to each other and the mind is liberated."[1] The subways, the neon signs in Times Square, and the Brooklyn Bridge are of little interest in revealing the manners and mores of people in New York, who are, after all, only Americans. But the pneumatic jackhammer is a marvel.

The title Le Corbusier chose was not entirely a caprice: to love the jackhammer, even when wielded by American hands, is to express a faith equivalent to the medieval cathedral builder's striving for structural perfection. But Le Corbusier has given the act of faith a new substance: people can virtually erase nature through invention. At this point in his life, Le Corbusier loved fast, chrome-plated cars, chrome-and-leather chairs without a betraying seam or stitch, as well as elevators that ran so smoothly you weren't aware they were mov-

---

[1] Le Corbusier, *When the Cathedrals Were White,* trans. Francis Hyslop, Jr. (New York: Reynal & Hitchcock, 1947), p. 47

ing. These objects transcend the body's errant powers, or they erase
the resistance of wind, hide, and gravity.

Had during his stay in New York in 1935 Le Corbusier visited some
movie theaters, he would have seen a popular, uncomfortable reflection of his sleek urbanism. Many of the films of New York made for
audiences desperate to escape the privations of a worldwide economic
collapse were also filled with chrome cocktail shakers and automo-
biles. In these films witty people assemble for amusing parties in that
peculiarly New York palace, the penthouse high above the city, its
walls of glass giving onto terraces filled with plants, the sounds of the
street below drowned out by someone playing a grand piano painted
white. The machinery of staging and props was self-consciously elaborate and often, as in the Busby Berkeley shows, display was the
point; the furnishings and the sets, the white piano and the penthouse
terrace, mattered more than the dialogue or the plot: stylishly designed, self-consciously modern things were used knowingly. These
films were an escape from the breadlines on the streets. Economic
cataclysm prompted the desire for sleek, perfect things as relief. The
architect and the unemployed, both driven, if for different reasons,
by a desire for transcendence, shared the dream of a city of chrome.

The modern architecture Sigfried Giedion championed was a revelation, he thought, of the unity of space and time. We have seen the
unintended consequence of seeking for this unity: an object endowed
with inner coherence seems cut off from the world around it, a world
that is necessarily messy, incomplete, and disorderly. The contrast
between the aesthetics of unity and the character of society is marked
by constructions like those of Mies van der Rohe, the sublime divorced from the social.

The machine of Le Corbusier's dream takes this divorce a step
further. Le Corbusier set himself against the ways in which time is
usually felt in urban space. The façades of old buildings and worn
paving stones offer evidence that our own lives are no more and no
less than an addition to the past. Le Corbusier rejected this evidence;
he wanted modern architecture, which seeks for freedom of movement in a perfectly coordinated form, to expunge historical time from
the city.

Probably Le Corbusier's most notorious proposal to replace the historical by the sleek is the Plan Voisin, which he contrived in 1925 for Paris. The Plan Voisin would have gutted the medieval quarter of the Marais, leveled it flat to the ground. In place of this thousand years of haphazard building, Le Corbusier would have placed enormous X-shaped towers on a grid plan. To Le Corbusier it little mattered that the forms of this Plan Voisin required so much human destruction: "the principal aim is manifesto."[2] The X-shaped towers are meant as architectural expressions of mechanical production; they can be repeated again and again and again. In this they compose a grid in its modern, indeterminate form; the Plan Voisin has no necessary boundaries, it could be the Marais or all of Paris. The act of design is opposed to the record in stone of human habitation.

The machine entered in another way into this plan. Le Corbusier makes an extreme use of perspective in order to render the towers; the perspective on this city is drawn from someone in an airplane. While the architectural convention of looking down on a big built object to see it whole is commonplace, Le Corbusier has so stretched this convention, by positioning the viewer so high in the sky, that it is impossible to see much detail in his buildings; one notices more the way the X's look when mechanically repeated. There is thus a loss of historical relations and of concrete details in Le Corbusier's manifesto; the Plan Voisin is the very emblem of a disembodied, neutral city.

This Plan Voisin was the prototype for the grade-flat-and-build urban development that has defaced cities all over the world. Le Corbusier's destructiveness in this plan has, it must be said, a sympathetic source. Architects of Le Corbusier's generation wanted no more quoting of the past, of modern buildings made to resemble Gothic castles or Renaissance palaces. Moreover, the nineteenth-century insistence on sweetness and light was as deadening in architecture as in literature. The English garden city and greenbelt communities of Ebenezer Howard and his followers were a defining instance of this deadweight; they were worthy, healthy, organic, and boring quasi-suburbs, dedicated to the proposition that coziness is life. Jackhammers and the "Cartesian eye" were a release from that well-meaning provincialism.

[2] Colin Rowe and Fred Koetter, *Collage City* (Cambridge, Mass.: MIT Press, n.d.), p. 72.

The "antihumanism" Le Corbusier described himself feeling at this revolutionary point in his life had an urban enemy: the street. In the Plan Voisin the street is a place for trucks and taxis, but not for people. In 1929 Le Corbusier declared, "The street wears us out. And when all is said and done we have to admit it disgusts us." A few years later Sigfried Giedion would declare, "The first thing to do is abolish the rue corridor with its rigid lines of buildings and its intermingling of traffic, pedestrians, and houses."[3] When Le Corbusier came to New York, he was, naturally enough, looking for confirmation of his manifesto. He remarked to a young friend when he first arrived, "Yours is the first truly abstract city." New York's lack, in his eyes, of a durable architectural past, its instant towers, its grid of block after similar block, its streets filled with buses, elevated trains, trucks and cars, all seemed to have permitted the design of an *urbs* cut free from the claims of a dead European *civitas*. It should also be said that after the Second World War, and I think because of it, Le Corbusier changed: the builder of the soft city of Chandigarh in India was not the designer of the Plan Voisin, the builder of the church of Ronchamp was not the author of *When the Cathedrals Were White*. However, when people speak of the architect as a ferocious modernist they have in mind visions such as Le Corbusier harbored earlier in his life that deny the legitimacy of the past or the impasto of different forms in a city made by successive waves of habitation.

In discussing the work of the grid planners or of contemporary builders of the neutral city, I used the term "compulsive neutralizing" to describe their work, a phrase which may seem to characterize the neutralizing impulse psychologically. In fact this compulsion to empty in order to build reflects a belief the modern artist holds about his or her social status as an inventor. The inventive person stands in a hostile relation to the existing society. When we use words like "provocative" or "arousing" to describe a modern invention of an artistic sort, these words carry the implication of a challenge to, a negation of, what already exists. Le Corbusier could be said to make these implications visible in his Plan Voisin. The desire to create is burdened by the belief one must in the process negate; indeed, the

[3] Both quoted in Michael Dennis, *Court and Garden* (Cambridge, Mass.: MIT Press, 1986), p. 213.

act of creation produces an image of this denial, a picture of the very possibility of creating a blank canvas, a clean emptiness—these spaces of negation which seem the promise of freedom.

This is the promise of the Plan Voisin, one not accounted, I think, by its many critics. "His city was a wonderful mechanical toy," Jane Jacobs remarked.[4] "His urbanism . . . is dominated by a conceptual poverty that inevitably minimizes the complex problems inherent in the contemporary city and countryside," according to Manfredo Tafuri.[5] Or again Le Corbusier's revolutionary Plan Voisin has been called to account as a new kind of city center well suited to international business.

A downtown made of glittering office towers reflecting the power of multi-national corporations . . . [is] based on the very forces with which Le Corbusier had hoped to put his Plan Voisin into action.[6]

The rhythm of creation and negation in Le Corbusier's work is significant at a more profound level precisely because of what it aims at, an aim of others also moved by a similar desire of freedom. Le Corbusier hoped to erect a new awareness of time, the sense of *now*. You have to fight off the deadweight of the past, as a young person must overthrow the presence of an overbearing parent. This destructiveness can be redeemed by the quality, indeed, the perfection, of form one can create once one is free. The literary critic and theorist Harold Bloom describes this sense of time as a result of "anxiety of influence." In urbanism, the result of this anxiety about past and present, as represented by Le Corbusier's early work, is to destroy the differences which have accumulated in space for the sake of affirming this difference in time.

And it is here, I think, that Le Corbusier has to be answered, in

[4] Jane Jacobs, *The Death and Life of Great American Cities* (New York: Random House, 1961), p. 23.
[5] Manfredo Tafuri, *"Machine et memoire": The City in the Work of Le Corbusier*, in H. Allen Brooks, ed., *Le Corbusier* (Princeton: Princeton University Press, 1987), pp. 207–08.
[6] Stanislaus van Moos, "Urbanism and Transcultural Exchanges, 1910–1935" in Brooks, *Le Corbusier*, p. 225.

this necessarily destructive vision of time in space. By what alternative urban means could people be provoked? Negation is a trap; like the young Le Corbusier, the artist can wind up representing only his own act of denial. How can the work of visual design become more *arousing*, beyond the terms of this adolescent confrontation?

Some suggestion of how one might arouse others in an adult way came from Le Corbusier's travel companion, Fernand Léger, who made the voyage to New York with Le Corbusier. They had shows together in 1935 at the Museum of Modern Art, though Léger had come before in 1931 and would spend the war years here in exile. Léger perhaps as well made fuller use of his ticket: he went to movies, rode the subways, haunted bus repair shops after midnight, practiced English in bars, and generally made himself at home.

The sense of living time in Léger's work appears in his imagination of machines. In Léger's paintings men and women are thoroughly at home with machines—human arms, for instance, become in these paintings mechanical armatures; a pleasing if chunky body can be made of metal and glass as well as bone and muscle. Léger's visual friendliness toward the machine traces back to the bridges and factories in the paintings of the Parisian suburbs by Pissarro and other impressionists. Throughout his career Léger had a much more intimate relation to machines than did Le Corbusier. Léger's study of mechanical elements began during the drawings he made at the front while a soldier in World War I; his welding of mechanical and human forms first became apparent in works like *Pont du remorqueur* (1920) or *Les disques dans la ville* (1920–1921). By the time he began *Composition aux perroquets* and his extended visit to New York in 1935, the figures in Léger's paintings are thrust into odd, gravitationally impossible relations to one another; the collagelike spaces he makes are not elements pasted on a flat plane but volumes within which the arbitrary becomes perfectly plausible because we suppose some mechanical support has made it possible—the mechanical-human whole that supports people within a volume is greasy rather than gleaming, and does not alienate. Human relations are implied in the clanking, awkward objects that are most real machines.

Léger's paintings of machines are suggestive precisely because they address the issue of immediacy. Immediacy comes from a sense of seeing something *used*. The evidence of this use is the fragmented condition of the object, a piece of broken pipe or a worn valve become part of the human world, altered and worn down like the human body. When he declared "the object has replaced the subject, and abstract art is like a total liberation," or more fully, "each object, whether a painting or architecture or system of ornament, has a value in itself, strictly absolute, independent of what it represents,"[7] Léger was far from imagining his mechanical-human objects as symbols of power and control.

The modern temper, as Baudelaire conceived it in the nineteenth century, accepted the fragmented character of everyday life. Experiences of immediacy became intertwined with those scenes on the street that tended to fragment one's vision, to focus on the part. To accept this constantly shifting scene, rather than look for someplace fixed, stable, and whole, was to become involved in the life of the city. Léger painted that involvement. Léger expressed his love of the fragmented in his last American picture, *Adieu New York*, a painting he described thus:

> You know, the USA is a country where there are innumerable pieces of refuse. One throws something out rather than repairs it. Thus you see in this painting that there are pieces of iron, machine arms, and even neckties. What I liked to do in America was make paintings out of all that.[8]

It is this very art of things fragmenting in use that places the canvases in the immediacy of the present.

Modern urbanism has not learned how to incorporate such a painterly sense of time into building. When we think of representing usages— that is, the fact of buildings having a historical life—we easily slip into nostalgia and the quoting of past forms. Nostaglia is the mirror opposite of Le Corbusier's *now*. This nostalgia was given voice, for example, by the late-nineteenth-century urbanist Camillo Sitte in his

[7] Fernand Léger, quoted in Musée national d'art moderne, Centre Georges Pompidou, "Parcours des collections permanentes: Léger," p. 7, p. 5.

[8] Léger, "Parcours des collections permanentes," p. 10.

longing for the unruly medieval alley choked with animals, children, and adults, for the square filled with stalls of fruit, spices, and meat. As Carl Schorske has evoked Sitte's hope for return of street life,

> In the cold, traffic swept modern city of the slide-rule and the slum, the picturesque comforting square can reawaken memories of the vanished burgher past. This spatially dramatic memory will inspire us to create a better future, free of philistinism and utilitarianism.[9]

Léger's painting makes a more profound suggestion about spaces full of time. These would be, first of all, overlays. The architects Colin Rowe and Frederick Koetter have imagined a whole city built in this way as a "collage city." A collage, however, is not a random pasting together of elements, and a space full of time supposes more than simply the impress of flux, the register of things appearing, breaking, altering, and messing up as they are used. Léger gave his machine parts an expressive relation to one another, as in his writing Baldwin gave fragmented time a shape. And shaping the physical elements which accumulate on the street is also necessary. It is by sensing the form given to time in space that we perceive the street as a more arousing experience than a mere record of what has happened in and to it.

It is by recurring to the Renaissance again that we might understand how this adult time might be shaped in space. The Renaissance designers found, indeed, urban forms for the present tense. Again, rather than copying the forms of the past, we need to understand the principles of their inventiveness.

Fortune's Machines

The Renaissance first invented machines that aroused in the city a sense of present-tense, fragmented time. However, these machines

[9] Carl Schorske, *Fin-de-siècle Vienna: Politics and Cultural* (New York: Knopf, 1981), p. 72.

made the present tense fearsome. Two machines refined in the Renaissance first gave people the power to fragment time in cities: the clock and the cannon. One cut time into meaningless fragments of deadly routine, the other created fragmentary moments of blind violence.

By the nineteenth century, when cities began to be built according to the relentless extensions of the mechanical spatial grid, time had long since submitted to a kindred process; the clock had already imposed a grid on time. The modern mechanical clock as we know it began with a discovery made toward the end of the thirteenth century. Renaissance craftsmen came upon one way to regulate evenly the escape of energy from a spinning wheel and applied this discovery to time. The escapement of these first clocks was a device called verge and foliot, a weighted bar (the foliot) that seesawed up and down as it revolved on a spindle (the verge); the up-and-down motion equilibrated the turning motion of the spindle. The clocks first built in the Renaissance using this escapement are clumsy by modern standards, requiring regulation every day; in 1656 or 1657 the physicist Christiaan Huygens found a better solution to the escapement problem by replacing the foliot bar with the pendulum, creating clocks that measured precisely equal minutes for a week at a time.

Throughout the Middle Ages people had known of time divided into equal portions, by the hourglass and the water clock, but mechanical time divorced from the natural ebb and flow of day, night, and seasons had little meaning. According to Marc Bloch, feudal society showed "a vast indifference to time."[10] The Benedictine monks began to give precise time meaning, allotting particular spiritual tasks strictly to each hour. The Benedictines might have been the first organized medieval group to "give the human enterprise the regular collective beat and rhythms of the machine," but they did so in the interests of strengthening monastic life.[11]

The public clock mounted at the center of a town high up on a building created a different order of discipline. These clocks were

[10] Marc Bloch, *Le société féodale* (Paris: Albin Michel, 1940), p. 116, and developed on pp. 116–20.
[11] Eviatar Zerubavel, *Hidden Rhythms: Schedules and Calendars in Social Life* (Chicago: The University of Chicago Press, 1981), p. 32.

first used for the regulation of bodily functions rather than spiritual rhythm, telling people when to rise and when to sleep, when to eat and when to rest. It was the effect of subjecting the human body to a grid of physical discipline that eventually would be made use of economically, to pay for labor by the hour. Then, at that point, clock-time became a time of power in the city, "an instrument of economic, social, and political domination wielded by the merchants who ran the commune."[12]

Clock-time was brought to a technical conclusion thanks to a further invention by Huygens. Some time in the winter of 1674–1675, he devised the spring balance as an alternative to the pendulum; now clocks could be made very small. This was the birth of the watch. The time of the watch was a luxury time, as these objects were highly expensive; when the watch became relatively cheaper and more practical, it diffused no further than the burgher class. Among the burghers watch-time became an instrument for self-regulation; it was individual time. From the advent of the verge and foliot until the invention of the watch, mechanical clock-time was a necessarily more public, spatial experience.

The monastery was a closed world in which the hours and their parts were reckoned by listening to the bells, and this same marking of time through bells of course continued in the churches of the Renaissance cities. These ringing bells marked the ritual moments during the day, the amount of time lapsing between one sacred duty and the next. The machinery that produced little mechanical dramas when the hours struck, in Venice or other cities—such as a bell ringer popping out of a concealed compartment to pound on a drum while the church rang out its hours—reinforced the ritual of the moment. Practical time required instead reckoning how much time was passing between these little dramas. The quantification of the time in between, of time elapsing in units, was the time shown on clock faces; in this sense, secular time meant *visible* time without ritual.

This secular time required a clock face clear enough to be read by people making practical use of it, which is why the design of clock faces and hands became a specialty. Moreover, to be usable by large numbers of people, clock time needed to be visible at a distance. The big clocks in the Renaissance therefore tended to an enormous scale. A great clock maker like Isaak Haprecht was able to build clocks for the cathedral tower at Strasbourg and the town hall in Ulm that were highly accurate; most clock makers, however, for the sake of making quantified time visible, constructed clocks larger than they should have been to make the most efficient use of the verge-and-foliot. And in the very size of the clock lay its effect upon urban space.

One of Haprecht's greatest clocks is located on the town hall of Heilbronn. He set it up above the wall of the town hall, into the sharply sloping roof, so that from any entrance to the square the time is visible. The precision of its inner works is matched by the attempt to site it so that, indeed, it is visible, if at an oblique angle, from points on streets farther away than where they give upon the square. In a clock mounted on the square in Weinsburg, the buildings lining the square were shaved on their façades and reorganized so that this clock would be visible from the side streets flowing into the square. Seeing the time became one of the first ways post-medieval planners defined what it meant to lay out a market square efficiently.

Moreover, the building of these clocks created the desire (realized in different places in different ways, of course) to take down the temporary shelters and storage sheds that were often built up two or three stories in the medieval squares and markets; these tall sheds interfered with easily seeing the time. By the time of the completion of the old Place Royale in Paris, now the Place des Vosges, this connection between unobstructed people and the visible time that cooks, carpenters, and footmen needed to tell as they went about their business in the city had become a space-time for kings; in the old Place Royale an elaborate silent clock was placed on the eastern face. The square was designed to be ordinarily empty, the people using it hidden under its street-level arcades.

The history of urban clocks is an instance of what, in our culture, exactness and precision came to dictate: they came to dictate acts of clearing away obstruction so that a mental operation can be performed autonomously. In this case, the simple operation of telling the time. In part, for the sake of that temporal precision, urban volume was emptied.

In the tasteful glass-and-steel tower with its simple furniture carefully placed, we experience an emptiness that does not duplicate the
experience of the Renaissance planners, for whom clearing way was a
positive act of making-room-for in the midst of the clamor and mess
of the squares and markets. Creating empty volume was the way
these planners diffused the knowledge of time. Still, the Renaissance
clock maker's derivation of empty space from mechanical time inter-
sected with the later grid form, with its own economic and psychological logic of emptiness. Clock-time came to be complemented by
grid-space. This space/time relationship is anything but the beneficent conjunction Sigfried Giedion imagined. Rather than surprising
discoveries, the clock seemed to offer its users only monotony.

In the Renaissance, one contrary force to clock routine appeared in
the evolving technology of warfare, and in the effect of machines for
war upon cities. To understand the effect of warfare on the experiences of time of the first modern city dwellers, one has to understand
something about the strength of medieval city walls.

The walls of the medieval city were the physical guarantors of the
inscription above the medieval gates, *Stadt Luft macht frei* ("city air
makes free"). The practices of medieval warfare had determined the
form of city walls, particularly their height. Arrows, even when fired
from crossbows, were relatively harmless projectiles to those behind
a moat and wall; the catapult of stones was a similarly ineffective
means of harming many people sheltered. Instead, the wall itself was
in medieval warfare literally the "field" of battle in laying siege to a
city.

The logic of the siege was and is a contest of wills in time. The
hostile army surrounds a town; the populace and immediate countryside withdraws within. In medieval sieges, given the relative futility
of arrows and scaling, the actual struggle was who could hold out
longest, less a matter of killing soldiers than of collective endurance.
One effect of this form of warfare on the cities themselves was to
increase their density. Marketing was an activity that swept large
numbers of people in and out of towns for short periods of time. The
fear of unprotected attack encouraged people to settle more permanently within, and sieges required them to do so. When density

increased to the bursting point a new set of walls would be built concentrically around the old. The density and the centralization of the medieval town were thus partly products of its necessary time, the time of endurance.

The advent of the cannon changed this. First of all it rendered useless the old walls as protection. Instead of vertical combat at the wall, the cannon required the defenses of "ever increasing *horizontal* distances to be left between the city perimeter and the outer edge of fortifications."[13] The cannon could not have existed without the invention of gunpowder in the twelfth century (or more probably, its passage along trade routes, for the Chinese had known it for some time), but the military use of explosive power depended upon perfecting the metal tubing of firearms. Their erratic fabrication meant the "bombard" was as likely to blow up the bombardier as his enemy. Early cannons, like handguns, also suffered from the defect of taking a great deal of time to clean and reload; due to their screwed-in breeches that required hours to cool, the guns could only be fired a few times a day. It wasn't until the Ottoman Turks attacked Constantinople in 1453, with cannons routinely throwing balls of 200 pounds, that this weapon was sufficiently developed to be useful in the siege of cities.

Until the middle of the fifteenth century, successful use of cannons was still oriented, however, to the urban wall itself as the field of battle. These more efficient cannons meant initially that the walls could be breached, the invading troops pouring into the city to fight the moment a breach was effected rather than slowly starving the citizens out. The balls used were still made of stone, for the most part, which shattered on impact with the walls. Gradually, though, metal balls were employed, and these relatively lighter balls changed the entire terms of battle. They could be fired with great propulsive force over the wall; a population within could not see where the danger would come from outside the walls; destruction became more instant; exposure became as well a matter of invisible threat, against which there were no longer physical barriers.

The terror of this change in warfare became first apparent through-

---

[13] A. E. J. Morris, *History of Urban Form before the Industrial Revolutions* (New York: Wiley, 1986), p. 130.

out Europe in the invasion of Italy by the French armies under Charles VIII in 1494. Political and religious intrigues but half explain how Charles was able to conquer Florence, Rome, and Naples without fighting a pitched, prolonged battle. His army of eighteen thousand deployed and serviced batteries of artillery even more efficient than those of the Turks. In towns like Rapallo and in fortified outposts in the duchy of Milan, this army of cannons was able to destroy in an hour or two walls that the inhabitants expected to shelter them for months. Moreover, the use of the metal ball meant that even where the walls were not breached, effective attack could be mounted against those within; the number of cannons made these interior attacks population warfare, the walls now like pens keeping people from running away. The city ceased to be shelter, a fact that traveled throughout Italy in advance of Charles's army.

The cannon erased the notion of sanctuary, and in ways that at first had to do with its defects as much as its force. The science of ballistics was then conducted upon elementary principles of geometry, and in theory it should have been possible after some trial and error to aim cannons precisely. In principle, good aim meant the gunner could avoid hitting churches or convents when shelling a town. In fact, the irregularities in the mounts for cannons meant that at the moment of firing the guns went frequently and wildly off course. Like modern military technology, what first frightened people about cannons was that those in charge of the weapons couldn't control them. In Rapallo, when the citizens sought refuge in the sanctuary of the one church, they were blown up by accident; a gun firing elsewhere had jerked off its wheel at the moment of detonation, the ball's trajectory veering forty degrees and smashing through the church window. In practice, such misfirings were frequent, and this meant that the entire city could become a free-fire zone.

The invasion of 1494 was one of the most culturally consequent in modern history: it was the first instance of terror created by a machine; it weakened the reality of sanctuary, thanks not to evil men meaning to bomb churches but to machines that they couldn't make work. Cannons changed the meaning of density and crowding, the adage of safety in numbers of the medieval commune countered by the experience of penned slaughter.

But of all the cultural consequences of cannons, the effect on time itself was perhaps the most profound. The mechanized moment of terror became the opposite extreme of labor ordered by the clock; it was the time of outburst. Though it is always an illusion to think broader changes in values have dates, the history of the cannon culminating in this invasion is the closest we can come to locating the birth of the modern sense of *spontaneity*. Spontaneous is dangerous; in the moment of spontaneity, eruption occurs. Moreover, there is no way to escape the force of spontaneity in the penned slaughter behind the walls. With the advent of clock-time, the pursuit of fortune might end in the drudgery of a shop, a counting house, or cutting room. With the advent of cannon-time, the pursuit of fortune no longer occurred in safety.

The creation of mechanical, spontaneous violence is the context in which the design of cities in the Renaissance took on a new urgency. The builder in the medieval city focused his powers of precision in construction on making churches. Even before the perfection of the cannon, long bows and other new weapons began to influence the conception of an entirely geometric city. The *cittè ideale* were star shape, perfectly geometric constructions, a form which itself predated the cannon. Around 1460 Antonia Filarete conceived the design of one such perfect, eight-point star-shape city that he called Sforzinda, in honor of the prince Francesco Sforza whom he hoped would finance it; "The outer walls," he wrote in his *Treatise on Architecture*,

> should form a sixteen-sided figure and their height be four times their depth. The streets should lead from the gates to the center of the town where I would place the main square, which ought to be twice as long as it is wide. In the middle of it I would build a tower high enough to overlook the whole surrounding district.[14]

Filarete imagined because of its very perfection of form the *città ideale* to be a stronghold. When the next generation experimented

[14] Antonio Filarete, *Trattato d'architecturra*, trans. Sigfried Giedion, in *Space, Time and Architecture* (Cambridge, Mass.: Harvard University Press, 1982), p. 47.

with star-shapes for cities, however, their minds were on cannons: how would the old urban geometry relate to the new geometry of gunpowder ballistics? Simply as a form, the star-shape city was practically useless against mechanized, quick violence, as vulnerable a form as the old medieval town. The size of the defensible city would have to be radically increased, as well, for people within to escape the power of the shells. Vincenzo Scamozzi saw the airborne projectile as the controlling term of new urban planning: it created a spontaneous, violent event coming from a source invisible to those behind the walls, or indeed up upon its pointed ramparts. From Scamozzi's work, to Vauban, to Haussmann, the exploding ball rather than prayer would govern the imagination of precision in urban design.

By the advent of the wristwatch, these were the extremes of man-made time: a time of labor and a time of war, a time of routine and a time of spontaneity. These times were spaces as well: a space emptied of confusion, a space wracked with it—the first a space vacated of life, the second filled with death; the space-time of clocks repressing adventure and the space-time of cannons destroying sanctuary. The result in urban design was to set in motion the search for forms which could defend people against their own powers of invention.

The belief that one's life must be invented, rather than inherited, is, as Lionel Trilling once noted, more than an artist's credo. The belief in making oneself is the very mark of modernity, opposed to living out the roles of a traditional society. Le Corbusier was an emblematic man of our age in this sense; to break with the past is to take control of onself. The way the Renaissance dealt with their inventions of space and time addressed what the critic Stephan Greenblatt has called the belief that one must be "self-fashioning."

The nineteenth-century historian Jacob Burckhardt gave a famous description in his study *The Civilization of the Renaissance in Italy* of the Renaissance idea of living in the present tense, an awareness he likened to waking up from a dream:

In the Middle Ages both sides of human consciousness—that which was turned within as that which was turned without—lay dreaming or half awake beneath a common veil. The veil was

woven of faith, illusion, and childish prepossession, through
which the world and history were seen clad in strange hues.
Man was conscious of himself only as member of a race, people,
party, family, or corporation—only through some general category. In Italy this veil first melted into air; an objective treat-
ment and consideration of the State and of all the things of this
world became possible. The subjective side at the same time
asserted itself with corresponding emphasis; man became a spiritual individual, and recognized himself as such.[15]

For Burckhardt, this "awakening" from the collective illusions of faith
launched modern society. The moment Burckhardt chose for the
awakening seems no longer an accurate divide. The medieval world
was hardly the coherent whole he imagined; the Renaissance was
certainly more devout and mutually needful. But Burckhardt had
grasped what seems an indubitable fact: the Renaissance had a new
consciousness of time. One is responsible for oneself in the present;
it is one's *virtu*, one's powers of doing and changing things in the
immediate environment, that matters. God intervenes but men and
women act. Writers in the later Renaissance did seek for some image
that would represent this present-tense awareness. And even more
important, the writers sought for an image that would suggest how
much people could be held responsible for their actions in this new,
present-tense time.

As so often occurred in Renaissance culture, its writers reached
back into the pre-Christian past for a guide, for instance, to Ovid. A
contemporary translation of a passage from the *Metamorphoses* com-
pares the movement of time to the ceaseless, mindless ebbing of
waves:

The tyme itself continually is fleeting like a brooke.
For nether brooke nor lygthsomme tyme can tarrye still. But
    looke
As every wave dryves other foorth, and that that commes be-
    hynd

---

[15] Jacob Burckhardt, *The Civilization of the Renaissance in Italy*, vol. 1, trans. S. G. C. Middle-
more (New York: Harper & Row, 1958), p. 143.

Bothe trusteth and is thrust itself: Even so the tymes by kynd
Doo fly and follow bothe at one, and evermore renew.[16]

Just as antiquity furnished images of endless, meaningless time—
counter to the Christian story of a fate when time stops in judgment,
damnation, and redemption—so did the classical world furnish a symbol of time that seemed appropriate to their own condition. This was
the Roman goddess Fortuna.

In ancient times she presided over justice; Fortuna was thought by
Vergil to wear a blindfold; thus arrayed, she dispensed fortunes good
or bad impartially. In the Renaissance her blindfold was removed, for
the goddess had no longer a fate to give. *Fate* receded before the
more open-ended possibilities of history; *fortune* became equated
with *chance*. It is from the sixteenth century that our modern double
meaning of this word derives, chance as both the symbol of
opportunity—"We took a chance on it"—and the counterforce of circumstances or events that may defeat those opportunities. "This view
of *Fortuna*," the historian Felix Gilbert writes in a study of Machiavelli and his times,

> was the outcome of the experience that no single event has a
> clear beginning, and the investigation of causal connections only
> exposes the vista of an infinite number of further relationships
> and interdependencies.[17]

God had not reentered history in Roman dress, then, because chance
makes for us a puzzle instead of a fate, the puzzle of how our lives
flow—as in Shakespeare's *Cymbeline*: "I that have this Golden
chance, and know not why,"[18]—nor did Chaucer's Christian equation
of "chaunce and destinye" now serve. To quote Gilbert again:

> Yet this notion of *Fortuna* did not lead to a return to the medi-
> eval concept of a world directed according to God's plan. Italians

[16] Quoted in Ricardo J. Quinones, *The Renaissance Discovery of Time* (Cambridge, Mass.: Harvard University Press, 1972), p. 13.
[17] Felix Gilbert, *Machiavelli and Guicciardini: Politics and History in Sixteenth-Century Florence*
(Princeton: Princeton University Press, 1965), p. 267.
[18] Shakespeare, *Cymbeline*, 5.4.132.

of the sixteenth century saw no straight course or rational purpose in history; man was driven by forces which he could not
fathom.[19]

Mankind was subject to chaotic forces of time, then—not the chaos
of storms or droughts only—this new sense of time encompasses also
chaos made by man. Renaissance writers came to believe history has
no catharsis, no moment of resolution. For these writers it would
seem an evasion of truth to dream, as Le Corbusier later did, of a final
and perfect form. Chance forces inevitably deface perfection. Spenser's "Two Cantos of Mutability" are perhaps the most haunting evo-
cation of the eroding power of time:

> For, she the face of earthly things so changed,
>   That all which Nature had established first
>   In good estate, and in meet order ranged,
>   She did pervert, and all their statutes burst:
>   And all the worlds faire frame (which none yet durst
>   of Gods or men to alter or misguide)
>   She alter'd quite, and made them all accurst
>   That God had blest; and did at first provide
> In that still happy state for ever to abide.[20]

Though to modern eyes the cannon looks the representative object
of time as chaos, to Renaissance eyes it was the clock that more
potently symbolized Fortuna's powers. The pendulum strokes that
compose nine in the morning are no more meaningful than those that
compose the evening hour of nine; mechanical time lacks any of the
characteristics of perspective, the ordering of relative distances and
intervals by virtue of human perception, which was the Renaissance
tool for establishing physical value: no matter how you look at it, the
pendulum ticks and ticks and ticks. And this is one reason why the
physical image of Fortuna that appeared to them was no longer a

[19] Gilbert, *Machiavelli and Guicciardini*, p. 270.
[20] Edmund Spenser "The Two Cantos of Mutability" in *The Works of Edmund Spenser* (Baltimore: Johns Hopkins, 1952), 7.4.5.

blind woman but something much more like a clock face. The mechanism of the wheel of fortune was also like a clock's; the wheel turns
without purpose, mechanically perfect, humanly indifferent. An
anonymous engraving of the Wheel of Fortune ca. 1580 shows indeed
a clockface with Fortune's pointer the hand of a clock: the figure
flipping the pointer into a spin is neither goddess nor devil. It is an
impish jester.

These Renaissance fears may seem far from the problems of a modern planner. Yet they address what it means to plan. If chance rules,
then the act of design must be conceived as a provisional act, even if
the designs one makes are as massive as Rockefeller Center. Accepting
the provisional quality of what one makes is truly living in the present.
What is to be learned from this Renaissance past is what is at stake,
culturally, if we resolve to break the habits of designing self-sufficing
or neutralizing objects. If the designer creates in a provisional spirit,
accounting the fact that one must struggle against one's powers of self-
destruction, accounting Fortune and chance as the only "higher"
power opposed to this self-destructiveness—what kinds of things will
one make?

The answer the past affords this question is that Fortuna is the
enemy of the sublime; to understand her powers is to conceive of
buildings as provisional forms. The idea of a provisional form sounds
agreeable enough, but for our forebearers "provisional" was a forbid-
ding word. The appearance of Fortuna did not comfort Renaissance
writers. Instead, they saw her power making their own lives ever
more problematic. Machiavelli's writings dramatize this power of Fortuna to overturn control of one's own life. The opposition between
fortuna and *virtu* is a drama played out in Machiavelli's *Prince*: will
was expressed as *virtu*, by which he meant the marshaling of forces
within the individual so that he or she might try to impose order on
the world which lacks any of its own. Machiavelli imagined the struggle between *fortuna* and *virtu* a matter of death versus life and therefore unending; at most, people can stop the wheel of fortune spinning
for a while through their own actions; they cannot break the force that
makes the wheel turn. Machiavelli's near contemporaries gradually
despaired that the will alone was sufficient against the forces of
chance. A modern historian describes Vettori's history, written a gen-

eration after Machiavelli's political tract, ending as follows: "Fortune is lord of the world and man the victim."[21] In *Henry IV, Part Two*, Shakespeare made Prince Hal into an emblematic political man of his age, one who perhaps would have been a more attentive listener to the strictures in Machiavelli's *Prince* than the Medici who now in the sixteenth-century became the puppets of foreign rulers; by the end of the play, a chastened Hal knows the virtue of his own struggle to live not in the outcome, but in the sheer effort of will. But that trial by fire has brought him no triumph; he is tired by the effort it takes to live, chastened and tired of life. The effort of living in the present tense through sheer will has proved an exhausting burden.

Time's Walls and Borders

The Renaissance man and woman literally saw time take shape in everyday life in the city; these shapes corroded human effort, as in the clock and clock-labor, or threatened the city, as in the cannon and its relation to the safety offered by the city's walls. The people who lived through the advent of these inventions deduced a new force beyond their control: Fortuna. Their lives came to be a struggle against the machine goddess of time. More than the forms of the star-shape city or the empty volume of the square in which a public clock has been placed, it is the character of their struggle that speaks to the present. If Le Corbusier's celebration of gleaming machines was foolish, a more humane kind of form-making—one like Léger's—has to acknowledge that in using and fragmenting and pasting together forms, the maker of them is engaged in a spiritual struggle against him or herself. It is a struggle against the human power to annihilate through regulatory order, to be sure; but if and when one

[21] Lauro Martines, *Power and Imagination: City-States in Renaissance Italy* (New York: Knopf, 1979), p. 312.

wins this struggle, a person makes things of no permanent value, no ultimate worth, only present meaning. This humane, limited value occupies, as it were, only a small corner of our imaginative and intellectual powers—the humane construction is a small building in a larger city of beliefs, truths, regularities, clarities, and guarantees. The humane is so much *less* than what people are capable of. That is what we are struggling for—not fulfillment but to be less than we could be.

Against the regulation of time in space, I will therefore propose another form for time in space, of which I shall call narrative space—a more limited relation of time and space than the grand unity Sigfried Giedion sought, but one capable of guiding more humane urban design. Spaces can become full of time when they permit certain properties of narratives to operate in everyday life. I will try to show how the narrative properties of space give value to two elements in the city, walls and borders. The experiencing of these elements as narrative scenes is not very satisfying, not very fulfilling, yet embodies humane cultural values.

Narrative space is a far less abstract idea than it may seem initially. During the great age of urban growth in the nineteenth century, men and women often resorted to the places evoked in fiction to make sense of the places in which they lived themselves. One critic has explained Dostoyevsky's passionate attachment to St. Petersburg as the novelist's belief in the city as "the ideal environment . . . for the acting out and working out of personal and social conflict."[22] Dostoyevsky's readers in turn sought to understand these personal and social conflicts through his descriptions of the city.

This was more than a matter of the novel holding up a mirror to life. The novelist held up a magic mirror. It showed images of the city that were more legible than they were to the urbanite using his own unaided sight on the street. The novelist singled out the relevant details that gave a scene its character, made people speak appropriately in these circumstances, changed scenes when something significant needed to happen. Ordinary experience never presents itself this sharply, but the cities of the nineteenth century were particularly

[22] Marshall Berman, *All That Is Solid Melts into Air* (London: Penguin, 1988), p. 245.

unclear. They had grown quickly, enormously, and messily; there
were few past models to explain them.

One way to hold this magic mirror up to social reality was to turn
places into characters. In Balzac's works we read of a police court
"speaking sadly." The room does or feels this, and the figures like
Vautrin who move in it take on the changing emotional color of their
surroundings, like Sarah Bernhardt's boudoir, a space more personal
than its occupant. Time also showed in this magic mirror.

Personifying specific places helped the nineteenth-century writers
in a task that falls upon all novelists, that of connecting events widely
separated in time. The labor of all long fiction is in part to work out
what a domestic quarrel, a boy's glance through a window, or a letter
announcing "You are ruined!" will lead to, much later. Long fiction
needs to make use of delayed reactions because the delayed reaction
is one way of assuring the reader that time has a shape, even though
the shape isn't immediately apparent. In the end things do hang
together, if a new event can come out of the seemingly dead past. By
radically changing the character of a place, the novelist could stage
this delayed reaction. Second-rate writers, from Elizabeth Gaskell in
the nineteenth century to her legion of sentimental heirs, often make
personified places do a particular work of delayed reaction in this
way. A successful man returns to the modest home where he was
born, surveys the dusty nursery where he used to play, notices his
stuffed bear now is missing its button eyes, and the man of important
affairs is overcome by the waste of his life in outer show. If only . . .
Regret is easy to manufacture. By contrast, there is a famous scene in
Balzac's *Lost Illusions* in which the Galeries des Bois, the old center
of prostitution, illegal financial trading, and street musicians (the
Times Square of nineteenth-century Paris) is ripped up and destroyed
by the authorities; Balzac's genius is to put us on the lookout for
where the "Houses of Sin and Laughter" will then, elsewhere, plant
themselves in the city, as though they were tenants forced to move,
tenacious in their habits. His life of places, personified, is the need for
more life, for a way to go on.

Since Kant it has been a commonplace among philosophers that perceptions of space and time are inseparable, and the commonplace has
applied to fiction. For instance, the Russian philosopher Mikhail

Bakhtin has explored the idea that all forms of writing contain junctions between space and time. He calls these junctions "chronotopes."[23] A chronotope is the relation a novelist makes, without usually ever thinking about it, between how long a kiss takes and how big the room is in which two people kiss. But for Bakhtin this coordination of space and time occurs only as an imaginative convention. A stolen kiss in a ballroom full of dancers may seem shorter than a kiss in an empty cloakroom, though the duration of the kisses in both spaces is exactly the same.

The personified places of the novel may hardly seem guides for the life of places in the real world. The places in which these novels were set lacked, often, the richness of character that readers sought from reading about them in fiction. Thus, the philosopher Hayden White asks a question that seems to answer itself: "Does the world really present itself to perception in the form of well-made stories, with central subjects, proper beginnings, middles, and ends, and a coherence that permits us to see 'the end' in every beginning?"[24] Of course this is the description of a very mediocre work of art. In bad art everything makes sense. Yet Hayden White's doubt could be put another way. In real life we know what the personification of place leads to: a legible, characterful image of the city. The modern planner's desire for places of sharply defined character might be said to be a form of bad art.

By contrast, Balzac's *Lost Illusions* clarifies the city by making the places of Paris into persons, but then what happens to the bourse, the brothel, and the police station is radically ill made by White's standards. These collective, sharply etched persons suffer inexplicable twists and unexpected turnings in their fortunes, revealed in changes of appearance, the revelation again sharply etched by the novelist. There is both contrived clarity and contrived obscurity. All good fiction addresses incoherence, admits it, and makes use of it. Baldwin's essay in autobiography is an apt illustration. But a narrative space can be more sharply defined. The novelist's secret is creating a

---

[23] Mikhail Bakhtin, *The Dialogic Imagination* (Austin: University of Texas Press, 1981); see "Forms of Time and of the Chronotope in the Novel," pp. 84 ff.

[24] Hayden White, "The Value of Narrativity in the Representation of Reality" in W. J. T. Mitchell, ed., *On Narrative* (Chicago: University of Chicago Press, 1981), p. 23.

space in which time moves forward. This movement in time also has non-linear characteristics.

Battery Park City is a sliver of land filled in at the edge of the Hudson River, its street plan laid out self-consciously in a grid so that this new place seems like the rest of Manhattan. It mixes housing stores and communal gardens in the midst of giant corporate headquarters; most of its inhabitants are upper-middle-class but come in all languages and colors. This new city is planned according to current enlightened wisdom about mixed uses and the virtues of diversity. Within this model community, however, one has the sense, in James Salter's phrase, "of an illustration of life" rather than life itself.[25] The house fronts look like movie sets with their clean, plant-filled windows, but the park benches along the waterfront are empty. In part this is so because a giant highway runs along the seam between the new earth and rocky Manhattan, a highway people can only surmount in covered walkways. People who have no business there seldom go to Battery Park City, however beautiful a riverfront scene it offers to a clogged metropolis.

Its playgrounds, therefore, are peculiar. There is too much room to play. The few infants cavorting are happy enough; older children seem at a loss for what to do. It is the same in another island community, this on the opposite side of Manhattan, literally an island in the East River reached by cable car suspended over the water, again well-provisioned socially and economically diverse. And again, Roosevelt Island, a place made for families, contains children who seem at a loss. When they take the tram to Manhattan, they are the most excited people in these boxes of nausea, though the journey has long ago lost the thrill of a voyage suspended over water. They are getting out.

Above the new art galleries, chic boutiques, and restaurants of downtown Soho, in buildings meant originally for light industry, are the lofts of artists and of artistic New York. It is a community surprisingly dense with children who have a healthy ragamuffin energy. They have colonized the loading docks, the empty lots, the roofs, a

[25] James Salter, *Light Years* (San Francisco North Point Press, 1982), p. 69.

half-size world at home in the most unsuitable surroundings. Once they can go out alone, these children also avoid a local "designer" playground made to give relief from the trucks; it is a ghost turf of swings, basketball court, greenery, and benches. These kids, too, like to be where things are happening.

The playgrounds that are full all the time in the city are like those at the corner of Sixth Avenue and Third Street, places kids reach by subway as well as on foot. Iron mesh fences frame courts for basketball, with only a few straggly trees. Trucks and honking taxis struggling up Sixth Avenue create a deafening volume of sound which combines with the portable radios turned to Latin or to rap beats. Everything in this crowded playground is hard surface. Here, though, is a space where time can begin. Linear spaces may be defined as those spaces in which form follows function. Narrative spaces are, instead, spaces like this playground, places of displacement.

Aristotle defined narrative as an "arrangement of incidents." The literary critic Edward Said draws a contrast between origins and beginnings, two very different arrangements of events at the start of stories. The origin of a war or a marriage can be traced in steps that infinitely regress to the past; the search for origins is an attempt at recovery, an effort to establish a clear line of events. "A beginning," on the contrary, "is a consciously intentional, productive activity . . . whose circumstances include a sense of loss."[26] This means, in the practical work of making fiction, contriving a scene that does not explain itself, in which necessary information is missing.

The simplest gesture can make this happen; at the opening of Thackeray's *Vanity Fair*, the poor and seemingly prim young Becky Sharp suddenly flings a book that her schoolmistress has given her out the window as her carriage drives away from school. This tells us more has gone on before than meets the eye; it equally makes us believe for Becky and her companion Amelia Sedley, as Thackeray announces:

The carriage rolled away; the great gates were closed; the bell

[26] Edward Said, *Beginnings* (New York: Columbia University Press, 1985), p. 372.

rang for the dancing lesson. The world is before the two young
ladies. . . .[27]

We have no sense of why she should have done this; we cannot make
her action "regress" in a logical chain of backward "becauses" to its
origin. Her flung book seems explicable only by more action, by
going forward. Indeed, had Thackeray made the reasons for Becky
Sharp's flung book clear even in one clear, explanatory sentence,
Vanity Fair would have been over; there would be no need for the
story.

A city playground is a place for beginning by escape, much as
Vanity Fair begins. And indeed it makes clear the sense of loss of
which Edward Said speaks. In a written beginning both the writer
and the reader observe a convention: the writer suppresses information that would immediately explain what is happening, and the
reader accepts the lack of it. To know too much might weaken the
desire to know what will happen next. In other words, time is endowed with the possibilities of the unexpected, the possibilities of
change; this is how a beginning builds up forward movement. In a
place beginning interest in what's going to happen is created in a
similar way. A game of basketball played among loading docks is not
like a game played in the family driveway. Kids in an urban playground cut themselves off in play from ties to their home and family;
they shun the nice places adults made for them. In these places a
conscious fiction is also at work. Kids at the "hot" playground behave
as if they were parentless, totally free agents. To some extent all kids
play with each other by behaving in this way, but city kids find places
where they behave without challenge as though fiction were fact, that
there were no reality before right here, right now.

A beginning is a displacement into the present; a place of beginning is where one can make this displacement happen. Time's
arrow begins to point forward. This in time suggests why Battery Park
City and Roosevelt Island are places from which children wish to
escape. These communities embrace difference in a logical fashion,
by mixing uses together. Housing is near shops, shops near schools,

---

[27] William Makepeace Thackeray, *Vanity Fair* (London: Penguin, 1986), p. 45.

schools near libraries, libraries near office towers; these additions should generate that traffic of living and of synergy that makes the whole greater than the sum of the parts. Good intentions, however, blind the planner to a truth that the novelist knows: you cannot begin something significant by creating immediate fullness.

How, then, to return to our original question about invention and discovery, does a planner invent ambiguity and the possibility of surprise? He or she needs to think in terms of what visually will make for a narrative beginning. To create the sense of beginning, a radical change will have to occur in the framework of urban design. The change must take two forms: a change in the way urban open space is dealt with and a change in the way buildings are made. The open space issue is a matter of boundaries. A boundary cannot serve as wall, because this kind of enclosure is literally deadly: the life of the enclosed place ends when the designer lays down his or her pen. Time begins to do the work of giving places character when the places are not used as they were meant to be. For instance, just as children make the loading docks serve as playgrounds, adults on Fourteenth Street appropriate parking strips for sociable spaces. For the person who engages in this unanticipated use, something "begins" in a narrative sense. To permit space to become thus encoded with time, the urbanist has to design weak borders rather than strong walls. For instance, a planner hoping to encourage the narrative use of places would seek to lift the burden of fixed zoning from the city as much as possible, zoning lines between work and residential districts, or between industrial and office workplaces.[28] An architect seeking to create a building possessed on narrative power would seek one whose forms were capable of serving many programs. This means spaces whose construction is simple enough to permit constant alteration; walls of brick are such weak boundaries, walls of plate glass are not. In a novel the beginning erases and effaces; space also comes to life in the present tense by being used to erase and efface—by acts of displacement.

[28] I have argued this at length in my book *The Uses of Disorder: Personal Identity and City Life* (New York: Knopf, 1970), passim.

However, a condition of endless alteration or smeared use would soon become meaningless, just as the sheer flux of events gives no shape to an entire story. In *Vanity Fair* the escape that met no contest would soon lose its meaning, and the young ladies would be reduced to traveling. "Character" in urban space, like character in a novel, develops through displacements which encounter resistance.

In the ecological structure of ponds or on wild land, the most intense activities take place at contested borders. On wild land, for instance, this intensity occurs in the zones where animals who live in fields come in contact with animals who live in forests; in ponds it occurs in the contact between organisms who inhabit the differing depths of water. Less conflicted spaces behind the borders are less active. The social center is at the physical edge.

In the walk I take to my restaurants, there is very little conflict at the borders between one difference and another along Third Avenue. These borders are revealingly called in urbanologese "zones of transition," the flat word "zone" conveying that the edges are empty of life. That differences do not interact in the zone is one sign of the neutralizing order of the grid. But there are other borders in the city that do indeed display the tense, intense life of an ecological boundary in the wild.

In Baldwin's youth these borders were sensed by blacks every time they crossed East Ninety-sixth Street. Above were the tenements bursting with families, the streets coated with broken bottles and smashed car windows on which children seeking relief from the inside played stickball. Already the monotonous housing projects built a generation before to relieve the physical degradation of Harlem had degenerated into something worse than physical squalor. The human pressure was going up in Baldwin's generation, Puerto Ricans after the Second World War crowding the American blacks who had come to New York in ever greater numbers since the First. As one walked south toward Ninety-sixth, one imagined this minimal life would never end, and then suddenly it did. On the south side of Ninety-sixth, the buildings sprouted white-gloved doormen.

A black child had difficulty crossing the border south because of these doormen. They frequently chased the children from Harlem away with policemen's nightsticks, which at the time were the standard issue of their trade along with the white gloves. All over the city at this time the borders of race had tensed. On the western edge of Central Park, the border was one building deep, between the palatial apartments on Central Park West and the side streets filled with Puerto Ricans; again the doormen carried clubs, and white people on foot seldom ventured behind where they lived. At the lower end of Manhattan, a new influx of Asians had begun. On the north side of Canal Street, Italians settled, on the south, Asians; the street was the scene of frequent fights between gangs of kids.

In "Urbanism as a Way of Life" Louis Wirth declared that "the juxtaposition of divergent personalities and modes of life tends to produce a relativistic perspective and a sense of toleration of differences."[29] The border realities in New York are nothing like this. What was left out in the Chicago school's belief in diversity is the undertow of conflict between differences. In modern society, verbal conflict in everyday life is treated as though something has gone wrong. Or conflict is repressed through a show of indifference, as on my walk in Murray Hill. Most of all, verbal conflict, especially between races and classes, seems threatening because it appears the prelude to physical violence.

In fact, mutual verbal conflict works much more often, as the sociologist Lewis Coser long ago noted, as a release-value, dissipating energies that could otherwise break out in violent form. By now Coser's insight has been well documented in studies of families and small groups. But it is equally true of relations between strangers; indeed, verbal contact between strangers plays a more positive role than release of energy. Strangers begin to *see* one another when they conflict in words.

In fiction, this sudden awareness of the other at a moment of conflict occurs in recognition scenes; these scenes are one way the novelist can create resistance to the sheer flux of events in a story. A recognition scene is, more concretely, one form of time's delayed consequences: something implicit in the past suddenly is forced out in the open. A recognition scene is like a border in that it organizes confrontation among previously separated elements. The novelist pos-

---

[29] Louis Wirth, "Urbanism as a Way of Life" (1938), reprinted in Richard Sennett, *Classic Essays on the Culture of Cities* (New York: Prentice Hall, 1969), p. 155.

sessed of art can make this confrontation in time an intensely visual experience as well, so that characters literally see differently than before.

In the tremendous recognition scene in *Great Expectations*, for instance, Pip suddenly understands his real relation to the convict Magwitch; the recollection from the past comes through a new awareness of how the other looks:

> Even yet I could not recall a single feature, but I knew him! If the wind and the rain had driven away the intervening years, had scattered all the intervening objects, had swept us to the churchyard where we first stood face to face on such different levels, I could not have known my convict more distinctly than I knew him now, as he sat in the chair before the fire. No need to take a file from his pocket and show it to me; no need to take the handkerchief from his neck and twist round his head; no need to hug himself with both his arms, and take a shivering turn across the room, looking back at me for recognition. I knew him before he gave me one of those aids, though, a moment before I had not been conscious of remotely suspecting his identity.[30]

Pip understands then both the truth about another person and the falseness of how he acted, based on an illusion; Pip suddenly understands at this moment, in the words of a modern critic, that he "has in fact misread the plot of his life."[31] The past and the present are now connected.

A recognition scene can work, however, in a contrary way, as in Flaubert's *Sentimental Education*, to make clear in a moment of conflict the limits of connection and coherence among the characters. The novel has come to the revolution of 1848, an event which has differently touched the three friends Frederic, Dussardier, Senecal in ways which, up to this moment, have been unclear:

> It was five o'clock, a fine rain was falling. Some bourgeois were on the sidewalk by the Opera. The buildings opposite were

[30] Charles Dickens, *Great Expectations* (London: Oxford University Press, 1975), p. 301.
[31] Peter Brooks, *Reading for the Plot* (New York: Knopf, 1984), p. 130.

shuttered. No one at the windows. Across the whole width of the Boulevard, dragoons were galloping, at full speed, leaning forward on the horses' necks, their sabres drawn; and the plumes of their helmets, and their large white cloaks lifted behind them passed across the light of the gas lamps, which writhed in the wind in the twilight. The crowd watched them, mute, terrified.

Between the cavalry charges, squads of police appeared, to push the crowds back into the sidestreets.

But on the steps of Tortoni, a man, Dussardier, recognizable from far because of his height, remained motionless, like a caryatid.

One of the policemen at the head of the file, his three-cornered hat down on his eyes, menaced him with his sword.

The other, then, moving forward a step, cried out:—"Long live the Republic!"

He fell on his back, his arms in a cross.

A howl of horror arose from the crowd. The policeman looked all around him; and Frederic, open-mouthed, recognized Senecal.[32]

Rather than a revelation of how much the past mattered, as when Pip suddenly knew Magwitch the convict was his father, in this moment the previous experience of the three young men is suddenly shown as a tissue of illusory connections. The moment when Frederic recognizes that it was Senecal who killed Dussardier, Frederic's "education" takes a significant turn: it simply didn't matter how they had lived before.

In their contrary ways *Great Expectations* and *Sentimental Education* portray characters who gain depth by becoming aware at the moment of recognition of how far they have come since they began. This same evolution occurs in James Baldwin's "The Fire Next Time." The scenes of recognition a novelist stages indicate the kind of self-understanding that occurs when suddenly a person becomes aware of crossing boundaries. Baldwin had that awareness when suddenly he realized he was no longer thinking as a black "should." At the bound-

[32] Gustave Flaubert, *Sentimental Education* quoted in Brooks, *Reading for the Plot,* p. 206. Original published in *Oeuvres* (Paris: Pléiade, 1952), p. 448.

ary one transgresses one's identity, as one had known it in the past: perhaps a secret reemerges to alter old ways of seeing, or perhaps the connections one had taken for granted simply fall apart. It is at these moments in fiction that we have a heightened awareness of the present through connection to the past. This is the artistic value of experiences of thrust, displacement, and resistance.

Faced with the fact of social hostility in the city, the planner's impulse in the real world is to seal off conflicting or dissonant sides, to build internal walls rather than permeable borders. Highways and automobile traffic, for instance, are used to subdivide different social territories in the city; the river of racing machines is so swift and thick that crossing from one territory to the other becomes virtually impossible. Similarly, functional disaggregation has become a technique for sealing borders; the shopping mall that is far from tracts of housing, the school on its own "campus," the factory hidden in an industrial park. These techniques, which originated in the garden city planning movement to create a peaceful, orderly suburb, are now increasingly used in the city center to remove the threat of classes or races touching, to create a city of secure inner walls.

The borders in fiction show what is lost in urban planning of open space by treating borders as though they were walls. People who live in sealed communities are diminished in their development. The wounds of past experience, the stereotypes which have become rooted in memory, are not confronted. Recognition scenes that might occur at borders are the only chance people have to confront fixed, sociological pictures routinized in time. It is only in crossing a boundary when people can see others as if for the first time. This experience of displacement and resistance we have in art and lack in urban design.

The legacy of the Renaissance experience of time and space is an unexpected one: the humanism of the Renaissance suggests that the sense of "natality" of which Hannah Arendt speaks, that same desire for present-tense life appearing in the designs of Le Corbusier and Léger, depends upon understanding the relation between places and events as in a narrative, a narrative fashioned around transgression and recognition, a narrative which evolves as people cross borders.

The planner of a modern, humane city will overlay differences rather than segment them, and for the same reason. Overlays are also a way to form complex, open borders. Displacement rather than linearity is a humane prescription.

This connection between the visual and the social focuses on the experience of limits; it is not, however, an ethos of weakness. Rather, Hannah Arendt's affirmation of the virtue of impersonality, the frustrations of catharsis and identity which appear in James Baldwin's essay, Serlio's invention of a scene of tragic limits, Léger's painting of the limits of how long things last, the restlessness of the outdoor pilgrimage planned by Sixtus V—all these point to a certain form that life can take in the dimension of the outside, an engagement with difference, an acceptance of impermanence and chance. The Christian dimensions must today be reversed in their value. The inside has come to be a destructive dimension; to flee within, in search of the permanent, the precise, and the guaranteed, is destructive. The outside could be the constructive dimension, as Baudelaire hoped. What the humanist tradition makes clear is that something like a tragic space will give the outside its constructive life, rather than this life coming from the relieving, urbane pleasures sketched by Constantin Guys, or the pleasures of leafy wholeness which animated the age of Thomas Jefferson.

Against the expression of the permanent and the precise, the immediate and the imperfect: a contrast between sacred and secular vision. This secular vision implies as well a certain way of making the things which are to be exposed.

The
Art of
Exposure

chapter 8

Making Exposed Things

The I and
the It

IN A CITY that belongs to no one, people are constantly seeking to leave a trace of themselves, a record of their story. In the 1970s, New York was awash with these traces. Huge numbers, initials, and nicknames identifying the writer appeared inside and outside subway cars, insignia made with cans of pressurized spray paint and felt-tipped pens. Neither obscene, nor political as in the posters of a previous decade, they were just names and tags like L.A. II written everywhere, the work of slum kids.

The scale of this graffiti was what at first made the impression: there was so much of it, and so much of it was big, covering doors and windows and bench backs and metal plates of subway cars, the functional parts of these walls ignored, all covered over as surface on which to write. From the walls of subway cars the names spread to the walls of buildings outside the slums, and the fixed walls were similarly appropriated. These endless monster labels might be rather grandly described as the making of a theatrical wall, the subway cars treated as a neutral backcloth to be brought to life by dramatic gestures in paint. The kids were indifferent, however, to the general public, playing to themselves, ignoring the presence of other people using or enclosed in their space.

Transgression and indifference to others appeared joined in these simple smears of self, and with a simple result. The graffiti were treated from the first as a crime. A marking pen with a two-inch-wide brush was the first tool kids used to write their street names or identifying numbers on moving or stationary walls; it was quickly taken off the legitimate art-supply market, as was its successor, a pen with a half-inch felt tip.

As the paints and pens became criminalized, so was entry into the yards where subway trains are stored. Before graffiti these yards were wastelands like the docks of New York, strewn with glass and beer cans, home to drifters who pried open the doors to sleep, and shelter to young people who had no place to go to make love. Some of these yards were out in the open, at the edge of the city, but others were subterranean, beneath the city's center, like the storage pit under the Brooklyn Bridge, where at three in the morning you could smell sausages cooking over the fires the drifters built at the edge of the tracks, and hear, over the sound of the crackling, sex moans from other cars but almost nothing from above, the hustling suits on Wall Street still asleep far away. When the graffitists invaded the yards, the places were gradually closed up with fences; at one point the police used specially trained dogs who patrolled the yards, prowling back and forth between a double fence, but now the ever-hungry, expensive dogs are gone, like the drifters and the lovers without beds; the trains are protected by fencing topped with razor wire. Far thinner and stronger than a medieval wall, these at last shelter the urban instruments of speed from writing.

One subway rider explained the offense of graffiti as arising from fear of the poor:

I am [a subway rider], and while I do not find myself consciously making the connection between the graffiti-makers and the crim-inals who occasionally rob, rape, and assault passengers, the sense that all are part of one world of uncontrollable predators seems inescapable. Even if the graffitists are the least dangerous of these, their ever-present markings serve to persuade the passenger that, indeed, the subway is a dangerous place. . . . The issue of controlling graffiti is . . . one of reducing the ever-present sense of fear.[1]

[1] Nathan Glazer, "On Subway Graffiti in New York," *Public Interest* (Winter 1979), n.p.

The reason others are afraid of graffiti, on this account, is that it is a writing of the underclass: we exist and we are everywhere. Moreover, you others are nothing; we write all over you.

And yet the signs of graffiti were inadequate to this meaning. New York graffiti of this time was innocent of obscene messages, or political messages, or indeed any message save one: *feci*, "I made this," this mark is me, I—158, Cam-Cam II—exist. An "I" declared.

I often saw this graffiti in my mind's eye when I listened to my son play the violin. The Suzuki violin method teaches a child to play music before he or she knows the names of notes; the method stresses beauty of tone and expression from the first lesson. When a pupil first begins the violin in the Suzuki method, the teacher therefore performs a generous act. On the neck of the violin the teacher tapes down two little strips of blue plastic, so that the student knows exactly where to place his or her first, second, and third fingers; the first finger on the upper band of tape, the second and third on either side of the lower band. The beginner is thus spared that excruciating experience of playing sour, out-of-tune notes. By converting the violin into something like a guitar, the teacher makes the student the gift of pitch.

At first the student accepts this gift without reservation. You put your fingers down exactly where the tapes are and that's that—you've solved the problem of pitch. In this early stage one of the tapes on my son's violin once came off by accident; he asked me to fix the instrument so that he could play again. I suggested, with the parent's knowing, infuriating helpfulness, that he find instead where the finger goes by listening to the sound it makes. This proposal would have robbed my son, however, of the certainty with which he began.

As the lessons went forward he learned more and more to listen to how he sounded, and in the process those little bits of tape began to annoy him too. There was the day that he learned that the violin, made of natural materials, changes its tone according to the temperature and humidity of the weather; some days the blue plastic bands were accurate guides, other days not. Then he learned that the same note has different shades, depending on the key in which it appears. Perhaps his most decisive experience in using these tapes was the month in which he found out how to create vibrato on a string. This rocking movement of the hand imparts warmth to notes by spreading out pitch, like the color that spreads in a watercolor stroke on wet paper. As he moved through each of these stages, hearing more, the plastic tape seemed an arbitrary answer, precluding the ear's discoveries. About a year after he began, he removed the plastic with which I once refused to "fix" the violin.

Such progress on the violin is what musicians call learning to listen with a third ear. It can be described more philosophically: the student learns there is a correlation between concreteness and uncertainty. In music concreteness means the student hears as if he or she were listening to another person playing; one's playing then becomes a tangible thing to be studied. Uncertainty means, in music, that the more the student can hear himself or herself in this way, the less satisfying musically are gestures that are at first easiest for the hand. My son, once he began to listen with a third ear, experimented with holding his left hand in odd postures that produce sour notes under some conditions and sweet notes under others; when he conducted these experiments on his left hand he was less concerned with problem-solving than with problematizing.

It was, as I say, as my secretarial self wandered over the relation of the concrete and the uncertain in music during those scrapings necessarily attendant upon executing "Twinkle, Twinkle Little Star," that the graffiti of the subway appeared in my mind. The metal subway walls or the brick walls of buildings had no inherent character for those who sprayed them; these were planes to write over, whereas my son was learning to explore things for their own properties. But the exploration of his materials had a disturbing result. What made him engage even more concretely with them was uncertainty about how to draw sound out of a wooden box fitted out with strings. This education was turning him outward, to judge his own expression, orienting his senses to results rather than intentions. It was an education in the "it," whereas the children making graffiti knew only the declarations of the "I." To speak of making things in an exposed condition, as we did at the end of the last chapter, is to talk about creating uncertainty and possibility in a thing. An untaped violin makes, in Hickeringill's diction, discoveries *to* its player. And there is a virtue to making something as an exposed, uncertain "it" rather

than a declarative "I": the violinist became more critical of the quality
of the expression than the graffitist, for he could judge the sounds as
things in themselves.

Our culture puts a great value on concreteness, at the expense of
abstraction. "Make it real, make it concrete!" is not only the artist's
command, but a command of everyday life. The emphasis on making
things concrete is a reflection of the value modern culture puts on
objects—objects endowed with solidity and integrity. Conventionally, the concrete seems solid, *terra firma*, the world is marble. The
uncertain seems to belong in the domain of insubstantial hesita-
tions and tender-hearted, inward subjectivity. But toleration of uncertainty is as much a part of scientific investigation as of artistic
creativity. A scientist who proceeds methodically from one self-
evident fact to the next discovers nothing. He has no feel for phenomena, no suspicion, no curiosity. Instead, a good cancer researcher
wants to find a cell that "shouldn't" be where it is, just as the third ear
of the violinist is listening for the odd, untaped sound. Of course a
violinist no more than a cancer researcher wants to sink into a mental
black hole. The goal is to find ways to make the violin work. But as a
player acquires the power to listen critically, solutions appear increasingly provisional; they will be revised or rejected as the player becomes a better listener. Focusing on the concrete is satisfied by
discoveries which reveal the unexpected and the problematic. It is in
this sense that there is a correlation between concreteness and uncertainty.

Power enters into this correlation. The implication in a Miesian,
sublime object is of domination by the maker over the eyes of those
who passively appreciate his or her creations, whereas a more uncertain object should invite reciprocal intervention. Graffiti on a New
York street reflects this power relationship: the walls of the "I" dom-
inate others who had no choice in their making, who cannot participate in their form, who can only submit to them—though with no
awe. The graffitist repeats over and over again his "I," his Cam-Cam;
he confirms his sign. This "I" establishes an aggressive rather than an
exploratory relation to the environment.

The genius of Sixtus V, Serlio, and Scamozzi was to create streets
and squares that lead from an "I" of perspective to a more puzzling

"it." About how this transition can occur graffiti also have something to reveal.

Paris graffiti a decade ago were usually made by stenciling: an image or slogan was cut out from the center of a piece of cardboard, then the board was pressed against a wall while the image was spray-painted on. Since the most ordinary materials were used just as they came from the manufacturer, there was no way to "criminalize" them. Even so, the public in Paris, as well as the authorities, was not aroused by the appearance of these graffiti, despite the fact that the slogans were frequently politically provocative and the images occasionally sexually explicit.

The medium in part explains the reason why. Stencils create images that are both small in size and clear in detail. Graffiti on the streets around the Bastille have been carefully positioned on the walls, and different graffiti makers avoided jostling one another's territory. In this part of Paris political posters are still common, but the groups making use of them now, mostly African and Iranian, have also taken care not to trespass on the framing space around the graffiti. Whereas in New York graffiti, the moment a tag or piece is smudged or altered, the rules of the game permit other graffiti writers to "write over," covering it with their own marks, an opportunity which is seized whenever it arises and which accounts for the thick impasto of painted IDs on the walls of New York. The Parisian graffiti incorporate the wall as part of what is to be seen distinctly, as framing space; the New York graffiti obliterate it.

The stencil images are of things: an insect repeated over and over, sometimes on the same wall so it seems to swarm; a banana transformed into a long face wearing sunglasses with the caption "Speedy Banana" next to it. On the walls of the new opera house at the Bastille are already repeated stencils of razor blades, to remind passersby of the guillotine and the revolutionary past here. The French graffiti writer makes his or her presence known by an image that does not name the maker.

These Parisian graffiti manage to experiment with the environment. This occurs in the play of the distinct images against the building surfaces on which they are placed. Some French graffitists have indulged themselves artistically in placing the images at odd or arresting angles; others have painted on the stenciled image to give it variety. The response of the viewer is to be intrigued with what is on the wall; the viewer answers their mark, looks to see what it is. Obviously, Parisians don't study these graffiti the way Chinese studied their freedom walls; here are simply signs that intrigue pedestrians who slow down and look. The same is true of the carefully designed *affiches* plastered on Parisian walls; they too help create walls people look at, walls on which things are juxtaposed rather than on which "I's" compete.

Anyone who lives a long time in New York easily becomes very angry about the waste of human life here. It is perhaps why, oddly, Parisian graffiti arouses a kind of hopefulness in the New York viewer. They suggest that the smudges of self at home might find a more independent, objective form. Among a few kids who made graffiti in the 1970s that passage did occur. For instance, Melvin Samuels, Jr., was a member of the "Death Squad writing group" in the South Bronx, and signed himself as NOC 167. Born in 1961, he began making canvases at the age of nineteen. Works like *The Letter NOC 167* make use of calligraphy like the letters on the subway cars of New York, but are truly "post-graffiti." The sprayed edges in yellow and pink of this canvas create a living wall of color; the magic-marker lines and spraying in brown and green on this wall are thought out in terms of color contrast, the black-marker writing itself carefully positioned within a field of yellow. The writing itself is two fragments, both in quotation marks; one, "the letter" announces the title of the painting, the other, "dreams of the holocast" [sic], is so unexpected a phrase nestling on its pretty background of ocher that one searches the painting to know why it is here, and finds a half-buried brown swastika in a jutting beam of green-and-brown. There are actually three writings on NOC 167's painting, not two. The third is his signature, but it is easy to miss, discretely placed at the lower right. His is the story one wants graffiti to tell, about how a mark beginning as a competitive declaration of self could become a sign explored for its own sake.

How can such an artistic evolution be related to the environment? In his *Art as Experience*, John Dewey sought to answer this question by identifying the conditions of exposure in an environment which

prompt an artist to pay attention to his or her materials. Struggle with
the environment, Dewey thought, can make any animal pay attention
to its surroundings. Dewey's view was not of endless warfare of each
against all, as Hobbes conceived the state of nature. For Dewey,
"only when an organism shares in the ordered relations of its environment does it secure the stability essential to living."[2] But resistance to impulse, and conflict with the impulses of others are primary;
they have to be experienced in order for the organism to seek stability. If a bear had been able to conquer its enemies, say by ripping
them apart with its claws, the nails of the bear's claws would matter
to it, so Dewey believed, only as means to an end, only as weapons.
If the nails had proved totally useless, there would be no bear. But in
a condition in which an animal manages to survive without dominating, reflection upon its resources may appear. Of course, it is difficult
to know how bears think about their paws, but what Dewey is getting
at is the value of frustration in the making of art. Frustration lies in
the middle between the artist's easy victories and giving up. The easy
victories make for bad art, Dewey believes, because the artist who
finds a quick solution is like the bear who never has to think about the
physical resources at its disposal. In frustration, in Dewey's elegant
phrase, the artist begins to "participate" in his or her materials: "when
the participation comes after a phase of disruption and conflict, it
bears within itself the germs of a consummation akin to the esthetic."[3]
Hegel had a century earlier the same sense of how engagement in
things for their own sake is born. At the end of the *Phenomenology of
Mind*, Hegel speaks of the need for "reconciliation" between con-
tending egos, "the 'yes' with which both egos desist from their existence in opposition . . . ."[4] It is after this frustrating struggle that they
turn to exploring the material conditions in which they live.

This is how both Dewey and Hegel might have explained how
NOC 167 began to experiment with his spray cans. Whether correct
in the case of Melvin Samuels, Jr., or not, this explanation well
articulates the nature of exposure in creative work; people are ex-

[2] John Dewey, *Art as Experience* (New York: Capricorn, 1934), p. 15.
[3] *Ibid.*
[4] G. W. F. Hegel, *The Phenomenology of Mind,* trans. by J. B. Baillie (London: Allen and Unwin, 1961), p. 679.

posed when they are frustrated, neither succeeding nor failing but caught in between. It is in that condition that they feel exposed *to* their materials.

It is a commonplace that artists are stimulated in cities as they are not elsewhere; this commonplace addresses something much more crucial to artistic creativity than bohemian decor or access to patrons. The frustrations of the city can serve the purpose of stimulating inquiry into materials. Since this enquiry is not limited to professional artists, it might better and more broadly be said the correlation we have explored between uncertainty and concreteness has a social dimension: exposure to difference, otherness, frustration. The plans of Sixtus V were designs which in retrospect can be seen as possessed of this power of exposure. They established limits on perspectival control of the street. To arrive at a sense of these limits means neither experiencing domination nor defeat in social life, but occupying the space in between; it is such a middling space, again, which is occupied by the poor on Fourteenth Street. In his urban designs, Le Corbusier certainly never occupied it, and the easy victories and total mastery of projects like the Plan Voisin show the result: a sense of materials, of textures and surfaces, is lacking. The Plan Voisin is all about control and not at all about sensuality. For an artist to feel exposed *to* materials occurs at a less comfortable, less satisfied moment.

In sum, there is a consciousness of material objects which can resonate to the consciousness people have of one another in cities. In the prior chapter, this space of exposure was set in a certain kind of time, which we called a narrative space to indicate that the productive experience of complexity doesn't just happen in a city but needs to be organized as an unfolding experience, much as the complexities of a novel are unfolded. There must be displacement across a border for the exposure to diffence to begin, as in a compelling narrative, and then there must be blockage and frustration to give the movement meaning, as in recognition scenes. The denoument of this process of exposure, to recur to the analogy of narrative once more, is not a satisfying catharsis but a concern for materials. Baldwin's elusive history intimated it might end this way, the story of exposure ends in the love of things.

The Art of
Mutations

I should like to show how this consciousness of things could transform what appears today the least humane of all urban designs: the grid. The modern grid is an organization of repeating elements on which nothing changes. The modern urban grid is centerless and boundaryless, a form of pure repetition very much like the workings of an industrial machine. The most austere painted grids, like Agnes Martin's *Untitled* of 1965, have been described by Rosalind Krauss as

> crowding out the dimensions of the real and replacing them with the lateral spread of a single surface. Insofar as its order is that of pure relationship, the grid is a way of abrogating the claims of natural objects to have an order particular to themselves; the relationships in the aesthetic field are shown by the grid to be in a world apart.[5]

Though Krauss calls the artistic grid "antimimetic, antireal," paintings like Agnes Martin's seem an eerie echo of the urban designs for Manhattan made in 1811 by the New York commissioners; her painting would be perfectly usable as one of the maquettes that divided land for sale in the age of High Capitalism.[6] But what Krauss is getting at is how the painter has transformed this seemingly simple, direct sign.

Much modern art has been involved with making grids expressive in a particular way. The logic of the grid is the repetition of an image. Many artists have attacked this logic by seeking to induce change in form by the process of repeating it. This kind of art is about mutation,

---

[5] Rosalind E. Krauss, "Grids," *The Originality of the Avant-Garde and Other Modernist Myths* (Cambridge, Mass.: MIT Press, 1986), "Grids," pp. 9–10.
[6] Ibid., p. 9.

the modern version of Spencer's idea of "mutability." Picasso, Mondrian, Jasper Johns, among many other painters have been obsessed by the relation of repetition to change, and are makers of grid forms that experiment with how to alter an image by repeating it.

How can mutations occur when an image repeats? In the silkscreen paintings of Andy Warhol multiple images of film stars or revolutionaries are repeated on canvas, echoing their endless reproduction in the press. This repetition of images seems to embody all the evils of the form: empty clichés mechanically reproduced. Warhol's multiples show the luminaries of a city exhausting itself in publicity. But what happens to the eye the more it looks is nothing so ideological. No one in a supermarket saw a stack of Campbell soup cans and began to ponder; contemplating the soup can requires a canvas, a medium in which looking is the point. In looking at sixteen Campbell soup cans or sixteen Mao Tse-tungs all at once, repetition forces you to consider the character of that repeatable thing, the put-down and the focusing inseparable.

Warhol's is the simplest way repetition in art can begin to do the work of mutation. What was unnoticed before now becomes worth studying; the image seems to change in value as one sees it all at once multiplied. In the portraits Warhol did during the 1970s, the image needed to be repeated triply or even doubly, and finally only singly, the single image reverberating with the expectation that elsewhere, endlessly, it had also been or would be mechanically reproduced. And this repetition summoned visual interest: the meaning of the image became less certain.

The word *mechanical*, used in its ordinary negative meaning, denies this is supposed to happen. The intricacy of early industrial machinery intrigued the Victorians; at the Crystal Palace exposition of 1851 in London and the Universal Exposition in Paris of 1887, great crowds gathered to watch machinery do human or indeed superhuman tasks. The robot made by Count Dunin, his "Man of Steel," inspired awe, and even so prosaic a device as the industrially manufactured porcelain flush toilet inspired enthusiasm. What the Victorians feared was the power of machines to repeat themselves, Count Dunin's robot going through its paces again and again and again without tiring, or they found offensive the results of machine labor when massed together. A thousand flush toilets appeared vaguely obscene, whereas one alone on exhibit was the herald of progress.

Had he lived to look at Warhol's pictures, the critic Walter Benjamin would have found in them a dire social significance based on this Victorian fear, these publicity photos or commercial symbols or similar visual junk repeated over and over again. Benjamin thought that the industrial process had entered into the artist's own mentality: "to an ever greater degree the work of art reproduced becomes the work of art designed for reproducibility."[7] Repetition can become a radical visual procedure, however, when it begins to play with simultaneity. This is what happens in Warhol's silk screens. The painter puts within one frame images that are usually experienced at different times: you have seen a thousand Marilyn Monroes but never sixteen all at once. The clichés lose their familiarity when put together; some other puzzling meaning appears.

A deeper arousal by opposite repetitive means occurs in the portrait photography of the New York photographer Richard Avedon. The setting in these portraits is always the same, an empty white background against which his subjects stand, facing full forward, gazing at the camera. And in exhibitions these portraits are presented in the same way, all printed on four-by-six-foot unframed panels so that by the environment of emptiness and the near-human size of the prints attention focuses on the subjects themselves, all that emptiness dramatizing the exposure of character.

Nothing is so fatal to an extreme gesture than then returning to normal, as it were, or even looking for some other, farther shore; the artist's daring then seems more like a virtuoso feat than an urgent need to perform a particular act. But in the course of thirty years of portrait photography Avedon has never varied. He has remained in the grip of an obsession about human character exposed by empty space, and this obsessive repetition has become like a guarantee of his integrity.

The peculiar American sense of place, which is that you are nowhere when you are alone with yourself, shows in these photographs.

[7] Walter Benjamin, "The Work of Art in an Age of Mechanical Reproduction," in Benjamin, *Illuminations,* trans. by Harry Zohn (New York: Schocken, 1969), p. 224.

The blank surround is puritanical; the unframed white represses any interest in the sitter's relation to the outside. Yet Avedon's photographs surprisingly manage to use their very visual severity to establish that human connection.

Recently, for instance, Avedon completed a group of portraits called *In the American West*. When these portraits appeared, both the exhibition and the catalogue of photographs were criticized for being a New Yorker's sense of the West, the critics not quite knowing what this phrase meant, but it came easily to them. Since the photographer's formal obsessions are displayed in full white force, the only way to know you are "in" the American West is by the clothing of the subjects—women in cowboy shirts, men in cowboy hats—but in many of the photographs even these props are gone—the men stripped to the waist, the women dressed in the kind of mass-produced clothes that could be bought in the shopping malls anywhere in America.

Through repetition, the viewer becomes engaged in these placeless persons, however, precisely because the anthropological clues are lacking. Avedon's photographs, in their severity of context, arouse their viewers to project and read in meaning. Moreover, they play with sequence, just as Warhol's do with simultaneity. Each frame becomes more consequent in a stream where nothing else changes; the viewer begins to invest himself in the differences he perceives. Avedon creates in these ways an intense involvement in his subjects.

These are ways a visual design can make use of the principle of the machine—repetition—to create expressions that aren't mechanical. This visual harnessing of the machine principle has a direct bearing on urban design. The late-Enlightenment urbanist Antoine Quatremère de Quincy was one of the first and still greatest writers on mutation. He sought to combat the notion that the traditional architectural orders of columns, or Palladian windows and doors, should be imposed as expressive building blocks, each expressive block repeated exactly as it came down from antiquity or from Palladio's practice—rather as the designers of Union Square imposed the forms of a baroque city upon a working-class New York street. To avoid this deadness, Quatremère de Quincy sought to distinguish between what he called "types" and "models" of expression:

The word "type" represents not so much the image of a thing to be copied or perfectly imitated as the idea of an element that must itself serve as the rule for the model. . . . The model, understood in terms of the practical execution of art, is an object that must be repeated such as it is; type, on the contrary, is an object according to which one can conceive works that do not resemble one another at all.[8]

A model is like a visual machine that repeats over and over. Quatremère de Quincy thought of a type as containing the ability to change itself by a process something like biological mutation or musical variation: "it is similar to a kind of nucleus around which the developments and variations of forms to which the object [is] susceptible gather and mesh."[9]

In making this distinction, Quatremère de Quincy hoped he could balance the claims of discovery and invention. On the side of discovery, he wanted to free the architect working with traditional forms from the notion that he was, or ought be, repeating classical motifs without change. If these forms are indeed vital, they will modify themselves in use; if they are not vital, then they will give rise to no variations. Quatremère de Quincy would surely have championed Louis Sullivan's search for new forms of ornament that grow out of the past. He would have been horrified by the doctrine, proclaimed recently by Carlo Aymonino, that urbanism should evince "singleness of theme . . . indifference to context . . . overcoming of local building code regulations" for the sake of the form.[10] He would have decried the mechanical quotations in Union Square, or in the plethora of other post-modern façades now pasted over shopping malls, car washes, and prisons.

However, Quatremère de Quincy thought of mutation as "varia-

---

[8] Antoine Quatremère de Quincy, "Type," quoted in Aldo Rossi, *The Architecture of the City*, trans. Diane Ghirardo and Joan Ockman (Cambridge, Mass.: MIT Press, 1982), p. 40. Passage originally published in Quatremère de Quincy, *Dictionnaire historique d'architecture*, vol. 2 (Paris: n.p., 1832).

[9] Ibid.

[10] Carlo Aymonino, "The Formation of a Concept of Building Technology," quoted in Rossi, *Architecture of the City*, p. 182. Original published in Aymonino, *Aspetti e problemi della tipologia edilizia* (Venice: Instituto Universitario di Architecttura de Venezia, 1964), p. 9.

tions" around a "nucleus." Practically, that would mean that on a street you could define the character of the place in terms of a core form; you would start with a house type, or façades at street level, or a tree variety with which you will line a street. This core form is the nucleus that will mutate when you repeat it, but you will always be able to say the houses were Georgian or the trees were columnar and deciduous in type. Because you can always place the form that started the variations, you experience continuity.

In more radical forms of repetition, however, once the process of change is in full swing you can't easily trace back to the point at which it began. Warhol's is a more drastic work of change in this way than Quatremère de Quincy imagined. Nothing in the actual image changes, but one's perception does, rapidly. Mao's level gaze becomes puzzling, arresting, problematic—you can't go back to it as an icon of revolutionary probity. By a different means, this erosion of the subject occurs in Avedon's portrait photography. Seen together, his photographs raise questions about the very genre of portrait photography. *In the American West* becomes at once an arbitrary and an intriguing label; the more one looks at young couples staring intently at the lens, the men and women holding nothing back from the camera, their pose its own icon of probity, the more uneasy one feels about understanding who these people are—the young woman's gesture of staring straight at you seems to mask her. Neither painter nor photographer is setting a subject in context; instead, each has found forms for subverting the acts of placement, resolution, definition. They are artists of the human face, of physiognomy, of character who connect viewers to these faces through inventing grid forms that mutate.

In this way, the more radical form of mutation is more humane; the eye explores the ambiguous and encounters the unexpected. Ours is an age of machines, but radical forms of repetition are not "mechanical." None of them recalls Le Corbusier's Plan Voisin. The principle of mutation suggests precisely why representations of a place—as Kevin Lynch sought in the ideal of "imageability" of the city—is no longer an expressive principle. A fixed, familiar image has no more value than a publicity photo—until something happens to it.

Making images mutate is a way of casting doubt on their representativeness. Instead one searches for other ways to make an image signify socially. Here, for example, are two evocations of strangers, the first from Hart Crane's "To Brooklyn Bridge," written in the 1920s.

> I think of cinemas, panoramic sleights
> With multitudes bent toward some flashing scene
> Never disclosed, but hastened to again,
> Foretold to other eyes on the same screen.[11]

The other, a half-century later, from John Ashbery's "As We Know."

> The light that was shadowed then
> Was seen to be our lives,
> Everything about us that love might wish to examine,
> Then put away for a certain length of time, until
> The whole is to be reviewed, and we turned
> Toward each other, to each other.[12]

Hart Crane uses the image of a crowd in a movie theater to evoke what it is like to be a stranger to others in the city. The multitudes "bent toward some flashing scene / Never disclosed, but hastened to again" are trying to get at something, to find out a meaning eluding them. The next line, "Foretold to other eyes on the same screen," says it is a meaning that was apparent to others before, a meaning with a parentage. The crowd of strangers becomes here, as elsewhere in Crane's poem, a mass in which each stranger seeks to find the source of the others' lives, where they came from, what they meant, before they, too, came into the darkened hall. They are looking for an explanatory image; these strangers want to undo being stranger to one another. They want to look like who they really are.

In contrast, Ashbery simply evokes what the awareness of another stranger is. When people no longer look in one another for "Every-

---

[11] Hart Crane, *The Complete Poems and Selected Letters and Prose,* ed. by Brom Weber (Garden City, N.Y.: Anchor, 1966), p. 45.
[12] John Ashbery, *Selected Poems* (New York: Elisabeth Sifton/Penguin Books, 1986), p. 259.

thing about us that love might wish to examine," then they become aware of one another: "we turned / Toward each other, to each other." It's a simple, sudden vision of a community of strangers, of people who have put aside the compulsions of love, the urgencies of intimacy, and so can see. In this moment, they defer "the whole" which is later "to be reviewed." And, in this moment of connection, there is no representation of each to the other.

At the beginning of another Ashbery poem, "Litany," which consists of two columns of different text printed parallel to one another on the page, the author writes in a note that "the two columns of 'Litany' are meant to be read as simultaneous but independent monologues." The poem begins thus:

For someone like me	So this must be a hole
The simple things	Of cloud
Like having toast or	Mandate or trap
Going to church are	But haze that casts
Kept in one place.	The milk of enchantment
Like having wine and cheese	Over the whole town,
The parents of the town	Its scenery, whatever
Pissing elegantly escape	Could be happening
knowledge	Behind tall hedges
Once and for all. The	Of dark, lissome knowledge.
Snapdragons consumed in a wind	The brown lines persist
Of fire and rage far over	In explicit sex.[13]
The streets as they end.	

"Litany" starts with a profane monologue on the left, a more "poetic" monologue on the right, but not for long. The voices switch sides suddenly, the last sentence of the left becoming suddenly a large vision of desolation, while on the right the last line of the first stanza, "The milk of enchantment," gives way by the last line of the second to "In explicit sex." From this beginning the two columns will mimic one another, or argue, or ignore one another for pages until the reader wonders why they have been printed together, and then sud-

[13] John Ashbery, "Litany" in *As We Know* (New York: Viking, 1979), p. 3; author's note, p. 2.

denly there will be another leap across. The meaning of an "independent" voice, as the poet first announces it, becomes clear. An independent voice exists only in relation to another voice. These mutually intertwined, unresolved voices together specify the poem—as they do a street.

These artistic creations of ambiguity challenge what seems a humane idea of relationship in urban design, the idea of designing in context. A design made in the context of other designs seems a sociable creation; it refers to the buildings around it. Quite modest acts of design can make this friendly gesture. In renovating a row of townhouses, for instance, one might keep the doors that were originally used while changing the windows that give directly onto the street, since ground floors work differently now than three or four generations ago. In adding new buildings, one might keep to the height of old ones, even though one does not keep to the same register of floor heights or windows. Such designing in context is like the work that goes on in a live street, a matter of negotiating and balancing. Its principle is change by mutation. In the awareness of differences of time expressed in space, in the respect for what others have done, *context* seems the key word in thinking of how to design a city of difference. Yet spaces regulated according to these gentle principles are not arousing the way an Avedon photograph or Ashbery poem is. Life on the modern street involves the capacity to provoke uncertainty, as well as to account gently the presence of others. In an elaborate but evocative way, the literary critic Frederick Jameson defines this experience as "our insertion as individual subjects into a multidimensional set of radically discontinuous realities."[14] This is the art of exposure.

New York offers a superb example of a building, radically out of context, which arouses the awareness evoked in Ashbery's poem. In this building, the elevator is put to a use that Serlio or Sixtus V would have well understood. The machine which creates the vertical grid mutates into an instrument arousing great uncertainty. The building in which the machine is put to this end is Frank Lloyd Wright's Guggenheim Museum.

[14] Frederick Jameson, "Cognitive Mapping" in C. Nelson and L. Grossberg, *Marxism and the Interpretation of Culture* (Urbana, Ill.: University of Illinois Press, 1988), p. 351.

Wright's friend and biographer Brendan Gill remarks how out of context the building is in relation to its neighbors on Fifth Avenue in New York:

> What could be odder and less expected than the primordial apparition of the Guggenheim Museum, coiled ready to spring skyward from its blockfront on upper Fifth Avenue? . . . Surely Fifth Avenue with its street wall of neo-Renaissance and neo-Gothic pastiches is the least sympathetic place upon which to set this gigantic wind-up toy. And one would be right to think so: the only reason that the Guggenheim stands where it does is no other site for it could be found.[15]

But this lack of outer context is part and parcel for what is happening inside: one becomes very involved in a very odd space. One enters an enormous atrium ringed in a spiral ramp. To get at the art, one has to take a hidden elevator up to the top, then begin a strange journey down the spiral, the paintings on view in nooks, resolutely hung to register as perfectly plumb in this world on the tilt.

In an earlier, companion construction, the Johnson Administration Building in Racine, Wisconsin, Wright made an experiment in the relation of light to height. He hollowed out the inner core of this tall building also into an atrium, then brought overhead light into the atrium through a glass roof, this light filtered by an inner layer of Pyrex tubing, the overhead light combined with light let in at strategic plays up and down the shaft from side windows. The effect of all this is that the direction of "natural" illumination is also ambiguous; you know the light you are in is directional, but not which direction. And the higher you go in these buildings, toward the glassed-in sky, the more confusing the light becomes. The object seizes you in its form by this vertical experience of uncertainty.

The art critic Leo Steinberg observed that in the 1950s, beginning with Robert Rauschenberg and Jean Dubuffet, something radical began to happen to paintings: they no longer were meant to be seen vertically, the surface of the painting confronting the eye, but hori-

---

[15] Brendan Gill, *Many Masks: A Life of Frank Lloyd Wright* (New York: Putnam, 1987), p. 429.

zontally, and thus at a more oblique angle to the human viewer in an upright posture. Steinberg calls these "flat-bed" paintings. "They no more depend," he says, "on a head-to-toe correspondence with human posture than a newspaper does," and he regards "the tilt of the picture plane from vertical to horizontal as expressive of the most radical shift in the subject matter of art."[16]

Wright's architecture proceeds by opposite means to the same end. The vertical becomes the dimension of radical disturbance and arousal. Wright's building is also radically out of context in this sense, since New York is the city par excellence in which the skyscraper functions like a nineteenth-century grid: it goes up and up, on and on. Wright's tall buildings force people numbed by the vertical environment to notice and think about height. The Guggenheim Museum forms a striking contrast to Rockefeller Center. Rockefeller Center is all about flow and relationship, and it is socially a disconnected place. But the comparison to Baldwin's essay is more telling: on the page and in the museum one experiences perceptual discontinuities and discovers a new sense of relatedness. At last the imaginative use of the machine is freed from the mechanical. Those artists who have experimented with the effects of repetition have sought in the same way to free the logic of the grid from merely mechanical results.

Sympathy and Empathy

A certain kind of city is implicated by the principles I have set forth. Indeed, this city could be given a fashionable name: a city of deconstructions. The movement which calls itself "deconstruction" puts a high value on difference and discontinuity. This movement believes that the sense of concreteness in physical things is tied to sensations of uncertainty. Finally, the deconstructive movement seeks to create

---

[16] Leo Steinberg, *Other Criteria: Confrontations with Twentieth-Century Art* (New York: Oxford University Press, 1972), p. 84.

experiences of radical disorientation of the sort created by the
Guggenheim Museum. For instance, in the bible of deconstruction,
Jacques Derrida's *Of Grammatology*, the author subjects texts by
Rousseau and other writers of the Enlightenment to a process of
mutation through repetition of certain ideas; these ideas are trans-
muted into ever more radical shapes every time they return.

Difference, discontinuity, and disorientation are also the principles
of a certain kind of architecture which calls itself deconstructive.
Constructions of this kind, like Peter Eisenman's Wexner Center for
the Arts in Columbus, Ohio, translate these three principles into a
building which challenges elemental assumptions made in the past
such as the belief that walls should join floors at a ninety-degree
angle. The Wexner Center has carried the tilted world of Wright's
Guggenheim Museum to a radical extreme. A deconstructed city
would carry the same visual principles outside; for instance, it might
create major arteries capped by dead-ends.

Yet the proponents of deconstruction would certainly scorn the
framework in which I have explored difference, discontinuity, and
disorientation. The word "humane" makes these proponents angry;
like Sartre or Arendt in an earlier generation, they think of "humanism" as denoting a kind of comfortable, bourgeois code. The spirit of
making a manifesto which animated Le Corbusier in his Plan Voisin
or in his writings on New York is much more in the spirit of deconstruction, though the means of deconstruction are opposed to the
perfections and regularities of Le Corbusier's own work. What the
deconstructive impulse particularly rejects is the idea that an ethical
sense of self-limits arises from the experience of discontinuity or the
creation of disorienting things. Discontinuity and disorientation figure
instead as opening the gates to a more *enraged* relation to the world.
To argue that the humanism of the Renaissance could be brought to
life again by such modern means would, as Derrida argued in *Of
Grammatology*, mistake just how powerful the experience of deconstruction is: it is too powerful to permit a merely liberal uncertainty.
A city of deconstructions would be full of aggressive objects.

Perhaps this vision has become, oddly, too comfortable by now,
the artist or critic knowing how to make those gestures which make
the signs of rage and disaffection, like a well-rehearsed ballet of sub-

versive gestures. Perhaps indeed a more truly uncomfortable idea is that difference, discontinuity, and disorientation ought to be of ethical forces which connect people to one another. Viewed this way, the ethics of difference, the moral value of exposure to others, the creative act of disorientation, recall the experience of sympathy, as it was championed in the Enlightenment.

The Enlightened champions of sympathy believed arousal and concern for others occurred by identification with another person, so Adam Smith maintained, as though one were the same as the other. Smith would sure have found nonsensical the idea one could care about another because he or she was different. Indeed, the idea is dismissed by the greatest modern proponent of sympathy in the Enlightened tradition. This is Simone Weil, the French ex-communist, near-Catholic writer who devoted her entire personal and writing life to the value of sympathy as a connective tissue between people. I should like to take her side, for a moment, since she would have seen the argument I have made to be condemned, as it were, to mere deconstruction. She disputed the value of relations among strangers, the street as a significant scene of life, the value of present-tense time, and the relation between objectivity and uncertainty.

Her attitude toward modern art is a good place to begin to understand these objections. She hated the art of her time, especially dada and surrealism. Fractures, ironies, contradictions—the modern artist's sharpest tools—were to her symptoms of "the enfeeblement of the sense of value," a charge she made in a letter in 1941, in the course of contemplating how the catastrophe of Nazism could have been accepted so passively by so many of her contemporaries. It is a letter that deserves to be read at length:

> The essential characteristic of the first half of the twentieth century is the growing weakness, and almost the disappearance, of the idea of value. . . . Dadaism and surrealism are extreme cases; they represented the intoxication of total license. . . . The surrealists have set up non-oriented thought as a model; they have chosen the total absence of value as their supreme value. . . . The other writers of the same and the preceding period have gone less far, but almost all of them . . . have been more or

less affected by the same disease, the enfeeblement of the sense of value. Such words as spontaneity, sincerity, gratuitousness, richness, enrichment—words that imply an almost total indifference to contrasts of value—have come more often from their pens than words that contain a reference to good and evil. . . . In a general way, the literature of the twentieth century is essentially psychological and psychology consists in describing states of the soul by displaying them all on the same plane without any discrimination of value, as though good and evil were external to them, as though the effort toward the good could be absent at any moment from the thought of men.[17]

For Weil the territory of unbridged differences, of mutation, of obscurity was a magic kingdom in which one could at last escape from being understood by others; the abstract language in this kingdom is a peculiar form of locomotion in which one drives other people away. To Weil the consequence of modernism is that one becomes blind oneself, can't see who others are, can't weigh reality. To deconstruct, for her, would be like wounding one's mind.

The modern city of strangers and differences she hated as the very enemy of sympathy. Simone Weil made a brief stay in New York during the Second World War, at the end of her short life; its competitive, raucous energies made no appeal to her. Moreover, its people were morally as well as nationally and economically uprooted. Instead, to communicate sympathetically requires the experience of what she called "rootedness," which she defined in *The Need for Roots* as follows:

To be rooted is perhaps the most important and least recognized need of the human soul. . . . A human being has roots by virtue of his real, active, and natural participation in the life of a community. . . . This participation is a natural one. . . . Every human being needs to have multiple roots. It is necessary for him to draw well-nigh the whole of his moral, intellectual, and spir-

---

[17] Quoted in Simone Petrement, *Simone Weil*, trans. Raymond Rosenthal (New York: Schocken Books, 1976), pp. 407–08.

itual life by way of the environment of which he forms a natural part. [18]

In entering upon this train of thought, Simone Weil might seem to exemplify the equal if opposite evil of her enemies. In place of an amoral art, here might seem a romantic-reactionary sentimentality, again in the name of wholeness and unity, her very word "rooted-ness" conveying that desire for the organic. She might seem to embody in our century the longings of Tönnies and others in the first industrial age for a simpler life. If only everyone had stayed just where they belonged and knew their place in their villages or small towns, in that never-never time when life had been so stable that its roots had grown deep. Human experience, in the ordinary expression of regret for a more unified time in the past, is taken as literally akin to certain forms of plant growth whose fragile root systems wither through the transplant shocks of history. "Homesick for the past, seeing nobody but their own congeners on the neighboring estates and the peasants who worked there," Patrick Leigh Fermor writes of a group of Romanian aristocrats in the years before they were killed or driven into exile during the Second World War, "they lived in a backward-looking, a genealogical, almost a Confucian dream."[19]

Weil was not an observer in this mold. She came to dispute the value of difference from her own passionate power of sympathy, which lacked the exuberance and the decor of the eighteenth century. If one had to put a date to her enlightenment, it might be in August 1935, when the young philosophy professor stopped working on the assembly line at the Renault factory in St. Denis. About the year she had just spent attempting to do factory work, she wrote: "the capital fact is not the suffering but the humiliation . . . the feeling of personal dignity as it has been formed by society is *shattered*. One must forge another kind . . . [of connection between people.]"[20] In that conviction began her quest to understand how people could root themselves

---

[18] Simone Weil, *The Need for Roots,* trans. Arthur Wills (New York: Harper Colophon, 1971), p. 43.
[19] Patrick Leigh Fermor, *Between the Woods and the Water* (New York: Viking-Penguin, 1987), p. 97.
[20] Quoted in Petrement, *Simone Weil,* p. 244.

in the world. Communication and sympathy could not depend on everyone sharing the same life. Yet she did not begin to conceive of the virtues of these differences, she did not become more pluralist in her vision. Instead, she thought that consciousness of the dignity of other people had to arise from a consciousness of insufficiency in oneself. Instead of turning outward, one has to go farther inside, not for shelter but rather until one confronts one's inadequacies.

When Simone Weil is called the first existentialist, it comes from this formulation of conscience that she made in the middle and late 1930s: we cannot contain within ourselves the necessary strength to live, we are each fragments in a pattern too ill distributed and short supplied for us alone to provision our lives. The recognition of personal frailty is the foundation of reaching out to others and needing to trust in their responses. Perhaps they will betray our trust, perhaps not: that is our existential uncertainty, which we must come to accept calmly.

The powerful attraction Weil, born a Jew, felt for the Catholic church was its recognition of the need to ground life in modesty and trust, but she stopped short of converting because she could not accept the concomitant doctrine of submission. In one of her most moving essays, "Profession of Faith," Weil speaks to other workers in the French Resistance about the belief that will sustain them even under torture:

> There is a reality located outside the world, that is to say, outside space and time, outside man's mental universe, outside the entire domain that human faculties can reach. Corresponding to this reality, at the center of the human heart, is a longing for an absolute good, a longing that is always there and is never satisfied by any object in this world.[21]

Yet this "Profession of Faith" is no exhortation to believe; she says she hasn't the right to exhort others. For the same reason came her dismissal, expressed in the letter of 1941, of the values that have

---

[21] Simone Weil, *Ecrits de Londres et dernièrs lettres* (Paris: Gallimard, 1957), p. 74. My translation.

concerned modern artists. In Weil's mind, "provocation" is a form of
immodesty. No one has the right to serve as the provoking conscious
of another. Her struggles taught her a string of simple human facts:
when people give signs that they know their own inner limits, they
will be trusted; when people are trusted, they come to care about
those who trust them. The signs of this mutual trust are only to be
found in shared moments; it would be immodest to ask for longer
guarantees from other people. This is Simone Weil's idea of sympathy. Her testament to sympathy would deny moral value to difference, discontinuity, and disorientation—not that they are immoral,
they are simply beside the point of what happens when that rare
event that is sympathy happens.

Here, then, are two ways of experiencing the concrete and the
uncertain. One is through the making of a special kind of art, an
art better characterized as displacing than deconstructive. The other
way of experiencing the concrete and the uncertain is to surrender
to others, as Simone Weil did, to learn silence rather than assertion.

Each of these experiences of the concrete and the uncertain implies a special way of seeing, just as St. Augustine's convictions gave
to his visual perceptions a special character, different from hearing or
touching. When I think about the conscience of the eye, such as
Simon Weil might have exercised it in everyday life, I think of the
following: Thirty years ago, the Lower East Side below Fourteenth
Street seemed to be dying. Its synagogues and churches were boarded
up, the cafés where old men argued and the shops that gave credit
even for a box of tea were closed. Yet young people in need of a city
continued to come to this slum, whose rents became steadily cheaper,
and one meeting place flourished as a center for young and old. Aged
men from the Lower East Side—mostly Russians and Ukrainians and
Latvians—still made use of the Turkish baths for hygiene when they
had an extra fifty cents; these baths were a bit cleaner than the few
surviving public bath houses, and in the Turkish baths the old men
could get the kind of massage they liked. It was a gentle beating on
the back with birch branches, administered by ancient yet surprisingly strong crones dressed in rumpled white uniforms like those of
hospital orderlies. Young Americans and aged immigrants mixed in

this bathhouse, and the young Americans found here were of two distinct kinds.

One sort lived in the neighborhood, and came to the baths as did their older neighbors, in search of the pleasures of cleanliness. These young people had moved into the cold-water flats of the Lower East Side only to discover the phrase was a literal, rather than poetical description; most of them had come from homes where a parent was a parent, insofar as a child was smothered in toys, clothes, and opportunities. Needing to breathe, these children of affluence were now starting over; they wanted to mark an end and make a beginning at economic degree-zero. Of course, this was slumming, but then the point about really being alive when you are young is that you try on various lives, just like clothes, to see which fits.

Most of these young people were, even if bohemian in spirit, gainfully employed. They treasured the scuffed tables and cracked china they bought from used-furniture stores on Second Avenue, for this was also the time before scuffed tables and cracked china were antiques. If they could not properly care for their bodies at home, therefore, where the bathtub if it existed was next to the kitchen sink or was it, they did as their neighbors did and went out to bathe, just as people uptown went out to dine.

These were the old and young men cleaning themselves; there were other young men there in search of love. During the late-Beat–early-hippy era their illegal tastes were still anathema. Even though in "Howl" Allen Ginsberg, the Lower East Side's poet, had declared that sexual revolution was political revolution, changes in sexual attitudes appeared after the Beats had disappeared, the Hippies had gone back to school, and political radicalism was on the wane. Steam was therefore in this time often the protective mantle worn by desire.

The Turkish bath was packed with naked male bodies and clothed women (staff were added continually, though no attendant ever appeared to retire). Imploring eyes appeared and disappeared in the swirling steam, and as one moved from the hot tank to the cold tank, walking carefully on the slippery, slightly slimy tiled floor, one might feel a touch along one's spine that could be the accidental scrape of an old man's hide, the caress of a fingernail, or the tip of a birch twig limp from a tour of duty.

All of this led to a clock near the door. Steam baths, whether for health or from desire, are exhausting affairs. People leaving this Turkish bath would therefore frequently need to rest, and the management, in imitation of the genteel public spaces around and under clocks in uptown hotels, had arranged chairs and even a soggy sofa underneath a massive displaced clock. Now dressed, and exhausted, the men looked idly around, sprawled in the chairs with broken reed seats or on the wet sofa, surveying the faces that were all that remained of the muscle, fat, and bone revealed within. The old Slavs looked on all the young men, even those whom they knew, and knew to have girlfriends, with a kind of bewilderment.

On the street it was easy to tell at a glance which young persons in search of soap came from the suburbs. They were the ones who smiled frequently and purposefully. Friendliness was their way of showing respect: we are not hostile intruders. But now, preparing to return to their urban homesteads—the old American phrase for the frontier so neatly turned to account among these pioneers of the slums—the young men seemed perplexed. For the gay men these exhausted moments also formed a puzzle evident in the eyes, the puzzle of returning, of reclothing, of desire terminating in disguise. Daily, as one entered the Turkish bath, later razed for a parking lot, one witnessed this curiously immobile scene among those who were about to leave. It was a moment of mutual contemplation, a moment of passing at the borders of selves.

In his *Leisure, the Basis of Culture*, Josef Pieper remarks that "leisure is a form of silence, of that silence which is the prerequisite for the apprehension of reality; . . . it means not being 'busy,' but letting things happen."[22] Leisure is the opposite of will, as Arendt conceived it. At rest a body does work upon its own sense of limits. And this experience of a being at rest was Weil's idea also of the spirit in which people would look around them. The old man surveys the faces of these young people who have shared his bath and sees ever more clearly the son who does not share his house. As they slumped among the others, perhaps it was not exhaustion that had effaced the smiles of the urban homesteaders but calm consideration of the simple proposition, "I don't belong here." The gay man may equally feel

[22] Josef Pieper, *Leisure, the Basis of Culture,* trans. Alexander Dru (New York: NAL, 1963), p. 41.

that his place is not here; his desire, which cannot wait, which should not hide, dictates that he depart.

Every two hours on the hour in the Turkish bath, a gong would ring and the attendants, the old ones more exigent than the new, would comb the baths forcing people to leave the steam room, the cold tubs, and the toilets, driving them into the dressing cubicles so that on the half-hour a new group could be admitted; there were only a few minutes for reflection. Perhaps it was just as well; one left, not when one wanted, but simply when one's time was up.

This is the eye of sympathy, as I imagine Simone Weil might have seen in a later, less terror-stricken time. The other eye of conscience, exemplified by Avedon's photos or Ashbery's poems, is an eye of empathy. Though the word *empathy* is a modern one, this act of vision is dictated by the peculiar conditions of city life, and its terms go back to the very foundation of European cities, to the creation of the Greek polis.

Aristotle called the Greek *polis* the result of a *synoikismos*, a coming together for trade and mutual defense of households—*oikoi*—which had formerly been self-sufficient in the countryside. In contemplating this union, the first great urban historian of modern times, Fustel de Coulanges, noticed that each *oikos* worshipped in distinctive ways gods whose character was shaded somewhat differently in each household. The rituals of household worship among nineteenth-century Chinese families struck Fustel de Coulanges as practices that were long before familiar to the Greeks in the variations around the Mediterranean, say, of the worship of Apollo. The rites of Apollo differed in Asia Minor from those on the African rim, the god himself was possessed of a different face in Asia and in Africa. How were people who prayed to a diverging god, or to different gods, to live together in one city? People needed others whose beliefs they did not share. In the problem of *synoikismos* Fustel de Coulanges thought the Greeks left behind them an enduring puzzle.

The Athenians of Solon's time did not solve matters by repressing their divergences. Differences began instead to tinge everyday talk with silence and misunderstanding. Aristotle named this charged speech "discourse," which he thought of as the great secular event in the history of the city. He declared, "Of good and evil, right and wrong, just and unjust . . . it is the sharing of a common view in these matters that makes a household or a city," a declaration that would seem to speak against disjunction, and yet he follows this declaration almost immediately by declaring, "though we may use the same words, we cannot say we are speaking of the same things."[23] An urbanite knows these two declarations are both true rather than that they cancel each other out. And here is how the empathic eye makes an art of exposure from the condition of the city itself:

In a film-editing studio near Orso's Italian Restaurant on Forty-sixth Street, a small group are about to look at a film of *white lightning*. The phrase refers to the way landlords in New York clear buildings of poor tenants in order to tear the buildings down and sell the land, or simply to raise some money by cashing in on fire insurance. The landlords hire professional arsonists who specialize in quick and thorough blazes. White lightning strikes in New York mostly in the poorest parts of the boroughs of Brooklyn and the Bronx; recently however, landlords in mid-Manhattan, on streets once the province of prostitutes, have decided that cleared land is more profitable than vice, and white lightning has begun to strike in the center of the city. The documentary film is about this new phase.

In this kind of crime a certain code of honor is supposed to be observed: tenants or squatters living in the building are passed the word a few days in advance on the street, but occasionally the street telegraph is out of order, or a neighbor wants to settle scores with someone, so that the residents are caught in the blaze. In a recent fire one angry pimp had kept the word from a few prostitutes in an otherwise abandoned building in Manhattan, and they had burned to death, unable to organize themselves to escape the blaze, so the police believe, because amid the flames they were high on heroin. It was this horrific story that had caught the attention of the director who decided to film white lightning, and who asked me to help him write its story.

We went out to Queens, to learn more about burns from an expert who had treated many victims of white lightning in the boroughs. This turned out to be a youngish Vietnamese doctor, who, having

---

[23] Aristotle, *The Politics*, trans. J. A. Sinclair (London: Penguin, 1962), bk. 1, ch. 2, p. 28.

treated people sprayed with napalm jelly in his native country, now was putting his expertise to work on arson cases in his adopted country. At the sight of the Vietnamese doctor, the director grunted with satisfaction; the story was shaping up quite nicely. The doctor went carefully through each of the steps by which a person burns to death, his voice even, his features betraying nothing. Horror was recounted by a mask; the director gradually focused his eyes on the linoleum floor.

To make clear to us the progress of sensation in a burning death, the doctor described the gradual deadening of the neural centers on the skin as the burn passes from first to second to third degree. The nervous system during sustained contact with the flame goes into shock, just as after the initial burning sensation caused by napalm; the pain system of the body short-circuits consciousness as the napalm continues to eat through the epidermis into the fat and muscle layers below the skin. Though the victim in shock is not experiencing pain as someone who accidentally touches a finger to a candle does, still the traumatized body responds to the stimulus. The napalm victim will attempt to swipe at the blob of jelly in the initial place of contact, then try to clean the palms by rubbing them on other parts of the body; this involuntary motion is how the victim spreads the napalm jelly all over himself or herself. The fire victim, feeling ever drier as the heat increases and the burn penetrates to the subcutaneous layers of the skin, begins gasping for air. In a closed building this involuntary action is as usually disastrous as the body smearing itself with the acid jelly, because the building is filled with smoke. "Thus, they often suffocate before, technically, they die of their burns."

Now, in the screening room a hundred yards equidistant from the table-hopping and kissing of Orso's and the building that had most recently been set to the torch, we were to see the results of the director's work. The room was filled with perhaps forty people, many of them from the documentary film world, which is a world in New York of people who mostly fight with television producers who want life-in-the-raw documentaries that will offend no one. The doctor from Queens had been invited.

The film opened with a handheld camera tour of the area north of Times Square, showing interviews with bored porn-shop cashiers, with my-isn't-this-awful tourists, with tired social workers; then the subject of white lightning was introduced through interviews with officials, a mayoral assistant blaming the judges for being too lenient, a judge blaming the police. It was all just as one would expect, except that at the end of the tour north of Times Square the director had the grace to photograph a Japanese film crew also making a documentary. And then he focused his attention on one house, a house with some obvious traffic, both of prostitutes and drug dealers, the camera set up in a building opposite. There was now very little sound, save street noises, and the announcement that the street telegraph had predicted this house would "go up" that evening. The camera, fixed in position, recorded the goings on of the day.

As dusk fell, the voice of the Vietnamese doctor was heard, describing the process of burning to death in the same flat tones that he had used to us. Now at night, the house opposite was illuminated by street lamps. A light went out in the upper story; perhaps this was someone who had not heard, or who had not been told. On the film, the street noises of night gradually subsided, the camera remained fixed on the house. Minute after minute passed on film, as hour after hour passed on the street. Cars honked, a siren wailed and it seemed that at last the fire must have begun, but sirens cut into every night near Times Square. Then, as the audience was almost restless in its anxiety to see the fire, the light began to brighten on the front of the house; the street lamps went out; morning had come, safely. This was the end of the film.

At no time was Times Square in all its horror, all its dread possibility, more felt than during the final moments when the film revealed that there had been nothing to fear. The camera's inventive play with change and constancy led us to feel the whole of a terrifying city in a single thing. The film's powers were not deconstructive; rather, it aroused empathic concern from its very powers to disorient and to deny us our catharsis. This is the urban conscience of the eye.

chapter 9

Centering
Oneself

IN THE FAMOUS ESSAY he wrote as a young man, *The Birth of Tragedy*, Friedrich Nietzsche drew a distinction between Apollo and Dionysus as gods presiding over contrary forms of culture. Dionysus presided over a community of people sharing disruption, releasing themselves by drinking, making love, and fighting. Apollo presided over a calmer, more formal, and more balanced life. The arts of exposure and displacement might seem Dionysian expressions. But I believe they might instead serve the ends of a more balanced, Apollonian life.

Allen Ginsberg's poem "Howl" might be the voice of Dionysus in modern New York, as Nietzsche heard him. It is a poem of frenzied erotic bonding and ritual among strangers in the slums and shadows of the city:

> who bit detectives in the neck and shrieked with delight in
>   policecars for committing no crime but their own wild cooking
>   pederasty and intoxication,
> who howled on their knees in the subway and were dragged off
>   the roof waving genitals and manuscripts.
> . . . .
>
> who balled in the morning in the evenings in rosegardens and

237

the grass of public parks and cemeteries scattering their se-
men freely to whomever come who may.[1]

Dionysus is in ancient ritual the god of wine, a god half-goat, half-man
who spreads terror whenever he roams in the night. Nietzsche made
him into a symbol of release through ritual. "In song and in dance
man expresses himself as a member of a higher community; he has
forgotten how to walk and speak and is on the way toward flying into
the air, dancing. His very gestures express enchantment."[2] This enchantment cannot occur alone. It requires a mass of people who lose
themselves, who become a frenzied crowd. The rites of Dionysus, as
Nietzsche conceived them, were rites that could be practiced best
among strangers: the drinking, dancing, and fucking is more intense
if no one knows who you are or where you come from. Dislocation,
deconstruction, disorientation: these words can describe a frenzied,
Dionysiac city.

Nietzsche imagined wild release, however, as no permanent way of
life. The exhausted celebrants end, like the ancient Silenus, heavy
and disgusted with life. "Howl" is dedicated to Carl Solomon, a friend
of Allen Ginsberg's shut up in Rockland State Mental Hospital. Dionysiac frenzy has driven Ginsberg's friend into the prisonlike hospital where he is electroshocked daily. The first third of "Howl" is a
proclamation of the Dionysiac City; the acolytes declare their free
souls are dangerous, but never that, in freedom, they are in danger.
Even when arrested, they keep it up. In the second part of "Howl"
the suit-and-ties arrange for therapy. At the end of "Howl" the poet
promises his electrode-numbed friend to set him free, but the poet
can release him only in dreams.

It was in exhaustion Nietzsche believed the knowledge of tragedy
to begin; men and women at last empty of desire could look around
themselves clear sighted. Though in later years Nietzsche renounced
much of the youthful exaggeration in *The Birth of Tragedy*, he never
gave up the idea that the revelation of tragic limits comes as a result
of the shared, terrible experience of going wild. Those who have
passed through the rite wanted nothing any more—and so they could

[1] Allen Ginsberg, "Howl: for Carl Solomon" (San Francisco: City Light Books, 1956), p. 13.
[2] Friedrich Nietzsche, *The Birth of Tragedy*, trans. Walter Kauffmann (New York: Vintage, 1967),
p. 37.

see. This is Dionysiac exposure. "Howl" ends with weakened, exhausted celebrants submitting to the controlling hands of authorities who don't drink or smoke themselves.

Nietzsche thought that civilization masks such tragic knowledge. The mask shows the visage of a calm god, perfectly formed, untroubled, the image of Apollo. Echoing the attacks on civilized masks and the equilibrium of politeness made in the eighteenth century, Nietzsche believed this deity presides over a beautiful illusion. Nietzsche took his image of Apollo from a famous passage in Schopenhauer: "Just as in a stormy sea that, unbounded in all directions, raises and drops mountainous waves, howling, a sailor sits in a boat and trusts in his frail bark, so in the midst of a world of torments the individual human being sits quietly."[3] Apollonian calm and order derive, Nietzsche thought, from that self-sufficiency. Nietzsche suspected the human capacity to create whole, harmonious form; it was more superficial than of the experience of exposure, which was fraught by catastrophe like that recounted in "Howl."

By contrast, the composer Igor Stravinsky celebrated the human being as a maker of form. In his view, the conflict between Dionysus and Apollo represents an "eternal conflict in art between the Apollonian and the Dionysian principles. The latter assumes ecstasy to be the final goal—that is to say, the losing of oneself—whereas art demands above all the full consciousness of the artist."[4] To a friend Stravinsky once remarked that forms are better shared than selves. We might usefully conclude this essay by considering how the Apollonian temper might cope with uncertainty, displacement, and the loss of control.

The Two Bodies
of Apollo

We began this book by looking at how Christian ideals of innerness caused men and women to lose their balance in the world. To abolish

[3] Quoted in Nietzsche, *Birth of Tragedy*, pp. 35–36. Original passage in Arthur Schopenhauer, *The World as Will and Idea*, vol. 1 (London: Routledge, 1950), p. 416.
[4] Igor Stravinsky, *An Autobiography* (New York: Simon and Schuster, 1936; New York: M. and J. Steuer, 1958), pp. 99–100.

the distinction between inner and outer dimensions, as the Enlightenment did, proved no remedy—at least as a guide for our own time. There is a real difference between inner and outer life, between family and strangers, community and city; the outside has its own reality. The Apollonian ideal that speaks to this condition is an ideal of the centered human being. The ancient Greek word for centeredness is *sophrosyne*, which could also be translated as *balance* or *grace* or *poise*. This ideal in the modern world might indicate the condition of someone living out in the world; by being exposed to differences, the person could find his or her balance. To invoke the pagan ideal of *sophrosyne* would be to explain how a person might become centered in the midst of strangers on the street.

The Greeks conceived of Apollo as a healer of sickness and as a *mousagetes*, a leader of the Muses. The two powers, healing and making, were related. Creative effort produces calm and centeredness. By contrast, Dionysus makes nothing, he drinks and fucks and kills. Those under Apollo's sign are free to create because they have tamed their own self-absorption. This is the Delphic oracle's answer to what Baudelaire nearer to our own time called spiritual sickness: make things well. The ancient pagans literally saw this instruction, whenever they contemplated the statues or paintings of Apollo.

They found instruction in the modeling of Apollo's lips, the proportion of his limbs, his muscles and bone, the modeling of his nose and mouth; an ordinary mortal learned about scale, proportion, and grace by studying the form of a perfectly well-made man. From contemplating this technically perfect form, the Greeks, however, like those who recurred later to Greek ideals, deduced two meanings for balance. In one the person moved by the Apollonian ideal finds his or her way to stand, sure of footing, in opposition to ordinary life and the imperfections of most productions. In the other Apollonian ideal, oddly, a person attempting to make well is moved to a greater acceptance of complexity and imperfection, of fallibility and failure in the world. His or her own centeredness in work makes the gift of this acceptance. The maker is centered by a kind of craftsman's calm.

Undoubtedly the most striking attempt to invoke Apollo's form as reproach to the ordinary world is the eighteenth-century art historian Johann Winckelmann's description of the Apollo Belvedere:

Here there is nothing mortal, nothing subject to human needs. This body, marked by no vein, moved by no nerve, is animated by a celestial spirit which courses like a sweet vapor through every part. . . . His lofty look, filled with a consciousness of power, seems to . . . gaze into eternity. Disdain is seated on his brow and his eye is full of gentleness as when the muses caress him.[5]

It was with this passion that Winckelmann praised ancient art for *eine edle Einfalt und eine stille Grösse*—its "noble simplicity and calm grandeur." His is a poetry of ideal bodies that never age. In fact, Apollo could both summon plagues and banish them; like other Greek gods, his powers were dual. In the same way, he killed the young Achilles and was himself the god of youth. Yet as his cult developed he was seen more and more to be mostly a healer. His more sophisticated followers hoped to relieve themselves of sickness of soul by being made whole again, as when they were fresh and young. The engagement of ideal form with the ordinary world is one of stark confrontation. The force of Apollo's beauty is summoned against decay. The Apollonian spirit is here a force of renewal: the skin of the young Apollo is forever smooth; his healing will make the votary's skin likewise appear never to have been pierced or wrinkled.

The notion of effacing the marks time makes seems today tantamount to lying. Between Le Corbusier's gleaming, perfect machines and Léger's canvases of junk and broken axles, the latter looks the more truthful, in the sense of showing how what is made is used. Yet a poetics of renewal may seek by comparisons of the ideal and the actual to make the most radical social critique imaginable: what is, is insufficient. Recourse to the pagan past, especially to Attic culture in the sixth and fifth centuries B.C., is one radical way of declaring that what now is unworthy of what human life might look like. Such comparisons are radical engagements rather than detachments. For instance, from the twelfth century architectural recoveries of antiquity like the façade of St. Trophime at Arles (ca. 1150) onward, recourse to antiquity was seen to rebuke the present by building once again in the spirit of the first Europeans. These revivals sought, in Ruskin's words, for a universal human meaning rather than "other-worldly intimations." The

[5] Quoted in Hugh Honour, *Neo-Classicism,* rev. ed. (London: Penguin, 1977), p. 60.

young Le Corbusier was perhaps too pleased with his provocations to understand the drama of confrontation that attends this form of Apollonian ideal. Rilke's poem, "Archaic Torso of Apollo," renders this engagement in all its seriousness. The poem begins

> We cannot know his legendary hard
> with eyes like ripening fruit

and concludes

> for here there is no place
> that does not see you. You must change your life.[6]

The last line spoken in despair, as well as given as an absolute command—the combination of the ideal and the unattainable that reverberates as well in Rilke's "Third Sonnet to Orpheus":

> A god can do it. But will you tell me how a man can penetrate through the lyre's strings? Our mind is split. And at the shadowed crossing of heart-roads, there is no temple for Apollo.[7]

The god's body stages a bitter confrontation of the ideal and the actual. The god possesses the balance of *sophrosyne* and we poor mortals are constantly stumbling.

By contrast, above the door of Apollo's temple at Delphi is inscribed the most famous and least understood of Greek commandments: "know thyself." By which was meant: know your limits. This is not a recommendation to trim and compromise, to be diplomatic. Nor is it a radically confrontational nostrum about combat with oneself, as is implied in Rilke's poem. It is a proposal for another kind of engagement in the world.

The Delphic oracle warned against people seeking to imitate the perfections of the gods, a grandiose state the Greeks called *pleonexia*. Under its sway mere mortals imagined they could control their own destinies, and in particular, how they would live on in the memories of others. It was patently grandiose for people self-consciously to seek

---

[6] Rainer Maria Rilke, "Archaic Torso of Apollo," trans. Stephen Mitchell, in *The Selected Poetry of Rainer Maria Rilke* (New York: Vintage, 1984), p. 93.
[7] Rilke, *Selected Poems*, p. 230.

immortality; little better to attempt to determine what the children of one's grandchildren would remember, for the gods control the end as the beginning. Free of *pleonexia*, men and women can live in and for the present.

If Apollo's warning chastens people about mortality, the Delphic command of this, the most beautiful of male gods, also warns against spirituality—at least in the extreme form the Greeks knew it, Orphism, the belief that the "inner" soul is superior than the body, that the spirit matters more than the flesh, that truth hides, inaccessible to touch or smell. The worshipers at Apollo's temple rejected this spirituality, later absorbed into Christianity; they worshiped his body. The Delphic oracle found it immodest that a man under the sway of Orphic teaching should seek to transcend himself, his blood and bone, again as though a god.

The Dionysiac force released in Ginsberg's "Howl" is an Eros run wild. The cautionary dimension of Apollo's cult was a response to such self-destructiveness. The golden mean was not compromise but the act of standing in the center of forces which, at the edge, would make one collapse. It is the craftsman's occupations that will keep him centered in a world that cannot be made whole or redeemed by divine judgment, or culminate in historical destiny. All one can do is add to what already is. Making well is what keeps one sane, and how one finds a place in the world.

The first of these Apollonian ideals is about representing a universal, ideal human form. The second is not about representation at all—it is an attitude toward one's own productive powers that make one balanced and at ease among a crowd of people. Both the noble and the prosaic ideal of form are opposed to Christian suffering, the suffering that comes from turning inward in suspicion of the senses, believing one's soul the enemy of one's body.

Mark Rothko's Chapel

We began this study by examining Augustine's doctrine of religious vision, a doctrine which has translated into an enduring value in

Western culture given to interiors. The reason the interior has endured as a space of inner life is that this visual dimension seems to
promise spiritual, or as we would now say, subjective freedom—more
freedom of reflection and feeling and self-searching than is possible
among the contingencies of the street. In our culture, the free play of
subjective life seems to require an enclosed environment rather than
an exposed one.

Both visions of Apollo are inimical to this enclosed world shutting
out physical, and especially erotic, sensation. Apollo is a god whose
body is his divinity. The "Apollonian" is similarly a vision of spiritual
life which is open, exposed. Both severe and mundane versions of this
Apollonian spiritual life appear in the art of our time, as a rebuke to
the Christian conscience of the eye.

The greatest modern painter of the grid is undoubtedly the American Mark Rothko. Rothko's painting is in the Apollonian spirit as Rilke
conceived it; instead of the picture of an ideal body, however, Rothko
sought that of an ideal grid. In 1947 and 1948 Mark Rothko began to
make the grids which obsessed him until his death in 1970. In these
two years, his work shows a striking change; "Number 15" created in
1948 is closer to his last untitled paintings in 1969 than it is to "Per-
sonage Two" or "Aquatic Drama" of 1946. Thereafter, year after year
he repeated what the critic Robert Rosenblum called his "signature
format: tiered clouds of color magnetized before the symmetrical pull
of horizontal and vertical axes."[8] The color boxes given form by this
symmetrical pull of horizontal and vertical axes were, in Rothko's
mind, emblems of an ideal form. One of Rothko's critics says he became interested in writing about the painter because he wondered why
an artist who quested after "universal truth should paint more than one
picture."[9] The artist looked at grids in another fashion altogether. They
are put in the service of drawing the viewer out of himself or herself
through repetition, in the way we have previously explored.

At a late point in his life, in 1964, Rothko undertook a project that

[8] Robert Rosenblum, "Notes on Rothko and Tradition," in Tate Gallery, *Mark Rothko 1903–
1910* (London: Tate, 1987), p. 22. See also his *Modern Painting and the Northern Romantic
Tradition* (New York: Harper & Row, 1975).
[9] Michael Compton, "Mark Rothko, the Subjects of the Artist," in Tate Gallery, *Mark Rothko,*
p. 65.

would crystallize in visual terms the Apollonian ideal of a form that confronts everyday life by its very stillness. The painter, then sixty-one and at the height of his powers, had been commissioned by the de Menil family to create a set of murals for a new chapel in Houston, Texas. The de Menils were determined to give Rothko a space worthy of his art: the octagonal chapel would focus all attention on the murals, the light designed just as Rothko wished it, subdued and even, the only furniture in the space four benches from which to contemplate the paintings. After a series of mishaps, they succeeded in providing Rothko the space he wanted.

The proposed space reminded Rothko, with pleasure, of the Torcello baptistery. The chance to make a space of contemplation meant much more to him; it was a chance to make an entire environment from the kind of painting Rothko had been doing since 1948. In the Tate Gallery and in a room at Harvard University Rothko also sought to create a larger environment of paintings, the family of paintings finally transporting the viewer into a space greater than the painted objects. The chapel was to prove his last such project, the painter committing suicide before the paintings were installed. These paintings Rothko saw only in his New York studio.

He had as a young man read the early Patristic Fathers and particularly Origen; in the 1930s he painted a Last Supper, a Crucifixion, and Gethsemane, though he never converted. Soon after the de Menils made their offer to Rothko, Dore Ashton asked him what, if he had no specific desire to become a Christian, was the attraction of these writers. He appreciated, he said, "the ballet of their thoughts"; he found in them that thinking "went toward ladders," which is a nice way of describing Origen's mind: the play of it led him to climb higher and higher.[10] The paintings in the chapel were meant to inspire, as art critics never tired of calling his other works, "transcendent emotions," but his comments to Ashton about the Church Fathers suggest the necessary caution that requires those words to be placed in quotation marks. The play of Origen's mind inspired him, not Origen's love of God. And on view in this chapel are grids that serve that same ideal of contemplation and mental play.

[10] Dore Ashton, *About Rothko* (New York: Oxford University Press, 1983), p. 169.

Rothko came to believe that painting was an art of contemplating difference, as did his master, Henri Matisse. Rothko had once lived near the Museum of Modern Art in New York, where he had spent hours in front of a particular painting by Matisse, *The Red Studio.* The absences in that painting spoke to Rothko, the suggestion of a brush as a thing existing at all only because of its relation to a jug or a chair; Matisse had said "I don't paint things, I only paint the differences between things," a view that had an increasing value to the America painter toward the end of his life.[11]

Rothko's chapel shares little in spirit, however, with its twin in purpose, the chapel Matisse made in Vence. The buoyant forms and exuberant colors of the Matisse chapel declare the artist's faith. St. Francis had written of the liberation of spirit of those who believe, the faithful light like birds; Matisse painted that release. Whereas in Rothko's chapel, "it is as if the entire current of Western religious art were finally devoid of its narrative complexities and corporeal imagery, leaving us with the dark, compelling presences that pose an ultimate choice between everything and nothing."[12]

The paintings Rothko made for Houston are enormous in size, dark reds and blacks. His patron, Dominique de Menil, describes the chapel as it was finally built:

> In the apse; a triptych of monochrome paintings fifteen feet high. To the right and left: two triptychs eleven feet high which have black fields. All the other paintings are again fifteen feet high. The four paintings on the four small sides of the octagon are monochromes, and almost eleven feet wide. The one at the entrance, only nine feet wide has again a black field.[13]

All of Rothko's grids have the quality of self-transmuting, puzzling objects. The longer they are contemplated the more they change. These grids, taken almost to minimal differences, are the most changeable of all. Rothko found no release, he said, in contemplation,

[11] Ashton, *About Rothko,* p. 114.

[12] Robert Rosenblum, *Modern Painting and the Northern Romantic Tradition* (New York: Harper & Row, 1975), p. 218.

[13] Christophe de Menil, "The Rothko Chapel," *Art Journal* 30, no. 3 (Spring 1971).

indeed no end or consummation of any sort in it, nor do the panels for
his chapel offer it to others. Those who knew the weight of depression
burdening the artist during the time he worked were prone to make
a translation: the dark angel seemed to hover also over these somber
panels. Speaking to his friend Katherine Kuh a few years earlier,
however, Rothko declared that, "if my later works are more tragic,
they are more comprehensive, not more personal."[14] The somber-
ness of these panels may seem to earn them the title "tragic," but
again that is to make the artist's biography the meaning of his work.
Instead, they are tragic as Serlio's *Tragic Scene* is, a scene in which
no one is shown suffering.

Apart from its intrinsic greatness, the Rothko Chapel makes a
simple suggestion to our still-Christianized eyes. This is that subjective life can become more centered as it contemplates things, the
viewer at peace in his or her soul in this contemplation. Augustine
believed such peace could only come at the end of a long journey; the
wayfarer through life would renounce one worldly shadow after another, one pleasure after another, until finally the pilgrim felt in the
presence of a divine, otherworldly light. Renunciation of the world
remains in our culture associated with spiritual life; renunciation appeared in even so prosaic a form as Ruskin's dream of the hearth, and
the translation of this dream into the architecture of the home, a
refuge from the world in which subjective life was to flourish. Here,
by contrast, is spiritual experience generated by sensory engagement
in the icon of outer emptiness, the grid. A frequent comment on
Rothko's work is that it seems like Zen Buddhist meditation; a frequent criticism of the Houston project is that Rothko's paintings do
not really belong in a chapel, they are too impersonal, they arouse no
sense of comfort.

In this study, we have used the words "tragic" and "humane" to
evoke certain qualities of experience. These qualities have to do with
the relations people sense among themselves once they are no longer
protected, once they are outside. The life of a street is the urban
scene par excellence for this exposure; it becomes a humane scene

---

[14] Interview with Katherine Kuh, 1961, Archives of American Art, Smithsonian Institution, Washington, D.C. See Bonnie Clearwater, "Selected Statements by Mark Rothko," Tate Gallery, *Mark
Rothko*.

simply when people begin to look around and adjust their behavior in terms of what they see—a scene of mutual awareness. But this awareness can have, as we have traced it, a deeper structure. Turning outward implies a renunciation of certain impulses to wholeness and completion in oneself; this is the story told in James Baldwin's autobiography. Turning outward visually can also lead to renouncing wholeness and completion, or lead instead to another order of probing, restless vision; this is the story first told in the Renaissance when perspectival vision was applied to the making of streets. Turning outward can lead, indeed, to ways of seeing which make of the fragmented and the discontinuous a moral condition; this is the story told in the film about Times Square. The attractions of wholeness which are nearest us in time are those of the Enlightenment, but the pleasures of this age seem today much more distant, more foreign, than the sufferings of a much more ancient religious culture. All that is left of Enlightenment wholeness is the affirmation of the integrity of artistic objects, these plans and buildings which have acquired rights against those who must use and inhabit them.

Action without the need of completion, action without domination and mastery: these are the ideals of a humane culture. In the very rejection of the cathartic event, the moment of fulfillment, these ideals might seem to lack an essential dimension of tragedy, which is its heroic scale. Heroic tragedy appears in the Greek dramatists, in Shakespeare or Dostoyevsky. The limits on a person's control of the world stand revealed in this struggle. Tragedy can also be experienced as something "far less grand and mythic but more pervasive, immediate and intimate."[15] John Keats defined the more immediate experience of tragic vision, in a letter to his brother, as "negative capability": "when a man is capable of being in uncertainties, mysteries, doubts, without any irritable reaching after fact and reason."[16] On a heroic scale, tragedy consists in knowledge of self-limits gained searingly and in great pain; on Keats's more immediate scale, it implies knowledge that comes not through defeat, but rather in paying attention, contemplating differences. Rothko painted this Apollonian contemplation.

[15] Edward Joseph Shoben, Jr., *Lionel Trilling* (New York: Unger, 1981), p. 216.
[16] Ibid.

Balanchine's
Apollo

There is a less contemplative version of the Apollonian ideal which derives from the image of Apollo as the leader of the muses, as a *mousagètes*. In their book *Collage City*, the architects Colin Rowe and Fred Koetter argued that the visual accretion from generation to generation of buildings by different hands was a collective, urban process of composing dissonances like the collages which an individual artist might make. The "poetry" of such dissonant or fragmented objects seems to have little to do with Apollonian calm. It is not accidental, perhaps, that a book which makes use of modern New York as a talisman of modern culture should end with reflections on ballet. For the greatest modern artist in our city was the choreographer George Balanchine. And he, the most Apollonian of all artists, created a centered art from acts of displacement.

In a sketchbook he kept in May 1917, Igor Stravinsky wondered: "why is is that changes can take place within me from one year to another, and that these changes are considered legitimate phenomena resulting from man's constant and vital appetite for change—whereas in Art such phenomena are cause for reproach."[17] I was put in mind of this conundrum when, like other people at the New York City Ballet on May 1, 1979, I watched in stunned surprise George Balanchine's revival of *Apollo*, the ballet he had first made to Stravinsky's *Apollon Musagète* in 1928. This, one of the greatest ballets of the century, embodies in its original version what seems a form so coherent and controlled that it stood as a rebuke to the disorganizing, anarchic energies of the art of its time. Indeed, because the marble solidness of this creation, Balanchine declared in a 1948 issue of *Dance Index*,

[17] Igor and Vera Stravinsky, *A Photographic Album: 1921 to 1971* (New York: Thames and Hudson, 1982), pp. 13–14.

Apollon I look back on as the turning point of my life. In its discipline and restraint, in its sustained oneness of tone and feeling the score was a revelation. It seemed to tell me that I could dare not to use everything, that I, too, could eliminate. In *Apollon* and in all the music that follows, it is impossible to imagine substituting for any single fragment the fragment of any other Stravinsky score. Each piece is unique in itself, nothing is replaceable.[18]

Now *Apollo* had now been radically altered by Balanchine in his old age, the beginning and the end cut, Stravinsky's music cut.

All dance changes as it is danced. But *Apollo* was special. The role of Apollo is perhaps the greatest male dance role of the twentieth century; many in the audience in the theater that night had seen it essayed by nearly all the great dancers of Balanchine's own company. At one stroke, the role had ceased to exist in its full contours; nearly a third of the ballet was missing. How could a man not keep faith with something near perfect he had made? In the *Ballet Review*, Robert Garis called the production a "depredation."[19]

I found this broken promise, if it was one, provoking instead. In old age the choreographer was engaged in the project of breaking with the past; he wanted to make a ballet for now. But the provocation went further. Was there something in the very form of *Apollo* that invited its own remaking?

Though *Apollo* lacks an immediate story line of the nineteenth-century sort, it has a thematic, allegorical line. Stravinsky contrived this "play without a plot" for the music, in advance of Balanchine's choreography. From the nine muses of classical mythology, Stravinsky selects three: Calliope, who inspires poetry, Polyhumnia, mime, and Terpsichore, dance. Apollo is born to Leto; he discovers his own beauty and power; the Muses dance before him and he chooses the one among them he loves best; then the god grows into his full maturity, and the three arts all fuse within him into one; at the end, "Apollo, in an apotheosis, leads the Muses, with Terpsichore at their

[18] George Balanchine, "The Dance Element in Stravinsky's Music," in Minna Lederman, ed., *Stravinsky in the Theatre* (New York: Da Capo, 1975), p. 81.
[19] Robert Garis, *Ballet Review,* Fall, 1979, p. 6.

head, to Parnassus, where they were to live ever afterwards."[20] What Balanchine had done fifty years later was take away Apollo's youth and his apotheosis. No longer does the god learn his own nature; no longer do the god and his muses leave us in an elaborated ending, their consummated happiness revealed as our loss; there is mostly the play of dancing in the middle. On that May evening when Balanchine revealed this new version of Apollo, the narrower dimensions of the work were revealed by its props—namely one, the stool on which Apollo sat in judgment of the Muses.

Subtraction, elimination, purification of the present are among the strong critical motives for dreaming of the classical past, the assertion of simpler, purer forms based on the authority and morphologies of the antique. This ballet might simply be said to have suffered its own classical revival. But matters aren't quite so simple. As early as 1928 Balanchine had an intimation, in his corner of Apollo's kingdom, of a formal order that can submit to, indeed invite, radical change from within so as to remake itself again and again as the present.

Terpsichore's solo dance in *Apollo*, for instance, is a study in undoing classical movement: "We see leaps that do not advance, leaps that go *down*, back-front reversals that seem to maintain the mysterious constancy of a shape even as it changes."[21] At the Paris premier on June 12, 1928, the public reacted with confusion to the original precisely because of these self-generating contraries. There were visual echoes of Petipa, and indeed the ballet's provenance goes back even farther, to a production of *Le Pas de Quatre*, as staged in London in 1845, yet again not quotations. There were strangely disconcerting echoes of the eighteenth century in the music. *Apollon Musagète*, like Stravinsky's other great classic of this period, *Pulcinella*, presents materials from past eras and yet at the same time comments on them, throws them into relief, shows them in a reflecting, clarifying mirror. The harmonic progressions in *Apollon Musagète* and *Pulcinella* follow eighteenth-century rules—then suddenly these rules are turned on their head. The gentle modulations Quatremère de Quincy imagined are not to be found in this severely disciplined variation, which takes its own forms apart. In another

[20] Stravinsky, *Autobiography*, p. 134.
[21] Arlene Croce, *Going to the Dance* (New York: Knopf, 1982), p. 114.

variation for Calliope in *Apollon Musagète*, Stravinsky placed as an epigraph the poet Boileau's dictum

> Que toujours dans vos vers le sens coupant les mots
> Suspende l'hémistiche et marque le repos.

The play with silence in the score contravenes, too, this declaration of regularity.

The inner mutations of *Apollo* served Balanchine subsequently throughout his working life as principles of accent and phrasing. In this balletic work the eye focuses "on the full, classical positions rather than the infinite number of non-positions en route."[22] Balanchine's procedure was, as he said, to treat choreography as establishing a "family" of motions in time; these families were peculiar in that the younger generations of motion, though seeming respectful of their traditional parents, move so far away from them in a lifetime of fifteen minutes. The elements of rigorous form that first appeared in *Apollo* were organized into question marks of bodily movement or sound rather than strokes of the ineluctable consummating the graven; displacement is built into the forms, which are at the same time coherent.

That a perfectly made thing should then remain inviolate, timeless, as the proponents of Balanchine's first *Apollo* argued, has not yet accounted what it is to make something in a truly humane way. Balanchine invoked a distinctly humane knowledge of things when he created his own Apollo, as did Stravinsky when he gave the god music: a god of calm but not of permanence, a deity carrying within it its own seeds of change. This is an Apollo who ages. It is this deity, rather than the Christian god of suffering, whom we need to inscribe in the spaces of the city.

---

[22] Eva Resnikova, "The Mystery of Terpsichore: Balanchine, Stravinsky, and 'Apollo,' " *New Criterion* (September 1983): 24.

Index

255

ACKNOWLEDGMENTS

This book was made possible through a grant from the Chicago Institute of Architecture and Urbanism. I would like to thank its director, John Whiteman, for his encouragement and support. Parts of the book were first given as the 1986 Henry Luce Seminars at Yale University where my colleagues and students provided invaluable advice. An earlier version of Chapter Four appeared in *Raritan*, Spring 1988. I owe a special debt to Carl Schorske, my most constant, attentive, sceptical critic.

A NOTE ON THE TYPE

This book was set in Caledonia, a Linotype face
designed by W. A. Dwiggins (1880–1956). It belongs
to the family of printing types called "modern face" by
printers—a term used to mark the change in style of
type letters that occurred about 1800. Caledonia
borders on the general design of Scotch Roman,
but is more freely drawn than that letter.

Composed by American–Stratford Graphic
    Services, Inc., Brattleboro, Vermont
Printed and bound by Fairfield Graphics,
    Fairfield, Pennsylvania
Designed by Iris Weinstein